T0096574

In Sunshine
Or In Shadow

In Sunshine
Or In Shadow

A Journey Through the Life of
Derek Dougan

David Tossell

First published in 2012 by
Pitch Publishing Ltd
A2 Yeoman Gate
Yeoman Way
Durrington
BN13 3QZ

Email: info@pitchpublishing.co.uk
Web: www.pitchpublishing.co.uk

Reprinted in paperback 2018
Text © 2012, 2018 David Tossell

David Tossell has asserted his rights in accordance with the Copyright, Designs and Patents Act 1988 to be identified as the author of this work.

All rights reserved. No part of this publication may be reproduced, stored in a retrieval system, or transmitted in any form or by any means, electronic, mechanical, photocopying, recording or otherwise, without the prior permission in writing of the publisher and the copyright owners, or as expressly permitted by law, or under terms agreed with the appropriate reprographics rights organization. Enquiries concerning reproduction outside the terms stated here should be sent to the publishers at the UK address printed on this page.

The publisher makes no representation, express or implied, with regard to the accuracy of the information contained in this book and cannot accept any legal responsibility for any errors or omissions that may be made.

A CIP catalogue record for this book is available from the British Library.

ISBN: 9781785314056

Cover design by Brilliant Orange Creative Services.
Typesetting and origination by Pitch Publishing.
Printed in India by Replika Press.

CONTENTS

ACKNOWLEDGEMENTS

No book of this nature can proceed without the memories and opinions of those who knew, or shared a playing field, with its subject. Therefore I am greatly indebted to everyone who spared time to talk to me about Derek Dougan.

Among the football fraternity – and following the rough chronology of Dougan's career – teammates Ken Hamilton and Frankie Watters helped to complete the picture of his time at Distillery, while Bill Albury, Sammy Chapman, Ray Crawford, Tommy McGhee, John Phillips and the late Norman Uprichard illuminated his Portsmouth days.

For insight into the various stages of Dougan's Northern Ireland career I have Billy Bingham, Harry Gregg, Bryan Hamilton, Eric McMordie, Sammy Nelson, Peter McParland and journalist Malcolm Brodie to thank, while former teammate and manager Terry Neill was helpful in both Irish and PFA matters. Peter Dobing, Bryan Douglas, the late Ronnie Clayton, Mick McGrath and Matt Woods spoke about the controversial couple of years Dougan spent at Blackburn, and valuable Aston Villa contributions came from McParland, Nigel Sims, Bobby Thomson and Ron Wyllie.

A transfer to Peterborough brought the assistance of Graham Birks, Peter Deakin, Peter McNamee and Frank Rankmore, while thanks are due to Leicester teammates Gordon Banks, Davie Gibson, Richie Norman, Bobby Roberts, Peter Rodrigues and Tom Sweenie, as well as former club secretary Eddie Plumley.

Among colleagues at Wolves, I spoke with Mike Bailey, Kenny Hibbitt, John Holsgrove, the late Frank Munro, Geoff Palmer and Derek Parkin, while the story of Dougan's return to the club as chief executive could not have been told without Graham Hawkins, Doug Hope and Ian Cartwright. Gordon Livsey and Sean Suddards recalled historic times at Kettering, as did Alan Merrick, who, along with Brendon Batson, Bruce Bannister and Jackie Fullerton, was enlightening on Dougan's involvement with the PFA. Comments from opponents include those from Bobby Clark, Frank McLintock, Peter Simpson and Terry Conroy, who was also a big help in relation to Derek's involvement in the all-Ireland team and the latter years of his life. Bob McNab and Nick Owen shared memories of Dougan's broadcasting career.

Coreen Long and Josephine Long gave me great assistance in many areas, notably family life in Belfast, while friends and acquaintances who spoke about various elements of Dougan's life included Peter Bartlett, Peter Creed, Simon Dunkley, Stuart Earl, Robert Goddard, Alex Lattimer, Chris Westcott and Linda Westcott. As well as providing valuable background on his friend's campaigning for former footballers, Bob Runham played a vital role in getting this project under way.

Among my interviewees, final and greatest thanks go to Merlyn Humphreys, Derek's partner in later life, who offered me outstanding support, hospitality, contacts and insight into the man whose memory and legacy she continues to keep alive on a daily basis.

Many other people whose names may not appear elsewhere in this book deserve my gratitude for assistance given, with special mention for Haydn Parry and Richard Whitehead. Thanks to Alan Bennett, Adrian Bevington, Mike Davage, Matt Hill, Mark Hooper, Mike Jackman, Shaun Keogh, Paul Mace, John Nagle, Richard Owen, Neil Rioch and Dawson Simpson. As always, the written work of many other people has been of great assistance in my research and I have attempted to acknowledge as many as possible in the bibliography. Paul Camillin at Pitch Publishing ensured that this book came to fruition and I thank him for his support and professionalism.

AUTHOR'S NOTE

This book was researched and written between July 2007 and
July 2008, the 12 months immediately following
Derek Dougan's death.

Chapter 1

DOOG, RIP

The voice at the end of the line was unmistakeable, the introduction superfluous. "David," the uncompromising Belfast accent announced. "It's Derek Dougan."

What started out as a simple call several weeks earlier to request an interview for a book about Malcolm Allison had turned into a series of telephone exchanges and meetings in which we had discussed all manner of subjects, yet never been far from a return to the recurring theme of Dougan's passion for helping retired former footballers in times of trouble. Most of our discussions seemed to have taken place in between his appointments with lawyers, insurance companies or football authorities; engagements he approached with the same relish with which he'd attacked crosses from the wing during two decades as a centre-forward with Distillery, Portsmouth, Blackburn, Aston Villa, Peterborough, Leicester, Wolves and his beloved Northern Ireland.

That he had also shown an interest in – and asked for copies of – my previous books, I'd taken as little more than polite interest. Now it had all become clear. I had, it appeared, been auditioning. "What are you doing for the next few months?" Dougan asked, in a manner that left me in no doubt about the answer he wished to hear. "I want to get a new version of my autobiography out for my 70th birthday and I'd like you to work on it with me. You could come and stay at my house in Wolverhampton. We'd split any money 50-50."

It should have been an offer I couldn't refuse, but with several months of work left on another project and Derek apparently keen to work to a tight deadline, I had to suggest, with considerable regret: "I'd love to do it, but it depends on when you want get started. If you want to begin immediately I think you are going to have to ask someone else. Otherwise, let's look at it again in the summer."

Cursing the missed opportunity to work with an icon of the football era I grew up with and which, for me, retains an addictive fascination, I listened to Derek's parting comment. He laughed as he delivered his words, but I sensed the edge in his voice. "If I go ahead without you, I hope you read the book and wish you'd been involved."

A few months later, I discovered that his book would never be written. Turning on Sky Sports News to get the day's headlines, I learned that Derek Dougan, aged 69, had died from a heart attack at his home.

The tributes that followed in the next few days were fulsome, whether from teammates, opponents, friends, administrators or those who had simply stood on the terraces cheering or, in some cases, cursing the man they knew as "The Doog". Privately, those who have known him most closely over the years are in no rush to create a saint. Many had witnessed or been recipients of his extraordinary acts of thoughtfulness and generosity, but through their grief and their love they still recognised that Derek could make reckless, ill-judged decisions and, if he chose, be a bastard. By God, he could be a right bloody-minded bastard. John Holsgrove, a former Wolves teammate and a friend for four decades, would tell me: "If Derek fell out with you, or didn't like you, he would just shut you out."

The trick, it seems, was not to attempt to work out how you could reconcile the two sides of the man. You just accepted that the contradiction was as much a part of him as his long legs and gap-toothed grin. Take it or leave it.

The obituary writers had any number of themes to pursue, demonstrating the rich and varied texture of his life and the paradoxical nature of his character. Some reflected on the combustible nature of the young footballer who ventured from Belfast to the Football League, staying at clubs just long enough to get the management's back up before being moved along to the next one. Others, especially those with a geographical bias towards the Midlands, noted the legendary status the more mature Dougan acquired at Wolverhampton Wanderers, where he scored 123 goals and achieved his dream of a Wembley victory during eight years as a player before later becoming chief executive in one of the club's darkest hours.

Those focusing on his life away from the pitch paid tribute to his work as chairman of the Professional Footballers' Association, where his constant campaigning played an important role in laying the foundation for the contractual freedom today's players take for granted. Having worked towards securing the rights of the modern generation, he persisted – in his supposed retirement years – to badger the authorities for what he felt were the forgotten rights of football's older generation.

Another consistent theme was his Northern Irish roots; the pride he felt in wearing the green shirt of his country; the pain he had felt watching from afar as his homeland was torn apart by violence; and his dream of seeing a united team representing all the people of Ireland, regardless of religion or geography. The great friendships he struck up in and out of the game offered a further rich seam, whether it is recording the esteem of men such as Martin O'Neill or recalling that he had been a pall-bearer at the funeral of his great Northern Ireland colleague George Best.

What was not mentioned – because until now it has never been revealed – was that his feats on the field were achieved despite the considerable physical handicap of having only one fully operational kidney. Medical tests in his latter years disclosed that one of his kidneys had never developed from childhood, remaining the size of a walnut instead of reaching of reaching the usual length of five inches and weight of around five ounces. "The doctors asked him if he had been kicked there when he was a boy," Dougan's partner,

Merlyn Humphreys, explained. "For some reason it just stopped growing."

Derek Dougan might have been an antagonistic centre-forward, blessed with speed, strength and football nous more than flash-footed trickery, but no one could claim that he was an ordinary footballer. How many other players would begin a book by quoting Voltaire, as Dougan did in one of his three autobiographical volumes? Anything he lacked in flair with the ball at his feet, he more than made up for with unashamed showmanship and, away from the field, a mixture of easy charm and spiky combativeness, winning friends and creating enmity in equal measure.

Being around Dougan meant you were never far from encountering one of his deeply held beliefs, whether it was about the state of the nation or the way football should be run – to which he devoted another of his books. It was the reason why, when ITV constructed its revolutionary World Cup panel in 1970, Dougan was placed alongside Malcolm Allison in the vanguard. Televised football was never the same again.

Dougan never got to add that latest volume to a portfolio of personal work that even included a novel. Yet his story – which also illuminates a long and important period of development in British football – deserves to re-told, and not through a simple chronological account. The search for the real Derek Dougan requires the benefit of new insight from those closest to him; an understanding of his environmental and social influences; some attempt to rationalise the complexities of an often destructive personality; and a degree of impartial discussion of the man and the issues in which he became embroiled. Such a dispassionate assessment would never have been possible in a book guided by Derek's own words and opinions.

§

I am sitting at a polished dining table in the home of Merlyn Humphreys, the woman with whom Derek found love, happiness and contentment in his latter years and with whom he shared his life. Merlyn, previously widowed, strikingly silver-blonde atop her black outfit and with a ballerina's petite figure, explains that, although spending most of her time at Derek's place a few minutes away in Tettenhall, she has maintained her own detached house in the Wolverhampton stockbroker belt hamlet of Wightwick. She and Doog – as even she always called him – had, however, been planning to pitch in together and get married. He had even selected his best man. But then fate, and Derek's failing heart, wrenched such plans from the soil of Merlyn's existence.

"You know, you never would have got started on that book even if you'd been available," she declares. "He was all fired up about it and then, not long after he came off the phone with you, he received another call and he was off on another cause. That took every moment of his time for several weeks. He loved a cause." On this particular occasion it had been the case of former Wolves player Ian Cartwright, in dire need of funding for cancer treatment. One phone conversation later, Dougan was off in a whirl of auctions, dinners, celebrity football matches and legal documents.

Even on the morning of his death, he had been preparing to head to Hastings to represent former Portsmouth and Northern Ireland teammate Norman Uprichard in an industrial injury case relating to his days as a goalkeeper in the 1950s, an age when part of the job description was to accept a hammering from centre-forwards and then drag yourself back into action with anything from fractured fingers to broken necks.

Without invitation or cajoling, Merlyn describes the events of 24th June 2007. As she does so, a grey and sombre mood settles about us, conflicting with the late summer sunshine that has been dancing on the ornaments and picture frames.

Merlyn had been at home packing a bag prior to travelling with Doog to spend that night with friends Chris and Linda Westcott in Eastbourne. Having left Derek the previous evening so that he could sit up through the night watching Ricky Hatton's fight in Las Vegas, Merlyn was preparing to make the short return journey when the phone rang. "Doog at home" showed up on the caller ID window, but at the other end of the line all she could hear was the eerie silence of a seemingly empty room. "I thought my heart would stop with fear," she remembers.

As trembling fingers attempted to hit the speed dial button for Derek's number, her phone chirruped back into life. One breathless, painfully-delivered word will never leave her. "Merlyn."

The next few minutes passed in a blur of instinctive action, yet remain burned in horrific detail in Merlyn's memory: a mad dash by car; the sight of Dougan slumped, phone still in hand, in his armchair; the emergency call and the urgent order for Merlyn to attempt to revive him while the ambulance was dispatched. "They were telling me I had to get Doog out of the armchair and on to the floor. He was a big person and I was six and a half stone. They counted with me through 400 compressions to his heart and the perspiration was falling from my body on to his. I don't know how I did it, but you find the strength from somewhere."

Merlyn's faltering words, full of heartbreak, appear to require the same kind of effort that was called for in Doog's living room. Then, as now, she soldiered on.

By the time the emergency services arrived, she was close to exhaustion. Yet her efforts had counted for nothing. The briefest of examinations by the medics confirmed that Derek had probably died moments after his phone call. The colour Merlyn had seen returning to his body was simply the manually-achieved movement of blood around his body.

We get on to discussing this book and I tell Merlyn that my intention is to title it *In Sunshine or in Shadow*, a line borrowed from *Danny Boy*. She had selected the tune, one of Derek's favourites, to be sung at his funeral. It seems to encapsulate the light and dark of Dougan's life: the joy he derived from playing football set alongside the gloomy frustration he felt about important issues that affected players' rights; the glory and headlines that illuminated much of his playing career, and, in contrast, his campaigning away from the spotlight.

It also reflects the good and bad of the publicity he attracted right up to his death and, on the most basic level, the strictly defined black and white views of an opinionated man who even his closest friends sometimes wished would relax and accept that, in life, some things are simply the way they are.

Later, more than one former teammate will tell me that Dougan was an all or nothing kind of player, brilliant and committed when the mood took him, but prone to the odd day when enthusiasm and effort could go astray. Mick McGrath, a colleague at Blackburn, illustrates it by explaining: "We trained in pre-season at open-air school, which you could get to by road or through a field. At the end of every session the first person back to the changing room would get a yellow jersey. Derek was the type that if he wasn't first he would be last – there was no in between with him."

I ask Merlyn if Derek was truly a happy man. The books he wrote about his playing career seemed to focus much more on everything that he took exception to in his profession than the simple pleasure of being paid for playing football. Merlyn's own description of Derek turning down a relaxing Sunday spent walking and lunching in the countryside in favour of a day with his nose in his business files suggests a man who was too consumed by his passions and causes to stop and enjoy the good times.

On this point, Merlyn is quick to contradict me. "Derek was driven," she admits. "And he would go looking for things to get his teeth into. But those closest to him saw the funny side of him, the warmth and kindness and his love of life. Oh yes, he was happy."

§

Situated on rising ground in the north-eastern part of the city, the Collegiate Church of St Peter's has been at the heart of religious worship in Wolverhampton for more than 1,000 years. The small Saxon building that was erected in a forest in the tenth century has long since given way to the majestic structure that watches over a bustling city centre, with the ornamented tower rising from the heart of the building now one of the first landmarks to greet those arriving in town via its train and bus stations.

Extensive mid-19th century renovations have given it much of its present-day definition, but the fact that it has retained important architectural features dating back to the 1300s helps to make it a source of civic pride, along with its important role in offering a daily haven for prayer and succour.

There is no more appropriate setting for a public tribute to a man who bestrode Wolverhampton's sporting landscape for the best part of a decade and remained one of the city's most favoured residents more than 30 years after he left its playing fields for the last time. On Thursday 5th July, the golden Wolves replica jerseys stretched across torsos of all shapes, sizes and ages add a welcome dash of colour to the streets outside the church as Britain's dismal summer serves up a breezy, overcast lunchtime. The shirts are being worn in strict accord with the instructions of Merlyn, who has spent the last week filling numerous notebook pages putting together the funeral service that will bid Dougan his last farewell.

Inside the church, interspersed among family and friends, is the cast list of Dougan's career. The Wolves contingent is numerous, from current manager Mick McCarthy and Doog's old coach, Sammy Chung, to a list of teammates that includes Frank Munro, Jim McCalliog, John McAlle, Derek Parkin, Phil Parkes, captain Mike Bailey, Geoff Palmer, Barry Powell, John Holsgrove, Ernie Hunt, Dave Burnside, Gerry Taylor and Les Wilson, who has flown in from Canada.

Helping to represent Northern Ireland are Pat Jennings, Martin O'Neill, Peter McParland, Sammy Nelson and former teammate and manager Billy Bingham. Opponents such as Denis Law and Johnny Giles take their places on behalf of the wider football community, as do former colleagues from other clubs, while chief executive Gordon Taylor and his former right-hand man Brendon Batson signify Dougan's long involvement with the Professional Footballers' Association – the organisation that was once so close to his heart but which he spent much of his later life battling.

The conflicts that characterised one aspect of Dougan's life are best signified by the absence of John Richards. Over the past 20 years, Dougan has barely spoken to the man with whom, in the early '70s, he formed one of English football's most productive goalscoring partnerships. "I was very disappointed John wasn't there," Frank Munro tells me later. "It was a crying shame those two fell out."

Dougan, who would have abhorred the thought of dark introspection rather than vivid celebration being the dominant mood of the day, is to take his final bow in the colours that gave him his greatest fame. The hearse, decorated with old-style barred Wolves scarves, proceeds past the respectful applause of the onlookers. Their glimpses inside reveal a coffin of Wolves gold with "Doog", in his own handwriting, stencilled on the side, along with the number 10 – the figure he wore for the second half of his career at Molineux – and the distinctive club badge. Placed on top are two floral tributes: one in Wolves colours of gold and black, sent by the club's London supporters' club, of which Derek was president; the other, from Merlyn, in the green and white of Northern Ireland.

Amid the usual ungainly struggle, the coffin is hoisted onto shoulders. The pall bearers include Dougan's brother Dale and sons Alexander and Nicholas – strikingly like his father – which represents a temporary setting aside of differences that have undermined family relationships over recent years. In an accustomed outside-left position on the coffin is David Wagstaffe, the trusted winger whose understanding with Derek contributed to so many of his goals and who once called his teammate "the best header of the ball in England".

As the funeral party disappears beyond the ranks of photographers into the church, fans – Dougan would not have wanted them referred to as mourners – exchange expectant glances as they wait for the first notes of the service on the speaker system that has been set up around the forecourt of the building. *Bring Him Home*, from the musical *Les Miserables*, reaches them while, inside, the coffin is carried up the pillar-lined aisle and placed in front of the congregation. More than one teammate admits later they could not overcome the feeling that the lid was about to burst open to reveal that their friend had been kidding with them all along.

The tone of the spoken tributes is quickly set by broadcaster Nick Owen, a junior member of the production team when Dougan, at the height of his playing fame, hosted a sports show on BBC Radio Birmingham. Having thanked the attendees on behalf of the family he reminds everyone that Derek was "greatly respected and much loved – even if he did upset a few people", describing him as "controversial, fiery, humorous and passionate".

"I can't tell you how honoured I was," Owen confesses when I ask him about his part in the funeral. "I was absolutely thrilled, very touched and surprised. When Merlyn asked me to do it she said Doog had often talked about me, which was enormously flattering. I was very proud but also intimidated. Speaking in public can be daunting enough but even more so when you are speaking on behalf of someone at their funeral and especially in front of so many football icons."

The reading from the first book of Corinthians by Derek's niece, Josephine Dougan Long, falls between the official hymn of the football world, *Abide with Me*, and *Danny Boy*. Then Mike Bailey steps forward to recap Dougan's career at Wolves, where "his impact was immediate" after being signed from Leicester in 1967, the sixth occasion he was transferred to an English club. "He was big-name player who gave the club, the fans and the town a huge lift in status," Bailey says, noting that Wolves finally offered him the opportunity of "playing on the big stage to large crowds who adored him".

Bailey's contribution is significant, a generous gesture from someone who reportedly never got on with his outspoken colleague, although when we catch up later he says that the rift between the two men has been exaggerated. Yet others explain that for many years the Wolves dressing room had been defined along the lines of whether you were with Bailey or Dougan.

One of those in Derek's camp, John Holsgrove, who in recent years has grown closer to his former captain, reveals that Bailey "was a little embarrassed" to have been asked to play a formal role in the funeral. "But he handled it very well," Holsgrove comments. "He spoke because he was club captain and he spoke about Derek as a footballer. He didn't speak about him as a person because he didn't really know him."

Former Republic of Ireland and Stoke City winger Terry Conroy gets up to address the congregation, noting that his great friend had "a restless spirit" and emphasising the passion with which he pursued his beliefs and forced home his opinions. "He continued to hammer down doors to achieve the benefits he felt the players of his generation were entitled to," he says, closing with his vision of Dougan meeting St Peter at the gates of heaven and being shown the contract for entry.

Doog, he says, would assert: "That's not the way to do it. You listen to me, Peter, and you won't go far wrong."

The obvious nerves of Aston Villa manager and former Northern Ireland colleague Martin O'Neill are evidence of the honour he feels at being asked to represent Dougan's countrymen. "He was witty," he says. "He thought so himself." He recalls him dominating the squad for the entire duration of an end-of-season Home International Championship tournament early in O'Neill's own career, teaching him a hitherto unknown history of both football and his country. "He had the last word and the first word… he was iconoclastic in the sense that he broke the rules and didn't mind. He had tremendous courage to carry them out."

Leading the service, the Rector of Wolverhampton, David Frith, invites those inside and outside to sing along to the playing of *You'll Never Walk Alone* in order to "add a communal tribute added to those we have already received". As the music fades, chants of "Dougan, Dougan" reach the church, bringing a smile to the face of Merlyn Humphreys as she takes her place at the lectern.

Moving and dignified, her eulogy is based around an adaptation of the poem *He Is Gone*, beginning with the lines: "You can shed tears that Doog has gone, or you can smile because he lived." It precedes her introduction of Nat King Cole's *Unforgettable* – "because that's what Doog is and always will be".

After Derek's elder son Alexander has performed his own composition, *Praise the Lord*, introduced by his brother Nicholas, the Rev. Frith ascends the 15th century pulpit. He begins his address by relating the way Dougan ensured that his sister Coreen spent the Christmases after the death of her husband James at his home in Wolverhampton, "an act typical of his thoughtfulness, kindness and generosity".

As well as his love of his adopted home town, Frith highlights that Derek remained "hugely proud of his Belfast roots, yet also deeply pained by the hatreds and tragedies of his homeland". He continues: "I believe Derek to be an unsung hero of peace and reconciliation. The story of his off-the-field endeavours to put together an all-Ireland team [in 1973] ought not to be forgotten. He believed in the possibility of change, transformation and healing."

Admitting that he could display "waywardness" of character, he claims it was simply "part of the creative tension that goes with exceptional ability". Those close to him "knew that he could throw a wobbly sometimes" and, in an apparent reference to his estranged family, Frith acknowledges that Dougan knew "things could go wrong in relationships" but says he was open to the healing of hurt. "When the impulsiveness had passed, the kindness was still there, deeper and stronger," he says.

Here, the good reverend is perhaps being a little generous to Derek. One of his acknowledged failings was his willingness to hold a grudge; one of his biggest faults his failure, sometimes, to find forgiveness. The way he stayed away from his beloved Molineux for so many years speaks of someone quite happy to cut off his nose to spite his face.

The service over, the coffin is carried back down the aisle as *You Raise Me Up* is played. Dougan had been taken with the song the first time he heard it, at George Best's funeral. On that occasion he had been honoured to be chosen as a pall-bearer, commenting: "George carried us for enough years on the field so it will be an honour to carry him today."

Then Derek Dougan disappears, driven away to a private cremation. It is the final part of a journey that would have seemed incredible to the young shipyard apprentice from Belfast who looked across the water and saw visions of life in another world – the world of football – but whose personality would ensure he could never be constrained by its boundaries.

Chapter 2

BELFAST CHILD

George Best. The name on the airport sign greeting visitors to Belfast signifies many things. Not least, of course, is the place that the province's most brilliantly gifted of footballers continues to hold in the hearts of its population nearly four decades since he last wore the green shirt of his country and long after his death.

But it is also notable that it is someone possessing a unique gift with a ball at his feet after whom City Airport has been re-named; important that the power of football as a unifying force in a community torn asunder by strife has been so recognised.

Liverpool has its John Lennon Airport, which speaks eloquently about the role of popular music in developing the identity of that city, of establishing pride and a sense of belonging among its people. Belfast has Best and, therefore, football.

Derek Dougan might have had dreams that could only ever be played out many miles beyond the confines of his hometown, but he always knew the influence his sport could wield back home. One of the highlights of his playing career was captaining the Northern Ireland team that achieved a 1-0 victory over England at Wembley in May of 1972. The pure sporting satisfaction he felt was nothing compared to the joy of hearing that, for one evening, the threat of violence on the streets of Belfast had abated.

"The people of my homeland had been sitting by their radio sets glued to the game live and there was never a more quiet time in any Ulster spring since the commencement of the Troubles," he recorded. "The streets were virtually deserted. Ulster that evening was at peace and proud of a historic victory."

Not that he had needed such an event to remind him of the power of football in his home town. He had learned that fact of life early and had never forgotten it. After all, the sport had been at the core of his own existence throughout the 19 years he spent as a Belfast boy. "Derek was obsessed with football, football, football," says his sister, Coreen Long, whose home in east Belfast, coincidentally, is across the road to that of George Best's sister, Barbara. Eight years younger than her brother, Coreen adds: "My earliest memory of Derek is him playing football with his friends. He had one focus, and that was football."

As we speak, I am sitting at Coreen's kitchen table, below a framed picture of Derek in his Wolves days. Having picked me up at the airport in the middle of an early morning downpour, Coreen's daughter, Josephine, had announced: "My mum's cooking you Derek's favourite – an Ulster fry, with potato bread and soda bread. He would always have one when he visited us."

While I concentrate on endorsing Derek's culinary tastes, Coreen discusses family life. "Derek was on a pedestal to our father [Jackie]. He could have done no wrong. Derek walked on water to my daddy; he thought he was wonderful. In the early days after Derek went to England I remember him buying the *Newsletter* to see if Derek had been picked for the Northern Ireland team. It was a big excitement for him and if he wasn't picked he was not a happy bunny. And if somebody didn't give him a good write-up my daddy would have been angry."

Belfast had become the Dougan family home when Derek's grandfather Alexander decided to take advantage of its increasing employment opportunities. The population had been fattened by English and Scottish settlers in the 1800s and Belfast had been granted city status by Queen Victoria in 1888, while its commercial growth during the 18th and 19th century made it a beacon for all those looking for steady work in the northern part of Ireland. The established industries ranged from engineering and shipbuilding to rope-making and the linen and tobacco trades.

By the time Alexander Dougan moved his family from Comber, six miles outside the city in the direction of Dundonald in County Down, Belfast had overtaken Dublin as Ireland's most populated city.

Sandy, as everyone knew him, took up work as a boilermaker at the Harland and Wolff shipyard on the bank of the Belfast Lough, which sits at the mouth of the River Lagan and presents the city to the Irish Sea. At its peak during the Second World War, the shipyard, where the *SS Titanic* was built in 1911, provided employment to almost 35,000. Sandy, who eventually became a foreman, would be followed into the docks by his three sons, Sandy, James and John (known as Jackie). Even his grandson, Alexander Derek, would work there before he carried his dreams of a career in football across the water.

Derek, as he would be known, was born to parents Jackie and Josie on 20th January, 1938, second in a lineage that also included Pearl, Elizabeth, Coreen, Morris and Dale and which spanned more than a decade and a half. Entrenched in the heart of east Belfast, traditionally the Protestant sector of the city, the family moved shortly after Derek's birth from Susan Street to Avon Street, the kind of tightly-packed Victorian terraced housing that, throughout decade after decade, has served as a production line for inner-city footballers all over the British Isles.

Coreen explains: "It was next door to our granddad Sandy. The reason our family moved there was because the two houses had a big, shared pigeon loft. It was two-up, two-down and you had your outside loo. You came out the house at the back and that was where the pigeon shed was. Once the pigeons were there that was the big thing for my daddy. You couldn't go out the back if there was a race on, oh my God, no. He raced them every weekend and he was good, but going out there was a no-no because he was clapping them in."

These days, Avon Street has been expunged from the Belfast A-Z, a welcome victim of a city regeneration programme that has replaced it with a neat, comfortable estate. While today's children have colourful climbing frames on a lush-looking play area, Derek and his contemporaries had to make do with a patch of grassless waste ground that was coined, with due sarcasm, "The Meadow". Evenings and all day Sunday would be spent there in endless, multi-player games, participants breaking off to get changed for Sunday school or grab their tea before returning to the action with the scoreline running into the 30s and 40s. "It was rough stuff, a hurly burly," said Derek. "But I learned how to avoid crunching tackles and how to use my initiative."

Football courses strongly through the Dougan blood. Grandfather Sandy was a former Linfield half-back who had been good enough to be offered the opportunity to play professionally in Scotland by each of the Edinburgh teams, Hibernian and Hearts. Partly because he didn't know what to do with his racing pigeons, he remained in Belfast, playing for junior team Stormont. Six feet tall and with hair slicked back into a centre-parting, he cut an intimidating figure in the eyes of young Derek, especially when he continually nagged him not to be so reliant on his left foot – a trait the adult Dougan had still not rid himself of even when he was scoring goals in England's First Division[1].

Four of Sandy's five brothers had played at a decent level, with two – Bob and Bill – having been professionals for the leading Belfast teams, Linfield and Glentoran. Such was the sibling and team rivalry that they were once sent off for fighting each other in a Christmas encounter.

Derek's maternal grandparents, the Kitchens, also had a strong connection with the sport, his grandmother having had two brothers, Jimmy and Alfie Wishart, who played for the famous Belfast Celtic club. It was to his grandparents' home on the coast in Bangor that Derek had been evacuated during the war, starting school there at the age of three. Returning to Belfast, he attended Belvoir School, and developed a passion for Glentoran.

Although his father would not take him to their games at The Oval, he eventually found his way there anyway, forming vivid

---

1   Throughout this book, divisions will be referred to as they were known at the time – therefore First, Second, Third and Fourth Division, as opposed to Premier League, Championship, League One and League Two, when discussing Dougan's playing days.

memories of the team's forward line, including the elusive wing play of Sammy Lowry and the heading of Sammy Hughes. "I don't remember them playing to any particular system," he said. "I was aware of their individual skill and the way they complemented each other."

Such players fired the imagination. "If I had not seen Glentoran play in the late 40s and early 50s when I was at an impressionable age, my sense of football, the equivalent of what the poet WH Auden called a 'sense of theatre', would not have developed. The two had much in common because football is dramatic and has a relationship with theatre."

It was clearly in those visits to Glentoran and the awakening of the passions they aroused that can be found the first stirrings of The Doog – the man who would never miss an opportunity to play up to the crowd, who would go out of his way to provoke a response from the terraces, favourable or otherwise. The performer had been born.

It was at Mersey Street School, where he enrolled as a nine-year-old, that Derek received his first experience of playing competitive football. One of his teachers, a Mr Mawhinney, recruited him for a game after noticing the lithe youngster's natural stamina as he raced around the playground at lunchtime. Playing in boots borrowed from a lad called Billy Dickie, he played at centre-forward and scored a goal in a 1-1 draw, but, after continually drifting back towards his own goal, was swapped with the centre-half, whose own lack of positional awareness was taking him in the opposite direction. In the half-back line, Derek had found the platform from which he would launch a career.

As he progressed through the school's minor, junior and senior teams he admitted that "soccer became a life-force'" His father, who had previously paid for Derek to have boxing lessons, bought him his first pair of boots at the age of ten and took responsibility for their maintenance. Having bequeathed his son the natural speed that was to be so important in his career, he encouraged him to take his football seriously.

With such support, Derek practised for anything between four and eight hours a day, honing his ball control on cobbled streets that bore the indentations of so many years of young ambition and improving his heading with a rubber ball against the wall of the house. Such dedication saw him wear out countless pairs of shoes, but ensured the advancement of his game.

Mersey Street's fiercest competitor was Templemore Avenue School, an enmity Dougan said "meant as much as to other people as the rivalry between Eton and Harrow". Sammy Chapman – born within a month of Derek in the same street – was the star of the Templemore team. "We used to play against each other a lot," Chapman remembers. "Derek was one of the better players around at that time. He didn't play up front, he played in midfield. He always fancied himself as a midfielder and he would have been marvellous there later in his career. He had most things you would want as a player. He could play anywhere and he was left-sided, which was a great bonus. The other one wasn't much of a foot and it didn't do much, but it didn't need to."

Apart from football, Derek's other passion was his regular trips to the cinema to see westerns and the weekly newsreels, which injected him with a romanticised view of America and offered a grainy glimpse of events on mainland Britain. But it was football that offered him the chance to widen the horizons of his own existence in Belfast. Derek had never even met a Catholic until playing against Ardoyne School in the Belfast Schools Cup at the age of 11. Not that sectarianism was ever an issue in the Dougan household, where Josie would tell her children: "There is good and bad in everyone."

"I believe things are learned in the home," says Coreen. "Religion wasn't big in our house; we never spoke about Protestant and Catholics. Football was the religion of our house."

The only conflict that interested Derek was the usual battle that has confronted talented young footballers down the ages: the playing field or the classroom. It was no real contest. "I have often wondered if I would have developed my sense of football had I shone at classroom subjects," he said later. "It could be that a deep involvement in the game at its lowest level, making do with rags tied in a bundle and kicked around waste ground, was a way of compensating for seemingly lagging behind in academic subjects."

The advice of his mother – "the more you learn the better your chances will be in life" – went largely unheeded, even though Derek was no fool in lessons. Spelling and mathematics were his best subjects, but his headmaster, Mr Johnson, was a strict disciplinarian and Derek's palms were often warmed by the sting of his cane. On such occasions it was usually his grandmother, Lizzie, to whom he went for consolation and sympathy. On one occasion, when the cane had missed its target and caught Derek's wrist bone, Granny Dougan was round to the school at top speed to scold the headmaster.

In later years, Derek would admit that he regretted his ambivalence towards formal education and was determined to broaden his mind through voracious reading. His own writing would be evidence of having achieved worldliness beyond the average member of his profession. He would also warn young players coming into the game that "the better their all-round education the less likely they are to make fools of themselves in squandering their assets".

As much as the young Dougan was progressing in local schoolboy football, his mother, small in stature at just over five feet but huge in her impact on her son, was too much of a pragmatist to allow such dreams to blind him to the realities of life. "She was a woman of tremendous courage, and tremendous strength – a woman completely dedicated to bringing up her family," Dougan said.

Her priorities were making the family's limited budget last throughout the week, while ensuring that her children stayed away from those who could exert unhealthy influence. She once warned Derek that she would have no qualms in turning him in to the police if ever she heard he had been getting into trouble.

Derek, meanwhile, saw less of his father, who followed the usual routine of the Belfast working man. "My dad was a man's man," says Coreen. "He worked in the shipyards and he liked to go out and have a wee drink in the evening."

The Dougans were squeezed by the kind of poverty that can suffocate dreams. Later in life, Derek joked: "On the street where I lived, if you paid your rent three weeks on the trot, the police used to come and see where you got the money from." But Coreen stresses a point that Derek, too, always acknowledged. "Everybody was in the same boat. You didn't have material things so you played out in the streets. You played ball or skipping. When everyone has nothing you don't realise you have nothing."

Derek's ambition in football, therefore, was driven as much by the simple desire to be able to play the game all his life as any aspiration to carve out a better existence for himself. When, with his 14th birthday approaching, Derek chose to extend his schooling, he did so for footballing reasons, not academic. Remaining at Mersey Street would have meant leaving school in the March after his birthday.

By passing the entry exam for Belfast Technical High School he was able to spend the final year of his education at an establishment that would retain him until June – giving him the chance to represent the Irish Schools team in the spring internationals.

The location of the school, where Northern Ireland football greats Danny Blanchflower and Billy Bingham had been pupils, meant more of the city became familiar to Derek. Wearing uniform for the first time, his daily journey took him into the middle of Belfast. He would get down from the bus at City Hall and walk to the school building next to the Belfast Academical Institution, 200 yards away from Victorian architecture of the Grand Opera House and the Great Northern railway station.

Playing at centre-forward, his goals earned him selection for the games against Wales in Cardiff and England in York. Although he never felt that he was one of the better players in the team, he was retained in the side for the home game against Scotland at Grosvenor Park.

The school year completed and his games played, Derek was out into the adult world of employment, providing his family with welcome additional income through his job at the Triang toy factory on the Castlereagh Road. "If I had stayed long enough I would have been rewarded with unemployment in the end," he noted.

During his 18 months with the company he spent his time stuffing and attaching parts to a range of children's toys and animals. For his work he earned between £4 and £5 a week, the management allowing him to make a little bit more by ignoring the fact that workers under 15 were not officially qualified to do overtime.

Derek would never allow those additional shifts to get in the way of his football, which had now taken him into the competitive arena of the boys' clubs, a renowned breeding ground for future professional, even international, players. With Mersey Street Boys' Club having closed, Derek found himself playing for Cregagh Boys' Club, the same team with which George Best would come to Manchester United's attention a few years later.

Ever the tactician, Dougan chose Cregagh over Boyland Youth Club because he thought there was greater potential of getting a game. To increase his chances of selection he was smart enough to embrace other areas of the club, including table tennis and billiards. He knew that such commitment was considered important by Stafford Young, who organised the club and picked the football team. Derek was offered a place in the team, where he performed mostly at inside-left.

Selection to represent the Boys' Clubs of Belfast offered Derek his first trip south of the Irish border for a game against Dublin's representatives. He was, however, picked only as a reserve after playing poorly in a trial game when suffering from flu. "That was one of the great disappointments of my life. I would have travelled to the world's end for a game of football, which was all I was interested in from the age of ten."

Derek's knowledge of the south extended little further than the vague notion that it was mostly full of Catholics and that it offered better quality groceries than the north, hence his mother's occasional shopping trips whenever she had saved up enough money for the fare.

By now, Derek's first tentative steps towards senior football were being taken through two nights' training every week with Linfield, but his failure to break into any of the club's junior teams left him frustrated. Glentoran took a look, but their scout was unable even to offer the prospect of a game in their fourth team, ending Derek's hopes of achieving most east Belfast schoolboys' ambitions of playing for the Glens. But another club was waiting in the wings. Derek Dougan's career was about to take off at Distillery.

Chapter 3

OVER THE RAINBOW

So much of Derek Dougan's early life has been erased from the landscape of his home city. Avon Street has been rebuilt; the toy factory on Castlereagh Road where he first worked consigned to history. The building that housed Mersey Street School remains, even though the doors are now permanently closed, while the site of the Harland and Wolff shipyard, which once ebbed and flowed with the shift times of tens of thousands, is a virtual ghost town awaiting reinvention as Belfast's answer to London's Canary Wharf.

Most of that change can be explained by the natural passing of the years, a city evolving, improving itself or simply reflecting life in the 21st century. The disappearance of Grosvenor Park, Dougan's first home as a professional footballer, reflects an unhappier story: that of the Troubles.

Distillery Football Club used to sit just off Grosvenor Road, towards the west side of Belfast. Behind the ground was the Irish whiskey-producing Dunburn Distillery, from which the club took its name. Situated close to the Falls Road, the border between the Protestant and Catholic communities, the club was of mixed denomination, with a particular history of fielding Scottish players of both religious persuasions. Fans came from the two sides of the divide, in contrast to a club like Linfield with its firmly Protestant tradition.

When Derek joined Distillery it offered him the most regular interaction with Catholics that he would experience while living in the strictly segregated city of Belfast. Even when he went to work in the shipyards, there was little contact with Catholics, that part of Belfast's industry being dominated by the Protestant population from the east of the city. The degree to which the two sides of the religious separation maintained their distance from each other was noted by authors David McKittrick and David McVea in *Making Sense of the Troubles*:

The situation was summed up in 1971 by a Catholic observer who said: "If there is one thing which I have learned in my 30-40-odd years as a community social worker it is this: that, broadly speaking, two communities have lived side by side in Northern Ireland without really knowing each other, or without making any real, honest sincere and conscious effort to bridge the communications gap."

Distillery was one of the few institutions that crossed the divide, making it an ideal club for Derek, whose roots might have been Protestant but whose outlook on life continued to develop along strictly non-sectarian lines. A year before his death, Dougan said of his days at Grosvenor Park: "It was the happiest period of my entire footballing career and that was brought about by the camaraderie of the players. If you believe people who should know better there is a terrible conflict between Protestants and Catholics. I genuinely don't believe there is. I played on a team that was six Protestants and five Catholics."

Portadown-born Norman Uprichard, who played in goal for Distillery in the 1940s before forging a career in England, gives this description of the club: "It was a nice, friendly place and I enjoyed it there. I would finish work about five and on Tuesdays and Thursdays I'd get up to Grosvenor Park. We would train between 5.30pm and 7pm and then have a bath or shower. The terraces would be packed when we played one of the big clubs, Glentoran or Linfield, and really it was up to you if you progressed or not. If you did well you would be noticed."

It is sadly ironic that the club known for its religious impartiality was forced out of the city by the violence that increasingly erupted around it at the start of the Troubles, culminating in Grosvenor Park being firebombed in 1971. The decision was taken not to rebuild and the middle of the ground became the site of a peace-line barricade, mocking the spirit of the happily divided team in which Dougan had played. In one of his books, he recalled the heartbreak of visiting the remains of his field of dreams during a trip to Belfast with the Northern Ireland team.

Today, there is nothing to suggest a stadium had ever occupied the site. A busy main road connecting the M1 with the West Link bisects the ground where the old Grosvenor Park stood, while the team has moved south-west out of the city and now carries the name of Lisburn Distillery.

The oldest of its country's professional clubs, the original Distillery had become established as a force in the early years of the 20th century, but their last Irish League title had been in 1906 and only one of their ten Irish Cup triumphs, in 1925, had been post-1910. By the time Dougan arrived at Grosvenor Park, Distillery held a far less exalted place in the country's football hierarchy than the two major clubs who had just cast him aside. But not even the one-two punch of rejection by the city's major teams, nor the realities of life that were being drummed into him by his family, could sway Derek from the growing conviction that his future lay in professional football.

Even at a young age, he knew best. His change of jobs from toy factory to shipyard was, in his eyes, only a case of killing time in a more profitable environment. "Derek always had confidence in his ability," says Sammy Chapman. "We spent a lot of time talking about the future on various trips we went on and Derek was very clear about wanting to go and play professional football in England."

Billy Bingham, who began his career at Glentoran before signing for Sunderland, remembers that as being the natural progression of any talented player to emerge from the city's streets and playgrounds, although not all looked as far ahead as Dougan.

"Playing football as a schoolboy was what you did just after war and if you were good enough you got picked to play for your country. Then you might have a choice of Linfield or Glentoran or, if you were a Catholic, Belfast Celtic. But things just tended to happen; you were just stepping up to the next rung of the ladder without really thinking where it could lead – even though you knew that scouts would be there watching your games. The Irish League was a decent standard and had a mixture of older players who had come back from England and new ones coming through, like myself and Jimmy McIlroy at Glentoran."

In 1953, the year that the 15-year-old Dougan joined Distillery, Blackpool were providing the most romantic of stories in English football by finally realising the revered Stanley Matthews's dream of winning an FA Cup Final. Meanwhile, it was one of Stan's old teammates, Scottish international Jimmy McIntosh, who had played in the forward lines of Blackpool, Preston and Everton, who had been appointed player-manager of Distillery at the start of the 1952/53 season.

By the time the Irish Cup first round game against Glenavon arrived on 5th February 1955, McIntosh had decided that the tall kid with the decent left foot who had been impressing in the reserves was worthy of a first-team debut. Dougan had first worn the shirt of the Lilywhites in the third team and recalled scoring a hat-trick in his first game against the local amateur team, Chimney Corner. Playing at either centre-forward or inside-left he'd advanced to the reserves, where he was used mostly at outside-left and was able to pocket 15 shillings a week in expenses.

He admitted that he was "flabbergasted" when McIntosh gave him the news that he was to line up at centre-forward against the Irish League leaders. Ralph the Rover, the identity-protected reporter on the *Belfast Telegraph*, was caught unawares as well, not mentioning the possible inclusion of Dougan in his brief preview of a game in which he expected to see a comfortable Glenavon win. But there for the first time was Dougan's name in the "Teams at a Glance" section on the back page.

Unfancied Distillery held their opponents to a 0-0 draw before being beaten comfortably in the replay in Lurgan four days later after conceding a hat-trick to Johnny Denver inside the first 20 minutes. The *Telegraph* noted that Preston North End were represented at the game to watch Dougan, but said they could have learned little as "seldom did he see the ball, let alone gain possession".

After a couple more games in the first team, Dougan was back in the reserves, establishing a pattern of intermittent appearances over the next year or so. Derek was, however, making an impact at the club, not least off the field. Team captain Frankie Watters recalls a young man who, while yet to find the militant voice that would characterise his later career, displayed an air of confidence that extended into his personal appearance. His interest in the cultural contributions of America now extended to the fashions that Bill Haley and his acolytes were sending across the Atlantic via the rock and roll songs youngsters like Dougan picked up on stations such as Radio Luxembourg.

"Straight away we knew he was a character," says Watters. "He was a bit of a Teddy Boy. He was a big tall chap and he came into the dressing room one day wearing a black suit with a jacket down to his knees. We had a left-back called Gerry Brennan who was only about five-foot-two and he asked to try it on. It was touching his ankles. But Derek was a likeable person. He had no airs and graces and he fitted in well with the great camaraderie we had in the team, even though he was younger than the rest. He had a good attitude. It was when he put on his jacket he became very different to the rest of us. He was the only Teddy Boy in the team – the rest of us were common or garden working men. But he took us for what we were and he was happy enough with what he was. He never had cross words with anyone."

Future teammate Ken Hamilton, a winger who would join from Coleraine, adds: "Derek did not show any of those leadership traits at that stage. He was just a young fellow, a fun guy with a big jovial personality who enjoyed the *craic* and the dressing room humour."

Derek's sister, Coreen, whom he would dispatch to buy the biscuits whenever he fancied one with a cup of tea, recalls: "Even then he had charisma. What it was I don't know. You look at your own brother and don't know what it was. He had charm, but I realised it is only words. Derek would tell you something and you would really take it in – but it could be a load of old nonsense."

Enjoying the experience of travelling outside Belfast regularly for the first time in his life, Dougan would have been even happier had he been given the chance to settle in his favoured positions of centre-half or left-half. Instead he was continually pushed into the forward line, where he believed he was more exposed to the gap in the quality of play between boys' club football and the senior game. Watters, however, saw the same potential that was clearly identified by McIntosh and, later, Maurice Tadman, who would take over as manager in the summer of 1955.

"I always felt his best position was as a striker, in the inside-forward or centre-forward position," he says. "His height was an advantage to him and our wingers were able to get balls over to him. He never discussed with me that he was not comfortable playing there. He just seemed happy to be playing and got on with it. He became a tremendous player in that period. He won balls in the air and he was reasonably quick. Once of his greatest assets to our team was the ability to flick on headers. We had a long throw expert in Billy Twyman, whose throws were as good as a corner kick. He was ahead of his time because those were the days of heavy leather balls with big, fat laces, but he would target Derek and pick him out at the corner of the six-yard box and they created a lot of our goals."

Malcolm Brodie, the long-time sports editor of the *Belfast Telegraph*, clearly recalls his early sightings of Dougan in a Distillery shirt: "He came in as a lanky youngster and he seemed to be all legs. But it was obvious that he had a certain predatory skill. You could see that he was going to be someone who was going to get goals and he had a confidence about him."

Dougan's promise earned him selection for the Northern Ireland squad for the Easter Fifa International Youth Tournament, albeit as a late replacement when Crusaders winger Sammy Wilson withdrew injured. It presented him with the opportunity to spend 10 days in Italy, where his clearest memory was becoming claustrophobic in the Leaning Tower of Pisa.

His working life was also already beginning to give him the feeling of being hemmed in. True to the family tradition established by father and grandfather – and mirrored in the majority of east Belfast families – Derek had entered the Harland and Wolff shipyard, where his first six months as an apprentice consisted of little more than sorting cables. He moved on to the maintenance shop and finally, after 18 months, was entrusted to get on board and actually start fitting some of those cables.

"I'll never forget the first time I went on the boats," he told BBC Northern Ireland in 2003. "My mum got me a big pair of boots because of the safety aspect, protecting my feet from breaking a toe. I was standing talking and this welder sneaked up behind me – and welded my boots to the ship."

For another year or so he would work on cruisers such as the *Iberia* and assist with repairs, although he said: "Going into the shipyard was the biggest incentive I've ever had in my entire life to get out of it."

Of more interest to him than his work was the socialisation with the various different professions that made up the community of the shipyard. "I didn't work there, I went there," he recalled. "I used to sneak off in the afternoons a go training at Grosvenor Park."

As well as amateur Northern Ireland internationals Bobby Braithwaite and Maurice Masters, the workforce consisted of plenty of football fans eager to spend their days in discussion of the weekend's games and happy to cover for their young, increasingly well-known colleague when he clocked off early.

Billy Bingham, who had also started out as an apprentice electrician at Harland and Wolff, explains: "Most of the people there were from east Belfast and they were pleased for you. In my case many of them would come and cheer me on because they were Glentoran fans but in general they were very supportive of the footballers – there was certainly no resentment."

Dougan, who had only entered the docks in order to please his mother, felt that the work was just something he was forced to do between his hours at Distillery. And even this, he believed, was only for a finite duration. His conviction that his long-term career prospects were in England were unaffected by the fact that the maximum wage in the Football League made many of his Irish contemporaries think twice about such a move.

"There were not a big number of players going over," says Watters. "I had an offer, but players in England then were getting only £17 a week. In Belfast, the average weekly wage for people like me was £10 and I was getting another £6 for playing for Distillery.

I had a family so there was no point in me going. But Derek was always looking for the big time. He wanted to go across and would be boasting that he'd play for his country and play in England."

Brodie adds: "When you spoke to him he had great visions of how he would progress in football and become a Northern Ireland star. He was an outstanding youngster and you could see he was a class above. Clubs relied heavily on fees from English clubs so you knew it would not be long before he was on his way."

Looking back in his first autobiography, *Attack!*, Dougan would write: "I knew I could have no future as a footballer in Ireland. For generations the Irish have known that to better themselves they have to go abroad. We have become conditioned to packing our bags and travelling."

A major event in Derek's life, the death of his mother from cancer in June 1955, strengthened his resolve to move away from his home city. "This severed much of my kinship with Belfast," he recalled. "She had been the centre of my life there and now she was gone. I felt no pull from the grass roots. I wanted to get away."

The typical pattern of life for a Belfast working man was not for him: the factory or shipyard, the pub, the betting shop, a fight on Friday night, the football on Saturday and church or mass on Sundays. Derek was even prepared to consider a life in America, where two cousins had settled, if English football was not to offer him his ticket.

His sister, Coreen, however, adds: "Everybody has wee dreams but not everyone gets to fulfil them. Derek was lucky; he had two good feet. Otherwise he could easily have ended up in the shipyards, which he hated."

At Grosvenor Park, the performance of McIntosh's team during the 1954/55 season had been typically underwhelming – an eighth-place finish in the 12-team Irish League and little impact in any of the various national and local cup competitions. But the move of McIntosh to manage Glentoran while Dougan was in Italy brought about a change that young Derek believed helped his prospects of making progress in his career.

He was buoyed by the instant rapport he developed with Tadman, the former Plymouth and Charlton forward who had arrived to take the role of player-manager. He felt comfortable enough to ask if he could play at half-back, where he remained convinced he could make more of his ability. Tadman, who would himself score 35 goals from centre-forward in the 1955/56 season, acquiesced, although Dougan was still frequently asked to help out by moving back up front, either to left winger or inside-left.

Teammates were split over the role in which Dougan could be most effective. While some, such as club captain Watters, felt he was a natural forward, others felt his home was further back. Hamilton insists: "I'll tell you where he was absolutely brilliant – centre-half. He had the height for it and he was a good ball player, not a typical defender who just thumped it up to the forwards. He could bring the ball down, beat a player and glide it through to the inside-left or wing-half. I remember a game against Glenavon, who had a centre-forward called Jimmy Jones, an infamous centre-forward in the Irish League, a real old bustling bull type of a guy. Derek never gave him a kick. I always said to him: 'You were world-class at centre-half.' Derek was young and he was in senior football in Ireland and it was obvious that it was all there. He could move quickly for a big fellow and had ball control. In those days centre-halves and full-backs didn't have that so they kept playing him as a forward. But Derek had the potential no matter where he played."

The highlight of Dougan's four years at Distillery arrived in 1956, when the club won the Irish Cup for the first time in 31 years. Little did he know that it would be 18 years before he won the only other major club honour of his career.

Having seen the introduction by Tadman of several younger players, Distillery's league form had once again been mixed, with the team destined for sixth place in the table. But the cup was a different story. Drawn at Coleraine in the first round, Ralph the Rover made a gloomy forecast of Distillery's chances, only for Tadman's two goals to help them to a 3-0 win. "This may be the turning point," said the player-manager, who then scored twice more in a 4-0 victory at Crusaders to earn a semi-final place.

It was a busy and exciting time for Dougan, with important cup games interspersed with appearances for the Irish youth team, playing both in the forward and half-back lines. Early in the year he had scored in an international trial match, but had also "failed hopelessly on three occasions", according to the *Telegraph*. After a 2-0 loss in Scotland it was noted that Dougan and his pal Sammy Chapman had been the only source of attacking inspiration for the Irish, but had lacked consistency.

The Irish Cup semi-final at Glentoran's Oval was played as Devon Loch, across the water in Liverpool, was stumbling on the finishing straight with the Grand National at his mercy. Against Cliftonville, there were no such pratfalls for Distillery, who maintained their record of not conceding in the competition and were sent through by the prolific Tadman.

Powerful Glentoran awaited them in the final but a good omen had been Distillery's 2-1 victory over them at Grosvenor Park in the annual Mercer Cup challenge match, where Dougan made a powerful run to open the scoring.

In the showpiece at Windsor Park, a crowd of 20,000 saw Glentoran take the lead shortly before half-time. It was no more than Ralph the Rover had expected, having as usual predicted defeat for Distillery, who were without the injured Tadman. After retaking the lead following a Distillery equaliser, Glentoran were denied victory with less than five minutes to play when Dougan, who had recovered from an eye injury to take his place at outside-left, crossed for Jack Curry to head an equaliser.

It had been an exciting game, played, as our friend Ralph imaginatively pointed out, in "a real cup-tie atmosphere". The replay was vastly different, a dull 1-1 draw that merited only four paragraphs on an inside page of the *Telegraph*. Glentoran's goal after 11 minutes was cancelled out four minutes later by Andy Tait in "one of the most dreary matches of the season".

On the morning of the second replay, the lead story in the *Telegraph* would have helped remind Dougan why he saw his future away from Belfast. Opportunities for the workforce were dwindling as the city's industries contracted, prompting the Northern Ireland Development Council to court American industry to relocate to the province. Meanwhile, on the back page, Ralph the Rover was throwing up his typewriter in exasperation and announcing: "I am not making any forecast."

In the Distillery team, the injured Jimmy McEvoy was replaced by Hamilton, whose insertion on the left wing saw Dougan move across to inside-left. Hamilton, who had begun the season playing in Coleraine's reserves, recalls: "It was my first game in the Irish Cup so people used to tell me I'd stolen a medal! I'd played well against Linfield in the league and that was the reason I was in. It was a lovely night but in the first half I got a stitch in my side and never thought I would get through the game. Fortunately I ran it off."

After Glentoran squandered an early chance, Distillery gained control of the game, with Dougan making the most of his ability in the air and the defence remaining mostly untroubled. Watters adds: "We were a reasonably good outfit in them days. We had one of the best defences around, especially when Derek played there, and on the wing Kenny Hamilton was very quick and could give defenders a two or three yards start. He was a strong string in our bow."

The only goal of the game arrived with 30 minutes left when, with Glentoran keeper McMahon off receiving treatment, Curry chased a pass from Jon Dugan and buried his shot. Dougan, at the age of 18, was an Irish Cup winner, yet from reading his own life stories it is hard to gauge how much the achievement meant to him. As noted previously, the accounts of his off-the-field battles weigh more heavily in his memoirs than glorification of his triumphs. Hamilton, however, has an enlightening tale that demonstrates the importance of that medal won in 1956.

During our conversation later in the year of Dougan's death, he reveals: "Last year Derek phoned me up. We had remained in contact on an off over the years through my work with Ulster Television and we used to meet at different sporting functions. He called me, quite upset, to say he had lost his Irish Cup medal. He had given it to his sister and her house had been burgled and the medal was gone. He said: 'Would you lend me yours and I will get the Irish FA to let me make a new one.' I said that I would and I met him and Merlyn a few weeks later in Belfast close to Lunns, a very old and established jeweller. We went in there and they sorted it out for us. It is a precious medal. You could play for many years and never win an Irish Cup medal, so that was why he wanted to have it. It meant that much to him."

In the same year that he acquired his replacement medal, Dougan looked back at his Distillery career and said: "We were very lucky we were managed by Maurice Tadman. It wasn't until later on I realised I had such a wonderful bloke who was an advert for what a manager should be – honest, direct, speaking like a man to his players."

Dougan's skill and versatility continued to earn him honours from Northern Ireland's national selectors, although his first amateur international appearance was the result of injury to another youngster, Roy Gough of Crusaders. He took his place for the game against England at Bromley and, despite being part of a 5-2 defeat, was reported to have impressed the watching manager of Portsmouth, Eddie Lever. Four months later he was selected for the game against Wales at Ebbw Vale, where Phil Woosnam, a future professional teammate, scored in the home team's 3-1 win. The third goal stemmed from Dougan being robbed when in a good position for the Irish.

Having delayed signing him as a professional so that he could play in the game, Distillery offered Dougan his first contract, meaning he was adding another £6 to his Harland and Wolff pay packet instead of the 25 shillings per week expenses he took home as an amateur. "I was very grateful to Distillery," Dougan said. "They gave me many opportunities, to travel all round Northern Ireland… to see something of the world and to learn how I could use my skills to belong to that world."

However, as for improving those skills, Dougan felt that he was still largely on his own – although his first experiences of English football would make him appreciate the Distillery set-up more than he did while he was there. "I never had an individual coaching session in my life. I have always been self-taught and had more or less mimicked other footballers since I was ten years of age. I also developed a lot of probably bad habits which I found it hard to get rid of even under the more or less disciplined training we had when Mr Tadman came."

Dougan's insight into the demands that would be placed upon him in English football gained extra clarity when Distillery travelled to London to play a friendly at West Ham, where he was struck by the greater speed at which the game took place.

Derek's last full season at Distillery, 1956/57, was made memorable by taking the captaincy for a match against Hibernian in which the Irish team's line-up was strengthened by guest players from Linfield and Ards, adding to the pride Dougan felt in his appointment.

Distillery won 2-1 and his strong performance at centre-half prompted rumours of interest from Rangers and Celtic, as well as Hibernian themselves. In addition, Wolves and Blackburn had now been added to the English clubs said to be monitoring his progress.

Distillery finished runners-up in three competitions. They began the season by finishing second behind Linfield in the Ulster Cup, played under a league format; lost a play-off against Glentoran for the City Cup; and were beaten by the Glens in a replayed final of the County Antrim Shield. They did beat Glentoran after another replay to retain the Mercer Cup and repeated their sixth-placed Irish League finish of the previous season.

Spending the season in his preferred location in the half-back line, Dougan scored 11 goals and was sent for a trial at Preston North End, although his only reason for accepting the invitation was because he enjoyed the travel and the opportunity to escape Belfast for a few days. Despite playing in a couple of trial games, he had no intention of joining the club. He was no more enthusiastic when he journeyed to Bury to turn out for their reserve team.

Clearly, however, the time was fast approaching when Dougan would be leaving his home town for good. He little thought it would occur at the start of the 1957/58 season when, because of injuries, he again found himself pushed up front for the opening Ulster Cup game against Linfield, player-managed by the Newcastle legend Jackie Milburn. He argued against Tadman's selection but was assured it was only for two games. "I went along with this because I respected [Tadman] very much, but at the time I did have my say, so we knew where we both stood."

§

Now fate began to move quickly. Dougan would never make his return to the defence.

A scout from Portsmouth, former manager Jack Tinn, saw the

1-1 draw against Linfield and current boss Lever and chief scout Bob Jackson arrived for the next game against Bangor, in which Dougan felt he gave a sub-standard performance. Also in attendance was Leeds manager Raich Carter, the former England international, who was said to be ready to offer £4,000 for Dougan's signature.

Although becoming desperate to move to England, Dougan refused to get his hopes up and knew that the Irish newspapers were littered with stories of transfers to England that never happened. Kenny Hamilton confirms: "I was to be transferred to Fulham, Luton and Falkirk at different stages. None of them materialised."

When Carter made his official approach, Distillery, who began the season with an £8,000 overdraft, were keen to realise their most valuable asset, while Leeds were prepared to promise a place in the first team for their opening Second Division game of the season at Blackpool the following Saturday. Dougan, despite his impatience for a deal, felt he was being rushed into a decision, especially when Leeds made it clear that the nature of their offer was "now or never".

Lever stayed on for the next game, against Ards on their windswept Castlereagh Park ground in Newtownards, and saw the object of his affection score from 20 yards in a 3-0 win. Dougan got out of the post-match bath and was put in a taxi with club secretary Fred Duke for the ride back to Belfast. Along the way, they discussed a possible transfer to Portsmouth, a First Division team trying to regain the heights of their consecutive league championship victories in 1949 and 1950. The two clubs had agreed a £4,000 fee and Dougan felt no need to consult his father before ending his Distillery career after 76 games and 17 goals. "I was so excited I would have agreed to anything," he said.

§

Hamilton remembers hearing of Dougan's transfer the next day. "On that Sunday morning I went back to the club because you went in if you had an injury. Derek always came to the ground on Sunday morning and he was just sitting there, explaining that he had just been transferred to Portsmouth. He said to me: 'I hope that you will not be long here either.' He'd always had a desire that he would get away."

Frankie Watters, too, had known it was only a matter of time before Dougan left them behind. "You could see Derek was destined to make it. He was good on the ball and his anticipation was excellent. I always judge players by their anticipation and he could tell where ball was going to be when he didn't have it. I was pleased for Derek when he made himself into a star. It was something you saw in him all along, that attitude to get on."

Eddie Lever had witnessed the same thing when he tried to encourage Dougan by suggesting that he could continue his apprenticeship at Portsmouth's own shipyards over the next two years. But it was the last thing Derek was interested in and he told his new manager: "I am going to be a full-time professional footballer or nothing at all."

Lever had made the proposal with the suggestion that "Johnny Phillips will look after you". Phillips, a wing-half at the club, had been two years into his electrician's apprenticeship at Portsmouth docks when he signed for his local club as a part-time professional in 1955. He was making strides in the first team despite the demands of his day job.

"I was working full-time in the dockyard, a 44-hour week, and then training on Tuesday and Thursday nights," he explains. "At that time football was a risky business. If you broke your leg it could be the end of your career, so if you didn't have another trade you were a bit stuck. Many clubs encouraged their young players to have other skills, but, looking back, for me it would have been better if I had been playing football full-time at that stage of my career. Derek knew that and you could understand why he wanted only to play football."

Dougan's new manager left him with an instruction to report to Fratton Park the following Thursday once he had tied up his affairs at home. That involved going to Harland and Wolff on the Monday to hand in his notice – which came as no surprise to those who had been following events in the newspapers – and selling the Ford Prefect he had bought six months earlier. Then it was down to the ferry company to buy a one-way ticket.

For most of the people of Belfast, content to restrict their boundaries and ambitions, the Lough was an important bearer of trade and commerce into the city. For Derek Dougan, his sights set on grander horizons, it was his exit route. As the ferry carried him through the waters that helped define his home city, he looked to his right at the departing vision of the shipyards and gave thanks for the ability that was transporting him away. He had no regrets, no misgivings and no doubts. In comparison to the environment in which he had grown, everything ahead of him seemed like plain sailing. He never once imagined the stormy seas for which he was headed.

Chapter 4

POMPEY CRIMES

Sammy Chapman remembers the letter clearly. He thought nothing much of it when he saw that it was from his employers, Portsmouth Football Club. In the days before instant communication teams routinely corresponded with their players via mail, especially during the summer. He expected to find nothing more than the usual information relating to arrangements for the upcoming season. It was with some shock that he discovered the letter was from the new team manager, Freddie Cox, a man he had never met, and that its contents were directed specifically at him and Derek Dougan.

Chapman, who joined Dougan at Portsmouth shortly after his schoolboy opponent's own arrival at the club, has been introduced to me by another who found his way from Belfast to Fratton Park, goalkeeper Norman Uprichard. ("Remind Sammy he owes me a phone call," Uprichard has instructed in passing along his former teammate's phone number. "And if he wants to reverse the charges, that's fine. He can buy me a beer instead.")

Chapman is relating the story of what Dougan would describe as "the first time I officially rebelled". He explains: "This was a big problem for Derek and me. We had been back in Ireland during the summer [of 1958] and decided to get a flat between us when we got back to Portsmouth. Maybe it was a bit early for that kind of thing, but we had done it. I don't know how Freddie Cox heard about it, but he said in the letter that we had got to get back to digs."

The placement of young players in "digs" was standard procedure among professional football clubs. It usually meant two or three boys living with a landlady or family eager to supplement their weekly income by acting as providers and, to a certain extent, policemen.

Clubs felt that placement within a home environment meant their talented youngsters were less likely to be sampling the distracting delights of the local nightlife, as well as being fed properly morning and night. Parents, meanwhile, were more willing to release their offspring into the clutches of football clubs if they knew that their welfare was being provided for by a matronly landlady. The players received affordable lodgings and a couple of square meals a day, so the system worked well for all concerned – until someone like Dougan chose to challenge it.

He had been as disturbed as Chapman to receive his missive from the manager, who expressed his disappointment that his player had chosen to move from digs at Prince Albert Road – where he had lived during his first season with the club – without gaining Portsmouth's permission. Dougan went to the club the next day to see Cox, the former Tottenham and Arsenal winger who had moved along the coast from a managerial position with Bournemouth. Cox commented on the "audacity" of the proposed domestic arrangements, to which Dougan replied by pointing out that as he was paying for his own accommodation surely he could live where he liked. He argued that the home he had been living in did not offer a desirable environment.

"I was old enough and responsible enough to find my own lodgings and I resented the club's interference with my liberty," he later wrote. He offered the same argument to one of the club's directors, telling him: "All right. If you pay for my digs I will go and live where you want me to live."

Unsurprisingly, Dougan's suggestion was not acted upon. Some sort of compromise was reached when the players agreed to move back into digs, but insisted on finding their own rather than go where the club was suggesting. Chapman continues: "That caused us a problem because the Portsmouth area was a big seaside place and it was difficult to find digs at that stage. We ended up finding somewhere in Samuel Road but Derek didn't like the way things had been handled and he had kicked off on the wrong foot with the new manager."

Another teammate, John Phillips, adds: "Derek had got a flat on the seafront somewhere and that didn't go down well. The rules of the club were that, after Tuesday and until Saturday night after the game, you had to be in by 10.30pm. But Derek was a single man and wanted to be out and about. The club told him he couldn't do that."

Rather than meekly going along with the club's demands, like most players of his limited experience would have done in order to remain in management's good books, Dougan, typically, had fought his corner – and now felt that the new manager had him marked him down as a trouble-maker. His stance at least indicated the self-confidence he felt after his relatively recent promotion to the ranks of full-time professional footballer.

Chapman, who had taken that step himself when he joined Mansfield Town in 1956, had seen evidence of that as soon as he signed for Portsmouth early in 1958. Dougan seemed born to life in the First Division. "Obviously he had numerous opportunities, but I think Distillery guided him right and put him to the right club," Chapman recalls. "Portsmouth were a big club but it didn't take anything for him to adapt to it. He had the physical attributes and he was never overawed – the complete opposite, in fact. He had confidence in his ability, the kind of ability that can't be coached into people."

It was Dougan's presence at Portsmouth that had helped tempt Chapman to the south coast. "I had several offers but I picked Portsmouth because they were a good club and Derek talked well of the place."

As Dougan came to terms with a town where "there are many ways of life in the same community, and where you can really see how other people live – in Belfast this was never encouraged", he had started to enjoy the lifestyle of his new home, especially its proximity to the beach town of Southsea.

In that first season he lodged with Scotsman Alex Stenhouse and

Irishman Jimmy Clugston, became good friends with Uprichard and welcomed the arrival of Chapman to the Celtic clan. "The weather was good and it was a seaside town with nice girls," says Chapman. "We were young and Derek was a big talent in Portsmouth. He took the place by storm. He was a good-looking lad, tall with a bit of the Cary Grant look, and was a very good dresser at the time. He had stitched collars, pressed and studded, and wanted to look the part."

§

Uprichard remembers his teammate "in his sports car, driving along Southsea front with his scarf flying in the wind". Dougan's automobile was a Mk I Ford Consul, the convertible predecessor to the iconic Cortina. "I used to think his head was as big as the Isle of Wight," Uprichard adds.

Phillips has similar memories: "I can see him and Alex Stenhouse driving around in that open-top Consul. He was a bit flash, had that style, and was a man about town. He liked to go to the clubs in Portsmouth. I had a flat right behind the Savoy Ballroom and Derek, and a lot of us, liked to go there quite a bit." According to Ray Crawford, another young Portsmouth striker: "Derek was very charismatic, very likeable and a bit of a Jack the lad. He could have had any girl that he wanted."

Dougan's brash self-assuredness had led him not only to the reasonable belief that he was big enough to decide for himself where he should live, but also into an earlier disillusioning experience. He had been somewhat dismayed to discover that professional players in England were very different to those part-timers with whom he had shared dressing rooms back home in Belfast. "When I was with Distillery we always had team talks and inquests and everyone spoke their mind," he said.

This was not the case at Portsmouth or, in truth, at many league clubs in the late 1950s, a time when players' careers were in the vise grip of the clubs to an unfair degree. Not only were wages restricted to maximum levels but feudal contracts that tied players to their teams meant that anyone falling out with a manager or board could be shipped off or, worse, left to rot in the reserves at the whim of his bosses, with no recourse to any form of industrial justice.

What Dougan, as a newcomer to his profession, without family or financial responsibilities, had failed to anticipate and, at the time, appreciate was the environment of fear that pervaded the dressing room. He hung his clothes among men who were struggling to pay their mortgages almost as much as any other working man of the time.[2] They had only a finite professional life ahead of them and were petrified of finding themselves cast aside. As he matured into a spokesman for his peers, it would be a memory that helped drive him through various negotiation sessions with those running the game.

Crawford explains: "Players had no rights at all in those days. You were governed by the clubs in all aspects of your life. They would come round to your house at night and if you weren't in you were fined. You even had to get their permission to have a car because they were considered dangerous. I remember going to Ipswich and Alf Ramsey had just given all the players permission to have a car. Under [predecessor] Scott Duncan only two or three players had been allowed to own one."

Bill Albury, a wing-half at Portsmouth at that time, recalls: "Most of us couldn't afford a car anyway. I was on about £16 a week, with £2 less in the summer. Come Christmas, if you weren't in the first team or established in the reserves you were worried you would be on your bike and not signed on for the next season. I remember once thinking I had done quite well during the season so I went to see if I could get a £1 rise. I was offered the same terms – but you took it and cleared off. You were made to feel it was a privilege to be able to play football as a living instead of being a welder or bricklayer. That is how it was and why many players, like me and Johnny Phillips, took apprenticeships at the shipyards so you had something to fall back on."

The greatest disappointment to Dougan as Portsmouth

---

2   The average weekly wage in Britain in 1957 was £10, while only the minority of footballers earned the profession's maximum of £17, which was reduced to £14 during the summer months. By way of contrast with another branch of the British entertainment industry, comedian Tommy Cooper was earning £350 for a week's residence in the West End of London.

blundered along to 20th position in the First Division in his first season with the club, avoiding relegation by one place, was Pompey legend Jimmy Dickinson – team captain, capped 48 times by his country and on his way to playing a then-league record 764 games for his club. When a team meeting was called to discuss another unsatisfactory performance, Dougan could not understand why he appeared to be the only one prepared to speak his mind.

"Our skipper was a well-known figure in the game and as a player I respected him; but I had less respect for him as a man," he would record. "Because of a lack of conviction all his playing experience went for nothing because he never voiced an opinion at the right time."

Albury describes Dickinson as being "laid back", justifying his nickname of "Gentleman Jim". He adds: "He was not a dominating personality. He was calm and would go with the flow. He was a lovely man and wasn't getting on his pedestal on behalf of the other players." All of which infuriated Dougan, who expected the club captain to take a greater role as a spokesman for the team – a shop steward, if you like.

Dougan noticed that his Portsmouth teammates would look uncomfortably at the floor when a member of the management asked what had gone wrong on the field. The assumption was that all such questions were rhetorical, with players unqualified to offer any tactical opinions. "It was natural for me to speak up," he said. "What I said may not have been helpful but I put in my two cents worth. The looks of astonishment from the other players made me feel I had spoken out of turn."

He felt he was considered an "Irish upstart", although his fellow-countryman Uprichard can at least understand why some of his new colleagues would have held such a view. "Derek was a good player; there was no getting away from that. But he was so flamboyant. 'I am The Doog' he would say. I think he could have been better if he'd toned it down a bit."

It is hardly surprising, then, that Dougan would note that "some of the senior professionals didn't seem all that friendly". Uprichard, however, was his "safety valve". Married to an Irish girl and with his mother living with them, his home offered Dougan a little piece of Ireland. Dougan wrote of Uprichard: "He was one of nature's noblemen, a gentle anarchist with a great sense of the ridiculous and a capacity for never being riled by adversity. He liked to deflate the hierarchy and he was no respecter of important persons... But for him the frustrations at Fratton Park would have overwhelmed me."

The former Northern Ireland keeper says: "We got on well together all right. I lived right beside the ground and Derek would pop in most days and me and Doog and Sammy would have a cup of tea. We were all mates and I found a good bit of time to get out myself and we would go chasing, as it were."

Dougan could hardly claim to have got off to an auspicious start with his new club. On his first full day at Portsmouth, the Friday after his journey from Belfast, he had celebrated his new status as a full-time professional footballer with a cooked breakfast before launching himself with gusto into training, determined to impact immediately upon his colleagues. Before long he was fighting the involuntary tightening of his stomach muscles and battling against the irresistibly violent arching of his back as his eggs and bacon lurched into a half-digested slop in front of him. He had thrown up in front of his new teammates.

He claimed never to have eaten a big meal before training again, although fellow-forward Crawford remembers: "Derek used to throw up quite regularly. He wasn't the best of trainers, nor were a lot of the great footballers of the past. He didn't like to run around a lot and he sometimes used to eat too much at breakfast. I was living at home so would just have cornflakes or toast, but Derek had a lovely landlady who thought the world of him and used to look after him."

Dougan would find that training at Portsmouth failed to feed his appetite for learning his craft. In fact, his dissatisfaction with the professional side of Portsmouth juxtaposed directly with his increasing enjoyment of life off the field. "I was soon disillusioned by the training for the methods were far behind those that I had known at Grosvenor Park," he commented.

This was not an untypical situation in English football. The 6-3 victory of the Hungarians at Wembley in 1953 – and the 7-1 thrashing of England in Budapest that followed – was still only slowly permeating the self-satisfied mood of a footballing nation that had lived for so long off the fact that it had given the game to the world.

Forward-thinking coaches such as Arthur Rowe, Alan Brown and England manager Walter Winterbottom, who were attempting to create a new and challenging environment on courses at the FA's training centre at Lilleshall, and players such as the Malcolm Allison-led "West Ham Academy", who would rather dissect the game in the local café than spend the afternoon in the snooker hall, were still in the minority. At too many clubs training consisted of little that could be termed "coaching". Running round the pitch and a cursory game of five-a-side comprised the daily routine at many leading teams.

Of course not everyone shared Dougan's opinion on such new-fangled ideas. The alternative view is offered by Uprichard: "I was never one for tactics and never had much time for coaching – either you can play or you can't. We had a good team, one of the best teams in England, including the half-back line of Jimmy Scoular, Jack Froggatt and Jimmy Dickinson. We didn't need formations; we just went out and played. The only things we worked out were set pieces." Results that season might not exactly bear out Uprichard's memory, but it probably represents the majority view in the dressing room at the time.

Dougan's first Portsmouth performance was in a reserve game against Leyton Orient as an inside-forward, the position in which manager Eddie Lever had seen him play in Ireland. "Cheers for Dougan's neat work," was the headline in the *Portsmouth Evening News*, praising the way he linked with his fellow forwards, although a more considered view a couple of days later criticised his poor tackling. It was not until a few weeks later that he headed his first goal in a Portsmouth shirt against Brentford's reserves, by which time the local reporter was saying that he had not yet "developed the speed necessary for English football".

Injuries at the club meant that there was a need for a centre-forward and Dougan's fortunes began looking up when he was given the opportunity to audition for that position in the second team. Crawford, who would go on to play for England while at Ipswich, explains, however, that in the meantime Dougan had attempted to revert to his favoured Distillery position in the half-back line.

"I was in the team and Derek had not got in yet. We were talking in the corridor one day and he said he was going to see Eddie Lever to ask if he could play centre-half because he didn't think he would get in the first team at centre-forward. He played there in the reserves and after about ten or 15 minutes they whisked him back up front. He was a ball-playing centre-half and Portsmouth had no need for that – and he had given away a penalty."

After some impressive reserve team performances in the number nine shirt, he was selected for the first team in a Southern Floodlight Cup game against Charlton, with Lever explaining: "The fact is that we have to experiment." It proved a successful exercise, a 4-1 win earning Dougan the opportunity to make his Football League debut at Old Trafford, the home of reigning champions Manchester United. "They are worth another run," said Lever of his forward line in a newspaper report that praised Dougan for his linking play but noted his missed chances.

United's "Busby Babes" could hardly have offered a more testing introduction to the First Division, even with England's game against Wales on the same day robbing them of the services of full-back Roger Byrne, centre-forward Tommy Taylor and midfield prodigy Duncan Edwards. Yet it took only five minutes for Dougan to make his mark, heading the ball back for Jackie Henderson to score. The goal triggered a famous Portsmouth victory, with their new centre-forward later contributing to the third goal in a 3-0 win.

Dougan's positional play, passing and unselfish work on behalf of his fellow forwards was highlighted by the *Portsmouth Evening News's* reporter "Nimrod", who might have been speaking for Dougan's entire career to come when he wrote: "Fratton Park fans must not expect an orthodox centre-forward game from the 19-year-old Irishman."

More rave reviews followed a home win against Leicester seven days later, after which Lever attributed Dougan's adjustment to the rigours of the First Division – faster than he had expected – to his decision to pursue football full-time rather than taking the option of training part-time and pursuing the completion of his electrical apprenticeship.

Dougan's characteristic self-confidence, however, had led him to believe that he would have taken English football by storm even more easily and he confessed to finding the games more physically arduous than he had anticipated. He felt that Irish players had a greater desire to be skilled ball players, especially those who made it across the water, and noted that Irish football did not have as many defenders who styled themselves as "hard men" as the Football League.

"I was not at all happy that I was not able to score," Dougan recalled of his first three weeks in the first team. "I wasn't, I think, playing badly and the way I managed against the players of great experience sometimes surprised me. But the fact was that I was there to get the goals that were needed."

Ironically, the game that provided the turning point was the visit of Wolverhampton Wanderers, the club that was to feature in so many milestones in Dougan's career, even before he signed for them. Facing him in the old gold number five shirt would be England's Billy Wright. "He was immortal even then and I was pretty overwhelmed at the prospect," said Dougan.

Dougan's hope was that his extra height and speed could get the better of Wright's experience and skill on the ground. If there was one single moment that announced to the nation Dougan's arrival in English football it came in the second half, with Portsmouth trailing by one goal. He drifted to the right in the six-yard box and spun round Wright with a piece of pure cheek, only to see his shot saved by Wolves keeper Noel Dwyer.

Dougan later described it as "the most wonderful thing I had experienced up until then in English football", adding: "How I swivelled past Billy Wright was one of those things that comes by pure instinct." Dougan described the moment as leading to his first Portsmouth goal, although he appears over time to have mistakenly amalgamated the two moments. The goal came after 54 minutes when he fired the ball past Dwyer after Phil Gunter helped on a clearance.

The local paper, reporting on the 1-1 draw, said of Dougan that "often his wiles were too much for Wright", while teammate John Phillips recalls: "The game I always remember is when Derek did a nutmeg on Billy Wright. Billy went into a tackle and Derek slipped the ball through his legs and went round him. The crowd loved it. Crowds everywhere respond to clever players like that. Derek loved it as well." Crawford was sitting in the stands that day and remembers Dougan "giving Billy a right going over – he tore him to pieces".

Even Wright had to praise Dougan, who said: "Something happened to me. It got rid of a few inhibitions." But such a freedom of spirit was not to everyone's liking. His reaction to scoring a goal, to raise both arms to the crowd, was considered "non-English" and showy at a time when a manly handshake and a brisk jog back to the halfway line was the usual practice.

Daily Mail journalist Jack Wood took him to task for his "arms akimbo display of histrionics", although Lever defended him by describing it as a natural show of emotion by a happy young man. Wood, incidentally, was the first writer to coin the nickname Doog. "Over the weekend I read these reports and I had an impressions that if a star had not been born, at least a personality had emerged," Dougan recalled.

He had quickly come to enjoy the way that Fratton Park responded to his style of showmanship and was unperturbed by journalists who responded by telling him to play it straight. Dougan's view throughout his career was that a "few clownish antics" were justifiable if performances were not compromised.

During my discussion with Sammy Chapman he explains that he saw enough promise in his colleague's early Portsmouth appearances to suggest that his subsequent career could have contained even more success and glory had a few different corners been turned along the way. I concede that, having only seen Dougan in the latter stages of his career – when the stifling defences of the late 1960s and early 70s were attempting to strangle sophisticated forward play – he had come across more as a blunt, awkward and combative leader of the line than as a possessor of any notable grace.

Chapman believes that was a product of the prevailing on-field environment. "Derek always had a nice touch on the ball and could see things in the game," he argues. "He was a beautiful athlete.

Running wasn't a problem to him, which didn't always come across late in his career. He was very quick off the mark and he could sustain it. He could not only get away from somebody, he could keep away. I always felt he was going to be as good as he wanted to be. He made silly mistakes along the way, like we have all done. It would be easy to say he should have been a better player in the end and probably should have made more of what he was given. When he was coming to the end of his career at Wolves people were inclined to forget the tremendous start he had at Portsmouth."

Crawford confirms: "He had great touch and was very mobile. They rave now about Cristiano Ronaldo doing all these step-overs, but Doog was going them back in 1957. He was not an out-and-out goalscorer, but was a good link-up man and a very clever footballer."

One teammate, though, remembers Dougan as having some way to go before he could consider himself the finished article. Full-back Tommy McGhee says: "He was only a young lad when he came to us. He was quite a useful player but for a tall boy I thought at that stage he was not very good in the air. He improved out of all recognition later and he proved me wrong."

By the time the season ended, Dougan had done enough, with eight goals in 26 games, to put himself in contention for a place in the Northern Ireland squad for the 1958 World Cup finals in Sweden. He also qualified for a meeting in the manager's office, a visit he made with some trepidation.

On joining Portsmouth, he had signed a contract that earned him £13 a week, well below the £17 maximum of the time – a sum he noted, with resentment, was earned by several reserve players while he performed for the first team for £4 less. By the time he had paid for accommodation and lunch every day, it left him with little for the luxuries of life, such as good clothes and pretty girls.

Unsure of what to expect when summoned to his meeting with Eddie Lever, he was relieved to hear it was for the purpose of giving him a rise, but dismayed it was only an additional £2 a week. The explanation was Dougan's age, an argument he countered by stressing his belief that he was the team's best player, responsible for much of the current interest being shown in the team by fans and media. As years went by Dougan would come to look back on this particular negotiation with more affection. It was the only time in his career he was given a pay rise without having to ask for it.

He'd scarcely had the chance to figure out how many new items of clothing he could buy with his windfall, however, when Lever called the players to a meeting to inform them he had been relieved of his duties. Despite their difference of opinion over the appropriate compensation for a young First Division centre-forward, Dougan was sorry to see him depart. "It was his straight-talking, his fair dealing and integrity that I admired. He respected other people's views and did not try to subvert them to his own," he wrote in *Attack!*

After making his international debut in the opening game of Northern Ireland's World Cup campaign and failing to get another game in the tournament (discussed in detail in Chapter 6), Dougan made a return trip to Belfast. Intending to stay for almost two months until reporting back for pre-season training, he stuck it out for less than three weeks. He had been away less than year, but already Belfast no longer felt like home.

Chapman reveals: "He and I had sent home a great big packing box and then we followed on. But neither of us were romantic Irishman, we left that to John Wayne and people like that. Belfast did not have much of an attraction for Derek – it was just a family thing really. His sister, Pearl, was looking after them so Derek felt obligated to do his part and go and visit. We left as early as we could and went back to Portsmouth."

Derek was quickly loosening his domestic ties. Coreen, the sibling to whom he remained closest in later years, is accepting of the fact that her brother was simply growing up and moving into an environment that did not encourage familial closeness.

"It wasn't like today when the clubs look after the young players. He was more or less on his own. Nowadays clubs look after the parents and the young players often earn enough to have their family around them. It must have been difficult for him; he just had to survive. He was delighted to get to England and get into full-time football and the only time I saw him was when he came back on international duty. If he was doing his life again I think he would make sure his family would be a bigger part of it once he went to England. Also, when your mother goes it is the heart of the family, and maybe if she had lived it would have been different. But we as a family were very proud of him so it didn't matter. Everybody has their own life."

Derek, it must be stated, did not simply forget his family. Coreen explains: "He actually paid the deposit so that we could afford to move from Avon Street into Orangefields, which was a little semi with garden front and back – a little more up-market. If you were over a certain age you couldn't get a mortgage so he and my daddy's names were on the deeds. And he always sent letters and cards on birthdays and Christmas. On your birthday it was great seeing this letter coming up the street for you because you knew it was going to have money in it. He was very kind."

Back in Portsmouth for the 1958/59 season, Dougan and Chapman had those first dealings with new manager Freddie Cox over the matter of their living arrangements. Dougan's relationship with his boss was never to get any better and he even asserted: "There was no doubt that the trainers and coaches who stayed on at Portsmouth when Eddie Lever went gave the new manager a dossier on each player. And there is no doubt that Freddie Cox was well aware of my character and reputation."

Dougan also believed that certain players would pass on information about their teammates to the coaching staff, letting them know who was saying what in the dressing room. If it all hints at a touch of paranoia, then Dougan is at least supported in part by other players' recollections of the new regime.

Uprichard says: "Eddie Lever was a brilliant fellow but too nice to be a good football manager. He was a gentleman. I don't think he would last two minutes today, but he was a smashing fellow. Freddie Cox, on the other hand, was a dictator. It didn't go down well, whether it was me or Doog or a hell of a lot of the other lads. I remember playing in the reserves at Nottingham Forest one day and there were four internationals in the team, me and Doog and Tommy Casey and Alex Wilson of Scotland. Meanwhile, the first team were bottom of the First Division. I had nothing against Freddie personally and I had been with him at Arsenal, but he bombarded us, left, right and centre."

According to Chapman, Cox suffered because "the club was in transition". He points out: "A lot of the players were getting older and there were just a few remains left of the old, successful Pompey side. Jimmy Dickinson went to centre-back and the nucleus of the side had gone. Freddie wanted to do things his own way and he believed in the old ethic that you have got to work your socks off at all times, which the English love. Yes, you have to work, but you must have ability. Derek was real quality and, like all people with great natural talent, found it easy. Maybe Freddie thought he was not putting it all in at times, which was completely wrong."

Dougan found out that Cox's stance over his accommodation was symptomatic of the manager's need to lay down myriad regulations, which he helped to enforce by sending one of the trainers to players' digs on Friday evenings to check that they were at home behaving themselves.

One of the more bizarre rules was the "no driving to training" edict, inspired by the nonsensical notion that struggling to work on foot would produce greater levels of fitness. Dougan got round that one by parking his car in a nearby street and walking the final 200 yards. His take on the new wave of law-making was: "It had nothing to do with discipline. This was disciplinarianism. Players need to discipline themselves."

Albury's memory of rules such as "no dancing after Mondays and no long hair" were examples of what Dougan felt were implications that players were incapable of achieving acceptable levels of behaviour through their own professionalism. He adopted the same attitude when it came to Cox's insistence that all players participated in increased weight training.

"I had no desire to be another Charles Atlas," he commented, feeling that he knew his body well enough to judge what would be beneficial for his game. He believed the reason that he sometimes ran out of stamina late in games – remarked upon by journalists – was because he had left much of his energy on the training ground or in the weights room.

And where he had felt the freedom to discuss ideas freely with Lever, the unwillingness of Cox to welcome any exchange of opinions left him feeling "claustrophobic" and feeling that "a noose was being put around my neck".

In his book, *Doog*, he described his relationship with Cox as "one of mutual antipathy" and continued: "There was no possible way I could get on with Freddie Cox. We were worlds apart and as long as I stayed there was bound to be a collision. Eddie Lever had respected my views and judgements. He gave me faith in myself as a player. All he lacked as a manager was a hard-driving instinct and some luck, which is essential in a competitive game. [Under Cox] small matters became crises. Niggling worries were magnified and I thought there was no longer a sense of proportion at the club. I was on edge and tended to over-react, which probably convinced the manager that I had to be kept in check."

John Phillips' claims that "not many people got on with Freddie Cox" and that he created a queue of players wishing to get away from Fratton Park. "You could appreciate a manager being a hard taskmaster if you have respect for him, but Freddie didn't know how to handle professional footballers. He was OK with youth players but not with a player like Derek, who was too boisterous for him and liked to have his own way."

Phillips and Crawford both recount a speech by Cox which, in the league table of motivational messages, ranks in the same division as Brian Clough's infamous comment to the Leeds players in 1974 that they should throw away the medals won under Don Revie because they had got them by "cheating".

Cox stated at a team meeting: "I am out to prove to you that Third Division players possess the same skill as First Division players." Quite what Cox was hoping to achieve by his assertion is impossible to fathom, but he succeeded in insulting a group of players who had spent their entire careers striving to reach the most elevated level in English football. "It was utter nonsense," says Phillips, noting that eventually Cox would succeed only in taking his First Division team to the brink of relegation to the Third Division.

Albury claims that Cox was "two-faced" and would play individuals off against each other. "He'd tell me he reckoned I was the best wing-half in the club. Then he'd say to our right-back: 'That guy in front of you is letting you down.' It wasn't a good place to be."

Tommy McGhee says that "you couldn't speak to the man" and still bristles when he relates an incident before an FA Cup game at Burnley: "We went away to Brighton before travelling up there. On the Thursday night someone asked me if Freddie had said anything to me about Saturday as I was not in the side for Saturday. I phoned home and found it was in the papers. We went to the pictures that night and when we got back Freddie said it was coffee and bed, but I asked him for a word and said: 'Am I going to Burnley?' He said I was so I asked: 'What, as 12th man?' He said he hadn't decided yet. 'Don't lie to me,' I said. 'It's in the papers. You are not man enough to tell me.' Unfortunately, that was the end of me at Portsmouth. But he was the start of the ruination of Portsmouth."

Another of Cox's annoying traits was to keep the players hanging around for the posting of the team sheets. Phillips says: "On Friday morning, training was just a matter of a few sprints and exercises because we had already done most of our training for Saturday earlier in the week. It was a running down day. We would be out of the bath and dressed by 11.30am but by one o'clock we would still be waiting for the team sheets for the next day to go up. It was utterly ridiculous. Freddie Cox lost respect and lost the players very quickly."

Having reported for pre-season training in a less than positive frame of mind, Dougan had found himself and his teammates perfecting a new tactical approach. Cox, who Dougan said had falsely been labelled as a tracksuit manager by the press, then scrapped the system three days before the first game of the season, a 2-1 home defeat to West Ham.

Then came an injury that was to plague Dougan for five years after he twisted an ankle in a reserve game. The x-rays showed no break but for ten frustrating weeks he appeared to be getting no closer to fitness. "The management and the trainers thought I was trying to pull the wool over their eyes by not responding to training and maintaining that my ankle was sore." Finally, he was strapped up by the team trainer Sam Bernard and thrown into a third-team game, only to break down in agony after ten minutes. Further x-rays were ordered and this time a break was revealed. The fact that it had been missed first time around was, he was told, "just one of those things".

Dougan's anger over the way his injury had been mishandled was compounded by Cox's refusal to allow him to attend a ceremony in Belfast where members of the Northern Ireland World Cup squad were to receive commemorative medals. He believed that the mental rehabilitation offered by the ceremony would have left him in a better frame of mind for his fight to regain physical fitness. Instead, he received his medal by post. "I never forgave [Cox] for this and it made me more than a little bitter. I rebelled at this treatment because I thought it merited rebellion," he said.

The worst fears of everyone were realised as Portsmouth finished the season rock bottom of the First Division after winning only six games. Through the dark days it was friendship with Chapman, Uprichard, Ivor Evans, Basil Hayward and Stonehouse, who acted as his chauffeur when injury prevented him driving, that kept him sane. But Dougan knew that even such closeness would not be enough to keep him at the club for much longer.

Chapter 5

ROVERS REBELLION

The headline in the *Wolverhampton and Express and Star* is notable more for its tone than the bare numbers it introduces. "Estate less than £170k", it announces when probate records are released late in the autumn after Derek Dougan's death.

Clearly, for a professional footballer of note to leave only £168,177 once all the liabilities have been deducted is cause for raised eyebrows, especially when his modern Premier League counterparts take only two weeks to earn that amount. In isolation, straight comparison of money across such a span of time is a meaningless exercise, but its context and principle – the right of a footballer to earn market-rate wages and to have some control over his own life – is at the heart of a battle that Dougan waged for two decades, firstly on a personal basis and later as chairman of the Professional Footballers' Association.

Nothing illustrates the financial plight of the players of the late 1950s better than the case of the man who became Dougan's captain when he completed a £12,000 transfer to Blackburn. Ronnie Clayton had begun his professional career at Ewood Park in 1951 and was captain of the England team throughout the first of Dougan's two seasons at his club.

Dougan claimed to have sensed unease among the other Rovers players that Clayton was allowed to be half an hour late for the 10am training time so that he could tend to affairs at his newsagent shop. But over time his antipathy towards the indulgence shown towards Clayton was replaced by an appreciation of his colleague's need to provide for his family and the feeling that something had to be wrong in his profession when the captain of the England team needed to sell magazines and cigarettes to safeguard his financial future.

A maximum wage of £20 per week, reduced to £17 in the summer, and the knowledge that a club could simply retain without pay any player who refused to accept renewal of those terms was no basis for long-term prosperity.

I catch up with Clayton in the week that Dougan's posthumous value has been revealed. It's also a month after Minister of Sport Gerry Sutcliffe has sparked widespread debate about the salary of current England captain John Terry by describing the Chelsea skipper's £130,000-a-week pay packet as "obscene".

"The money wasn't that great in those days," says Clayton, although without any note of bitterness. "You had to look after your own future, which was why I had the shop. You can't imagine John Terry having to do that! You could never be sure when a club might decide they'd had enough of you and the players didn't have much of a leg to stand on."

In 1960, Burnley inside-forward Jimmy McIlroy, Dougan's teammate in the 1958 Northern Ireland World Cup squad and one of football's biggest names, admitted in his autobiography that "fear of retirement is constantly troubling us". He gave a bleak assessment of his future prospects by concluding: "I'll just scrub along and hope things turn out for me."

Dougan, the wide-eyed kid from east Belfast, was quickly awakening to the realities of life as a professional footballer. It was an environment where one of the best in the business had to "scrub along", where the England captain awoke early up to mark up the morning papers. By observing the work of Rovers' PFA rep, Harry Leyland, and attending player meetings as his industry faced the threat of a strike, Dougan received the early part of an apprenticeship in the work of his union. Seeds were sown that would eventually lead to him playing a role in bridging the gap between Clayton's corner shop and Terry's millions.

It was a good game against Clayton in his first game back for Portsmouth after injury that, Dougan believed, had paved his way to Blackburn – although Clayton has no recollection of playing against him before he arrived at Rovers. The successful sportsman's ability to block out any less than perfect performance, I assume. Positive mental attitude, as the sports psychologists of today would describe it. "No, I just don't have a very good memory," Clayton admits.

Reports had indicated that Blackburn, in need of a new striker, had been chasing Newcastle's Bill Curry, but when he turned them down their attention switched to Dougan, who, in the meantime, had been linked by reporters to a possible transfer to a London club. "There was a strange aura at Fratton Park," he later wrote. "The spectre of the Second Division hovered over the club."

Portsmouth would win only six League games all season and when they lost 5-1 at home to Newcastle it further fastened their grip on bottom place in the table.[3]

The next morning, Dougan was in bed at his lodgings when his landlady came knocking on his door, informing him that there was someone from the football club waiting to see him.

Gordon Neave stood downstairs with a message that Dougan was to report to the club immediately. In a state of excitement, he drove to Fratton Park. Perhaps those newspaper reports had been accurate after all.

Not quite. Manager Freddie Cox greeted him with a smile and the words: "Blackburn Rovers want to sign you." At that moment, Dougan cared little that it was not the Marble Halls of Highbury or the "Academy" of West Ham that beckoned. Ewood Park would do just fine; a haven after the purgatory of Portsmouth. "I could not restrain a sigh of relief," he said.

Cox might not have had much time for Dougan, but he

---

3   They retained it to the end, failing to win any of their final 24 League games.

realised that he was the club's most saleable asset – and they needed the money his transfer would net for them. After an hour of discussion with Rovers officials, the deal was done. Blackburn manager Dally Duncan instructed Dougan to meet him the following day at Portsmouth's Queen's Hotel, where most teams stayed when they visited the city. The men then travelled to London to join the rest of the first-team squad for the next day's game at Arsenal.

Even those Portsmouth teammates who were aware of the frustrations Dougan had been feeling were taken by surprise by the sudden move. Norman Uprichard says: "Derek didn't talk much about [a possible transfer]. He kept it to himself. I remember I was playing a game of darts in a pub near the ground when someone said: 'Have you heard the latest? Doog is away'."

Sammy Chapman adds: "It came out of the blue and was done and dusted pretty quickly. But Blackburn were a good side and weren't the only team that wanted him."

Having left with Portsmouth with an overall record of nine goals in 33 league games, Dougan scored the equaliser in Blackburn's 1-1 draw at Highbury, a good way to impress his new colleagues. "He was obviously quick and could get you a few goals," remarks former Rovers defender Matt Woods. "That's what you want from your centre-forward."

After the game, Dougan returned to Portsmouth to retrieve his belongings and his car before embarking on the long drive north to his new home, getting himself lost around the Manchester area on the way.

Doubts about the wisdom of his move were playing in his head before he even completed his journey. He had already been struck by the bleakness of the region when he played there with Portsmouth and now that image was more clearly defined by the miles of stone walls lining the roads as he drove in frustration around places such as Burnley and Rochdale. "What have I done?" he asked himself as he neared his destination.

His new teammates had other questions. "Who the bloody hell owns this convertible?" England forward Bryan Douglas recalls thinking as he arrived at Ewood Park the next day. He remembers the car being a pink Cadillac, although it was in fact their new centre-forward's Ford Consul. "That was my first impression of Derek – quite a character."

Inside-forward Peter Dobing, who would share digs with Dougan, continues: "He would drive around in his pink convertible and always had the hood down so he could wave to all the girls. One time we went to Blackpool to go to a restaurant called the Lobster Pot and we parked outside a shop. We were about to walk down the road to the restaurant when this chap comes out and says: 'You can't park there. How long will you be?' Derek says: 'An hour and a half.' When we got back, the car was jacked up and the wheels and the engine had gone – the guy had wanted to know how long he had to work on it."

Later, the car was changed to a white Jaguar, which features in a story teammate Mick McGrath uses to illustrate the benevolent side of Dougan: "As the weeks went by we got to know him better and he was a generous character. I was involved in a crash and my car was out of action so he said: 'Borrow the Jag.' I was too scared to, but he was that sort of man. Anything you wanted he would let you have."

Dougan and his Jaguar would become a big enough feature of local life that when he was involved in a minor collision, in which his and another car suffered minimal damage and both drivers were completely unscathed, it made front page headlines in the *Lancashire Evening Telegraph*.

On the field, Dougan's early career at Blackburn faltered when he began suffering from a sore throat and struggled to get through a full 90 minutes. He'd had a bout of tonsillitis a couple of months earlier and this time his tonsils were discovered to be septic, necessitating an operation to remove them and limiting his appearances to a total of four in what remained of the season since his transfer.

After knocking about with Chapman on the south coast over the summer, he reported, fit and revitalised, for the new season, excited by the potential in his new team. "I had left a side that was struggling to keep in the First Division and went to one that staggered me with the natural ability it had."

Dougan spearheaded a forward line that included England winger Douglas on the right wing, Dobing at inside-right, Welsh international Roy Vernon at inside-left and Ally MacLeod, the future manager of Scotland, on the left flank. Promotion winners and FA Cup semi-finalists in 1957/58, Rovers had established themselves in the middle of the First Division table despite undergoing a change of manager when Johnny Carey took the job at Everton and was succeeded by Duncan, formerly manager of Luton Town.

Less enchanting to Dougan than the possibilities on the field was the grimy atmosphere of a northern industrial town compared to seaside he had left behind. On a practical note he found himself having to wash his hair twice a day in order to maintain the condition his level of vanity required. It was a chore he could do without so he went to the barber and instructed him: "I want it all off," believing it would also promote thicker growth.

Woods says he remembers it "as if it was yesterday", and adds: "We were training in the morning and at lunchtime Derek went and had his head shaved. We didn't know until he came back wearing a trilby and suddenly took it off to show us what he'd had done. He took a lot of stick for it."

McGrath, who recalls the headwear as being like "something from the Andy Capp cartoon", adds: "We were all laughing at him for the hat, but when he took it off... my God."

These were the days where a short back and sides sculpted into place with a blob of Brylcream was the standard style and Dougan would admit: "My shaven head created a great deal of amusement." He felt, however, that it did have more significant consequences in that some in the football fraternity thought he was "crackers" and said: "I suppose it did not always help when I expected to be taken seriously."

The crowds, of course, loved it. The scalped hair and the deep summer tan brought to mind one of those westerns that Dougan loved so much and the fans on the terrace had quickly nicknamed him "Cheyenne" after the eponymous, mixed-race hero of the popular cowboy TV series of the time. The main character, Cheyenne Bodie, is described in one recap of the programme as a "loner possessed of an implacable sense of justice who drifted around… changing jobs in every episode".

It was clearly more than just a haircut that made the name appropriate. According to Dobing: "One time he put a bandana round his head and another day he came out with a feather tucked into it."

Dougan's two goals in the opening game of the 1959/60 season, a 4-0 win over Fulham, helped to set the tone for Blackburn's fast start – four wins and a draw in the first five matches. By Christmas Day, when he scored the only goal against Blackpool, Rovers were in second place and Dougan had 11 goals to his name, including four in a 6-2 beating of West Ham two weeks earlier.

Dobing remembers that game as an example of how infuriating and frustrating his colleague could be: "We were winning 4-0 at half-time and after a few minutes of the second half Derek sat down in centre circle and said: 'I have done my bit for today.' I said to him: 'Get up, you daft bugger.' He used to try to be different just to be different. If all the players in team were ready to go out and the manager said something and everyone else said yes to it, Derek would have to say no."

Despite the good start to the season, not all was well in the Blackburn camp. Vernon, a mercurial figure whose temperament had been kept in check by Carey, was increasingly at odds with his new manager and in February Duncan transferred him to Everton.

Mick McGrath recalls: "Dally was a gentleman but I don't think he was a strong enough person to handle a few of the players who were volatile – and Derek was one of them. Roy was a great player, but he needed handling, needed someone to tell him who was boss."

By the time Vernon had fallen out irreparably with Duncan, Dougan was having relationship issues of his own and had already decided that his career at Blackburn would not be a long one. He felt frustrated that he could not get closer to Clayton, with whom his rapport was not much better than that with club captain Jimmy Dickinson at Portsmouth.

"My regret is that I did not get to know him better," he said, but he felt that he was not alone in his reservations. "From the day I arrived I detected a certain amount of resentment... unflattering remarks were at times made about Ronnie Clayton."

Douglas sees any differences between the two men as being nothing more than age and background. "Ronnie is a lovely guy," he says of his lifelong friend. "He was just the complete opposite of Derek. He was happily married and bringing up a family and 100 per cent dedicated to his profession. He was not one for going out socialising. You have got to realise that Derek was still young and finding his feet. The girls all liked him and he liked the girls. He went out and about, to Manchester and Blackpool, and he liked life and had his own special pals, like Peter Dobing and Matt Woods."

Woods adds: "It was Peter he was close to. They were the only single guys in the team. Derek just used to come round to our house when he wanted a meal."

And even Dobing is keen to point out that he did not attempt to keep up with Dougan's social activities. "We didn't go out a lot together. He was up for the high life and I was more reserved. I thought that if I go to bed at 10 and he goes at 12 then maybe I have got two hours' advantage over him. He was more naturally athletic player than I was."

He might have been living it up away from Blackburn, but Dougan would write in *Attack!*: "The dourness of the club matched that of the town. I could not shake off the depression that caused me to wake each day regretting that I had to go to the ground. Life was grey and monotonous. The road from Portsmouth to Blackburn was beginning to resemble a cul-de-sac."

Once again, preparation for games was leaving Dougan scratching his shaven head in bemusement and eventually speaking of "a great waste of talent and ability". After running round the pitch a couple of times the players would go to a small patch of land that was used as a car park on match days. It was known as "Little Wembley" – with the same heavy sarcasm that had seen Dougan's childhood playing field christened "The Meadow".

He felt such methods were "slap happy", as was the constant absenteeism of Duncan. "The only time we saw him was if we had reason to consult him in his office," he explained. "Most weeks we saw him only on a Friday morning or on a Saturday before the team went out, when sometimes he gave us a very short team talk."

Woods is a little more forgiving, saying: "Dally was all right. He did his best. Everybody has their style of managing – some are hands on and some are hands off."

Other little things upset Dougan, like the trainers putting two-inch studs in his boots, which he felt led to muscle problems. He ended up looking after his own boots. Dougan believed that the lack of direction started at the top and he recalled a director handing out boiled sweets to the players on an away trip, making them feel they were being treated like "a bunch of schoolboys". A request to be given club suits in which to travel to games was rejected because of the expense.

At least the FA Cup provided some excitement as Rovers collapsed in the league to win only three of their final 18 games. Vernon was the hero in a third-round replay against Sunderland, scoring two goals in a 4-1 win at Ewood Park and prompting Dougan to muse: "The club must have been suffering from brain damage when they transferred him to Everton."[4]

McGrath's late equaliser earned a draw at home to Blackpool before two goals by Dobing and one from Dougan secured a 3-0 win in the replay. On the basis of their disintegrating league form, Rovers were unfancied visitors to Tottenham in the fifth round but a pair of goals by Louis Bimpson helped them achieve a 3-1 victory.

East Lancashire was buzzing when Blackburn were drawn to play at Burnley, riding high in the First Division. Along with the fierce rivalry among the fans, the game was given extra edge by the resentment that simmered among the Rovers players about Burnley's enhanced status in the game. But any inferiority complex harboured by Blackburn appeared to have been justified by the opening stages of the second half.

---

4   Chris Crowe was signed from Leeds as a replacement for a club-record £25,000 – £10,000 less than the fee reportedly received for Vernon – but made only five unimpressive league appearances and was ineligible for the cup games.

Dougan had seen a header saved and had needed treatment after taking a knock during an evenly-fought opening 45 minutes, but his Northern Ireland teammate, McIlroy, set up a pair of goals after the break to put the home team in command, before England winger John Connelly lobbed a third.

Dougan shot wide as Blackburn attempted to launch a comeback, but even when Douglas converted a penalty – given for a debatable handball – with 17 minutes remaining it appeared no more than a consolation. Three minutes later, however, Dobing cracked in a hopeful shot from 25 yards and Blackburn swept forward in search of an unlikely equaliser. With four minutes left, Clayton banged the ball into the box and it fell to McGrath, whose shot squeezed inside the post. In front of almost 59,000 in the replay, Rovers had to wait until extra-time to capitalise on the superiority given to them by the outstanding Douglas, with goals from Dobing and MacLeod sending them into a semi-final against Sheffield Wednesday at Maine Road.

Apart from his one goal against Blackpool, Dougan's contribution to the run to final four had been marginal. "I liked to think that my patron saint, whoever he is, was saving me for the semi-final against Sheffield Wednesday. I was right."

Blackburn, wearing – according to the match programme – their change strip of "red shirts, white knickers", went ahead after 13 minutes when Dougan linked up with McGrath and hammered home after receiving a return pass. Wednesday applied considerable pressure throughout the rest of the match, but with less than 20 minutes to play McLeod released Dougan to beat England centre-half Peter Swan and shoot beyond the reach of goalkeeper Ron Springett.

Legend, admittedly of Dougan's own making, has it that after the second goal, he told one of the Wednesday defenders – Swan or Tony Kay depending on the version of the story – to write to him if he needed any tickets for Wembley. Invited to write about the centre-forward's art in *Soccer the British Way* a couple of years later, Dougan gave this description of his decisive second goal:

"Just over the halfway line, I got a great ball from Ally MacLeod and went through the middle at top speed. Speed was always my strong point for I was a runner before I was a footballer. Two players challenged me, one of them England centre-half Peter Swan, but I evaded their attempted tackles and sped on. Out of the corner of my eye I could see Ron Springett start to advance form his goal line. This is it, I thought, my chance to end Sheffield Wednesday's hopes and put Blackburn Rovers in to the Cup final.

"I knew what I had to do – hit the ball at a very acute angle with my right foot – and I am never so happy with my right as with my left. But just at the right moment I let it rip. Ron Springett leapt upwards, sideways and backwards at the same time, his hand clutching frantically for the ball, but he was too late. True as a bullet the all shot into the top right-hand corner of the net."

Blackburn held on after Jack Fantham headed a goal for Wednesday and Dougan left the field in tears. A revealing picture taken in the winners' dressing room shows an exhausted and drained Dougan sitting with a blank expression while celebrations swirl around him. Perhaps, as he later admitted, he was acknowledging to himself that "at no point during the season would I have considered this even a slender possibility".

By the next day he was being pictured walking happily with his girlfriend, Valerie Martin, as the *Evening Telegraph* began its countdown to the big day. "I now put on record that the Rovers will bring back the cup," stated reporter Alf Thornton, who also noted that Wednesday had been undone by Dougan's "unconventional interpretation of the role of centre-forward".

Dougan remained too completely wrapped in his own shroud of discontent to focus solely on Wembley, admitting to feeling "depressed and anxious'". He explained later: "Whatever the result of the Cup Final I would be unsettled. When the singing and shouting had died... I would be left wondering what I was doing in Blackburn." He spoke of there being "no means of alleviating the discontent that gnaws at one's life".

The sentiments are fine enough and well expressed, but his folly was in not even waiting for the "shouting and singing" before taking the course of action for which his period at Blackburn has forever been remembered. On the eve of the final he sealed the envelope on his transfer request and sent it to the club via registered delivery. His motivation was sound – "I wanted to be happy every day and not on one occasion in the season" – but his timing stank.

He admitted that "vanity triumphed over common sense" and never backed away in future years from confessing that it had been a grave error of judgement. When he first wrote about his actions he tried to mitigate them somewhat, although his explanation was self-serving: "I did not choose the occasion. It more or less chose me." It sounds like the "I didn't mean to" pleadings of an errant child. By the time he wrote *Doog* in 1980, he was admitting that it was an 'insensitive and indiscreet decision' and describing it as "the one action [in my career] for which I reproach myself".

In fact, that wasn't quite true. There had been one earlier when he passed himself fit to face Wolves at Wembley. Playing against Birmingham in the final game of the league season – which he finished with 13 goals – he pulled up two minutes from time with an injured thigh muscle. With the final six days away, he had an injection from a specialist and began to hope fervently for the best. So, too did the *Evening Telegraph*, which treated its readers to daily front page bulletins on Dougan's fitness. Only on the day before the game, when Princess Margaret's wedding ceremony with Antony Armstrong-Jones dominated, was he shoved to a single column away from centre stage.

Dougan had told the press, and his manager, that he would not know until Friday if he would be fit, but that was not good enough for the club chairman Norman Forbes, who pressed him for a decision by Wednesday. Dougan was gradually admitting to himself that he could not be fit enough for such an important game, but found himself leaning towards taking a chance, hoping that his teammates could carry him through the contest on the Wembley turf, infamously unforgiving on players' fitness. With substitutes still several years away, the gamble would be a reckless one.

Wednesday arrived and, inwardly wincing through a series of sprints, Dougan succeeded in fooling all onlookers at the Blackamoor School playing fields, and took his place alongside his teammates for the journey south. "The rest of the week was spent in agony, mental and physical," he said. He made his final decision on the day before the game. His natural speed, greater than that of most of his colleagues, prevented him from showing himself up in a game of five-a-side at Hendon Football Club and he informed Duncan that he could name him in the team for Wembley.

"I had made two decisions," he would admit. "Both were wrong. I did Blackburn a double disservice." In another account of the events, he called his action "an insult to a club on its way to Wembley".

The DVD of the 1960 FA Cup Final game allows for a study of Dougan's performance and a search for signs of obvious lack of fitness, although without the multiple camera angles and analysis of the modern era the overriding conclusion is that you don't actually see very much of him throughout the 90 minutes – which is probably telling enough in itself.

Within a minute of kick-off he is seen to visibly flinch in a tackle inside the centre circle and shortly afterwards BBC commentator Kenneth Wolstenholme notes that he is having trouble running because of injury. Interestingly, having described him as a "colourful character", it is clear that Wolstenholme does not have a vivid enough memory of him to avoid spending the remainder of the match calling him "Duggan".

Dougan admitted later that he knew as soon as he set foot on the Wembley grass that he was "in trouble" and admitted to a "pang of conscience". McGrath says it was "unfair on the lads" but can forgive his colleague's decision, while Douglas recalls: "It was touch and go. We didn't know how bad it was and we were hoping by the time of the final that he would be fit. You think you only have one chance of playing a Cup Final so I could understand him passing himself fit, but it was quite obvious after five minutes or so that he wasn't."

Despite their main striker's obvious problems, Blackburn play well for ten minutes, with Douglas and Peter Dobing to the fore. But unable to create chances against the Wolves offside trap, which Wolstenholme notes they have introduced this season, Rovers allow their opponents to take over.

Midway through the first half Dougan gets behind his marker, Bill Slater, for the first time but no one is on the end of his half-hit cross. He sends in one more centre from the left but offers nothing in the way of attempts on goal. He even seems to be moving slowly in closing down defenders.

Matt Woods comments: "Normally Derek would have been able to give Bill Slater a five-yard start and still beat him, but he played when he was not properly fit. It was a very hard decision and you think you can get away with it. You only find out when you start playing the match. I wouldn't have liked to have made that decision."

By the approach of half-time, Wolstenholme is becoming increasingly critical of the defensive nature of the game and the number of offside decisions. But finally he has some real action to describe as Wolves take the lead through a scrappy own goal off Mick McGrath. Moments later Rovers full-back Dave Whelan is carried off with broken leg after a challenge that looks more innocuous than others that have gone unpunished and caused no damage.

Peter Broadbent remains at the heart of most of Wolves' good work as Blackburn struggle to deal with being numerically disadvantaged on such a warm day. Dougan, meanwhile, is moving more gingerly as the game progresses, his socks rolled down to accentuate the slender legs sticking out of impossibly high shorts. There is little of note happening, however, prompting Wolstenholme to inform viewers that it must be "the quietest of all Wembley cup finals". He adds: "The reason? Well, you don't have to look very far for it." Strong words from the former RAF man who rarely has a bad word for anyone.

Dougan is anonymous for the second half, although it not obvious to what extent his lack of impact is caused by injury. He is playing badly, but then so are his teammates. And they are a man short. Yet Woods asserts: "We should have won. We were playing with nine and a half men. They got an own goal and another of their goals was miles offside."

McGrath adds: "We knew Wolves were strong and physical but knew we had a chance of beating them. If you look at the rounds we had before the final we were very much in control of all our games apart from the first half against Burnley. We were confident. We had a good chance early on – I don't know if Peter Dobing froze, but the keeper made a good save. Then it was downhill."

§

Interestingly, Dobing is less confident that his team could have won: "Wolves were a hell of a good side, perhaps the best in the country. I don't think we had any great expectations."

In the end, Wolves get home comfortably, with Norman Deeley scoring twice to make the final scoreline 3-0. As they parade the trophy, the Wolves players are pelted with apple core, drinks cartons and the Blackburn fans' other detritus from an afternoon on the terraces. The next day one newspaper, noting the missiles and the quality of the contest describes the game as "The Dustbin Final".

Dougan has done little to add to the quality of the offering and Slater, the man tasked with marking him, comments: "I never expected to play in the Cup Final against someone who didn't seem to be trying."

Back in the dressing room, Dougan felt embarrassment that he had been unable to perform and humbled by the fact that his teammates gave him an easy ride over it. "No one told me that I should not have played," he recorded. "There were no comebacks, no recriminations. This spirit of sportsmanship made my transfer request look particularly squalid."

Of course, the Rovers players still had no knowledge of that request – even Dobing, with whom Dougan lived, was in the dark. They discovered it only when Dougan revealed his actions to one of the newspaper men at Wembley.

Woods recalls: "He didn't say anything about it and we didn't know a thing. We got a shock when we read about it. We had a few words about it but not a lot was said."

Douglas, meanwhile says, with a touch of understatement: "It didn't endear him to the others," and Clayton adds with compassion: "It was very bad timing. But he seemed a decent fellow and it must have hurt him afterwards."

While Dougan explained that he simply did not like living in the north of England, the press accused him of timing his request to capture headlines, which, of course, they gave him. He would claim that he had made verbal requests on six occasions but not been taken seriously. For the Blackburn fans already angered by Rovers' chaotic ticket allocation process and disappointed at the display at

Wembley, it was cause for further disillusionment over what should have been such a memorable occasion. It is significant that average attendance at Ewood Park would drop by almost 8,000 to below 20,000 in the following season.

Even though Douglas says that "after the defeat I don't think I have ever been so depressed", Dougan's teammates have been more forgiving towards him over the years than Rovers followers of a certain age. Among the waves of tributes following his death, there emanated from the Ewood Park congregation some damning appraisals of his Wembley performance.

A typical post was by someone who said he watched Dougan play "in a manner that many thought showed less than reasonable interest" and felt it was "a serious defect in sportsmanship". One Rovers fan said: "I was there and still feel betrayed" and mentioned Dougan's "abominable behaviour", while another said he "played like he just did not care".

A further interesting, if unreliable, perspective on Dougan's infamous transfer request was offered to the readers of the *Lancashire Evening Telegraph*, when it printed an interview with Dougan's younger brother Dale shortly after Derek's death. Dale claimed that his brother told him he had been "betrayed" by teammates who went back on a pact to submit transfer requests en masse because of unpaid FA Cup bonuses. Given that this claim was unsubstantiated in the story, and that Dougan – never slow to defend his actions – omitted to mention it in any of his autobiographies, while none of the Blackburn players I have spoken to have brought it up, it is probably safe to dismiss this version of events.

In the aftermath of Wembley, Blackburn were clearly in no rush to aid Dougan's bid to leave the club and he was left to make a fruitless trip to Belgium on his own initiative to discuss terms with a team there. But while Dougan was struggling to find his exit route from Ewood Park, his manager, Dally Duncan, was presented with his in the form of the sack.

The omens had not been good for Duncan when club chairman Forbes made some less than flattering comments about the manager at Blackburn's post-final dinner and praised the contribution of his predecessor Johnny Carey in constructing the Cup Final team.

Reports of ill-discipline on a post-season tour of Germany increased the pressure on Duncan, who refused to resign his post. Dougan, in a rare moment of sympathy for any of his managers, commented: "I think he got a raw deal."

It would not be until six games into the new season that Jack Marshall, a cheerful, gag-telling figure who had been in charge at Rochdale, was given the post, leaving Dougan to try to persuade the chairman in the meantime that the club would be best served by letting him go.

Dougan did not do much to strengthen that case when, in the opening match of the season, he scored a hat-trick in a 3-0 defeat of Manchester United, which may have been why fans did not give him as hard a time as he expected at the first home game. He then scored in each of the first two matches at Ewood Park. "He set off like a house on fire," says Douglas. "But he always had itchy feet. I don't know why he wanted to go."

Dougan, who would score 16 goals in 30 first team appearances during the season, had withdrawn his transfer request after his fast start to the season, but he quickly formed the opinion that Marshall was a small-time manager unsuited to the rigours of managing in the First Division. Once again, he identified a reliance on petty discipline to mask such shortcomings and, inevitably, fell foul of the rules.

He protested at being fined £2 for one transgression – "an act of disobedience, trifling when I look back on it" – and was duly suspended for a day, which cost him £3 instead. "It was when I was at Blackburn that I saw the important of constitutional method," he would write. "Harry Leyland, our goalkeeper, was on the committee of the PFA and he always told players how vital it was that they should turn up for meetings."

Meetings during that 1960/61 season were particularly significant, coming in the heat of the PFA's fight to free its profession from the Victorian shackles by which it remained bound. The union's annual general meeting in April 1960 had formulated four demands from its employers, the Football League: abolition of the maximum wage; the right of players to receive a percentage of transfer fees; a new retaining system; and a new form of contract.

In June, the Ministry of Labour had been informed that an official dispute now existed within the football industry.

Meanwhile, Football League secretary Alan Hardaker had been maintaining that there was a need to keep the old system of retain-and-transfer and maximum wage in order to prevent a return to the "chaotic conditions" that existed before the League's formation in 1888. Such a position won little in the way of support among the public, who were sympathetic to the players. In November 1960, Member of Parliament Phillip Goodhart described the League as "inefficiently organised, semi-bankrupt and all too often a thoroughly bad employer".

In that same month, an extraordinary meeting of League teams made the following offer to the PFA: a rise in the minimum wage of £2; a wage of £10 per week to be paid to those on the transfer list; match bonuses for reserves; and the introduction of talent money. The PFA's two biggest concerns – maximum wage and the retaining system – having not been addressed, a series of player meetings were held in which the union was given membership approval to issue notice of a strike to take effect on 21st January, 1961. Mick McGrath recalls: "Derek had a lot to say in all of that. He was never stuck for words".

By 9th January, the League had offered longer contracts; the abolition of maximum wage; the setting up of a joint committee; a minimum retaining wage per division; and testimonials for players every eight years. The retain and transfer system remained untouched. The union held firm.

Three days before the strike date, League officials, including Hardaker and president Joe Richards, met at the Ministry of Labour with the PFA delegation, secretary Cliff Lloyd, chairman Jimmy Hill and lawyer George Davies. After two and a half hours of talks, overseen by the Ministry's conciliation officer Tom Claro, the PFA trio met with other members of their management committee and, at 6.45pm, Minister of Labour John Hare announced to the press that agreement had been reached on the issue of the retain and transfer system.

If a player refused the terms offered by his club he would be placed on the transfer list on 31st May. If he was still on the list on

30th June he would receive a minimum wage based on his team's division. If there was no transfer by 31st July, he would be on monthly contract while League Management Committee resolved the issue.

"Players win," screamed the headlines the next day, prematurely as it turned out. The PFA delegation had the power to agree a deal there and then, and believed that the League negotiators had exercised a similar mandate. Done deal, so they thought. But it transpired that the League Management Committee had no such authorisation, even though Hill always claimed that Richards had said they did.

The League clubs, unashamed about such an obvious U-turn, rejected the deal at their next meeting at the Café Royal. The case went back to the Ministry of Labour and by 16th May another version was agreed upon by the negotiating committees, with the new retain and transfer clause reworded but still, the players felt, maintaining its fundamental principles. On 3rd June, the League's AGM threw it out. The players, therefore, had to accept a partial victory.

Matt Woods says: "When you signed a contract at 17 it was binding for life. We were not fighting for more money – it was freedom of contract we wanted. I remember a meeting in Manchester where Jimmy Hill told us there was no way in the world we would get freedom of contract, but the clubs would get rid of the maximum wage. Blackburn offered us £25 a week."

The end of the maximum wage famously paved the way for new England captain Johnny Haynes to be paid £100 a week by Fulham, but the handcuffs of retain-and- transfer remained. The freedom of players to determine their own employment remained a dream, one that would be at the heart of the work of Derek Dougan as PFA chairman a decade later.

Combined with the injustices of Portsmouth and the stifling atmosphere of Blackburn, this introduction to the PFA's campaign for improved conditions for members opened up new possibilities for Dougan, offering the hope of a voice for his frustrations. And, perhaps still not politically aware enough to acknowledge it at the time, his Belfast background undoubtedly deepened the enthusiasm with which he would fully embrace the calling of the union over the next few years.

Eventually he would articulate that he saw, in his enclosed world of professional football, an opportunity – a platform – that had too often been denied those he had left behind in the shipyards and streets of Northern Ireland. "As an Ulsterman I can see how in my own country there never was proper machinery to attend to general grievances," he wrote. "There was nothing to help a citizen put a case to the authority. There is nothing sectarian about this." Dougan was discovering the means by which he could take up his own causes, and there would be no turning back.

Interestingly, Bryan Douglas remembers Dougan's conversion to the union cause as gradual, rather than as the subject of some kind of epiphany: "I don't think Derek was that much interested in the union to start with. I was the union man who had to collect the subscriptions and it was always a job getting the money off him. I had a go at him about that when he became PFA chairman!"

Dougan soon found out that the confetti-fluttering of pound notes that was being experienced in some changing rooms around the country was not intended to land on him. His new salary offer placed him on less money than more experienced players who were in the reserves. Dougan's belief that "they were trying to humiliate me or drive me away" might have been another touch of paranoia, but clearly the club had not matched his own self-valuation and he made his point with a melodramatic tearing up of his letter in the secretary's office. He said he would have had to be a "zombie" to accept the terms being offered.

Dougan faced up to what he was sure would be deterioration in his game if he remained at Ewood Park. "I was just turned 22 but a player knows his time is always running out in football… I had not found what I was looking for and I was getting desperate."

He later wrote that among the saddest stories in his sport were those that involved talented players stuck at the wrong clubs. He would later acknowledge the wisdom of Kevin Keegan abandoning the security of Liverpool in 1977 for a move to Hamburg. He did not want to follow those who had chosen to "linger on, sink into self-pity and fade out of the game through deterioration of their play that would not have occurred if they had shaken the dust from their boots and found clubs suited to their style".

So when Blackburn duly offered him a further rise in wages a few days later, he had already committed himself to accept a transfer to Aston Villa. His turbulent two years at Rovers were over, probably with the home fans never having seen the best of their extrovert, eccentric centre-forward.

Douglas sums up: "He was very well-liked and a popular player. He was very, very quick and could pop in important goals now and again, but I always felt he didn't play to his full potential. He was a bit young and immature and still learning the game."

McGrath echoes that view: "He was always talking in the dressing room and was never stuck for words, but he had not matured as a player or a person. He was a better player when he was older and teamed up at Wolves with John Richards."

But Dobing, whom Dougan described as one of the naturally gifted players he ever played alongside, concludes: "He had got everything. He was good in the air and on the ground and was terrific to play against. He was 50 years ahead of his time, a showman everywhere he went. And I thought he was a fabulous bloke."

Chapter 6

NATIONAL SERVICE

Five months after Derek Dougan's death I find myself being distracted by a pair of events in Durban while I am trying to read up on his first few games for Northern Ireland. On my laptop, via the BBC's web site, are live pictures of the draw for the qualifying tournament of the World Cup to be held in South Africa in 2010. Meanwhile, on Sky, that country's cricketers are trying to chase down New Zealand's total in a one-day international.

It is almost half a century since Dougan made his Northern Ireland debut in the opening game of the 1958 finals in Sweden. It really was a different world then. When Portsmouth's young centre-forward was first talked about as a possible international, the Irish were approaching the decisive stages of a tournament in which only 48 countries were competing for the 14 available places. This time, 205 countries are chasing 30 slots.

The draw, a bloated cross between the Eurovision Song Contest and a South African tourism symposium, is being seen live in corners of the world that barely even knew the World Cup existed when a 17-year-old Pelé helped Brazil to their first World Cup victory.

South African president Thabo Mebki talks about his nation's pride in staging the event. A World Cup in Africa? What would they have made of *that* in 1958? He is followed by a somewhat smug looking Sepp Blatter, president of Fifa. He says that the event can offer South Africa "a strong unity for the future". It might well be a valid statement, but it strikes me as inappropriate to be commenting on the political state of his hosts' country, in the same way that Dougan liked to cite the quotation, "only an Ulsterman can criticise Ulster".

Once proceedings start, the mechanics of the qualifying tournament are predictably convoluted. The Central American section manages to feature three pools that are all divided into four sub-groups. I can't find any record of how the draw was conducted for the 1958 qualifying tournament but I have my doubts that it was interrupted by a vocal performance by someone in a nice frock.

There is, however, one pleasing aspect of this pantomime. No matter how far technology has driven the evolution of world football in the past half-century, no one has yet come up with a better way of determining who plays who than someone sticking their hand into goldfish bowl and retrieving folded scraps of paper out of a circular plastic container.

As the draw for the European groups is introduced with an explanation of how 53 teams will become 13, I lose my internet connection. I could hit the red button on my TV remote and switch to the BBC's interactive coverage, but South Africa now need nine runs to win off three balls with two wickets left. Andre Nel, the fast bowler with the "what-you-looking-at" mentality of a 1970s English centre-half, demands my attention.

By the time he has smashed three consecutive boundaries to win the game, I reconnect with the World Cup to discover that Northern Ireland have so far been drawn with three countries that did not even exist in football terms when Dougan was bidding to win a place in the squad for the 1958 finals – Slovakia, Slovenia and San Marino. Finally, the two names that come out of the bowl to complete the group, the Czech Republic and Poland, have a satisfying resonance with the faltering early years of Dougan's international career. It was Czechoslovakia who provided the opposition in Dougan's first match for Northern Ireland, his one game on the world's greatest football stage, and Poland against whom he scored his first goal in a major competitive international match.

Dougan's move to England in the late summer of 1957 had made him even more closely scrutinised by the Irish than when he was playing on their doorstep. Not only had his transfer served as an endorsement of his potential and raised awareness of his name, but interest in the Football League was high in Belfast, where – as in so many British cities of the time – queues would form at newspaper stands in anticipation of delivery of the evening sports special, *Ulster Saturday Night*, with its blow-by-blow reports of all the big games.

There was also the pride of his former community to keep his name at the forefront. Former Northern Ireland and Middlesbrough midfielder Eric McMordie, another east Belfast native, explains: "People in Belfast seemed to have this great warm feeling towards people doing very well for themselves after leaving for England. Even now, my own family speaks of people complimenting others for doing well. They really do look up to you. Everyone where we were brought up thought Derek was a real hero. And they still do."

Days after his Portsmouth debut in October 1957, Dougan returned to Belfast to show his First Division talent in a B international, scoring three goals in a 6-0 victory over Romania. He was then selected for a Northern Ireland XI to face the British Army at Leeds, but gave a poor performance in a 3-2 defeat after he had been led to believe that a good display would earn him his first full cap.

Yet a month later he was in the party for his country's decisive World Cup qualifying game at home to Italy. To fellow Belfast exile Billy Bingham, established on the right flank of Northern Ireland's forward line, his selection was no surprise. "Knowing he was from the same area as me I had followed his progress," he remembers. "I saw him play for Distillery as a 16 or 17-year-old. He had height, although he was no great header of the ball at that time, and had speed, which was a little bit of a change for a tall chap. I saw his potential."

Northern Ireland's World Cup campaign had kicked off with a respectable draw against Portugal in Lisbon and an unlucky single-goal loss in Rome, but a 3-0 win in the return game against the Portuguese, who surprisingly beat Italy at home, resurrected their hopes. A win in the return game against Italy would send them to their first finals, prompting Burnley inside-forward Jimmy McIlroy to describe the game as "the most important 90 minutes of football every undertaken by the footballers of [Ireland]".

Thick fog on the morning of the match caused Hungarian referee Istvan Zsolt to be stranded in London and by the time of the afternoon kick-off the game had been put in the charge of a local official, Tommy Mitchell. Peter McParland remembers the team, in a heightened state of pre-game tension, being given the deflating news that the game would not count as a World Cup qualifier.

"We knew that the referee had been fog-bound and that the Irish FA had put forward the best referee in Ireland. It was only 20-odd minutes before kick-off when someone came in and said: 'I have got some bad news. The World Cup game is off. It is going to be a friendly'."

It was the most inappropriate description for any game as the teams drew 2-2 in a contest marred by Italian brutality and the ugly mood of a crowd incensed at the downgrading of the game they had paid to see. Wilbur Cush, scorer of both Irish goals, had his shin pad broken by one of the worst tackles of the game and an Italian was sent off for a two-footed lunge into the back of Billy McAdams. The final whistle saw thousands of angry fans invade the pitch. The home players, with the help of the police, ushered their opponents to safety rather than leaving them to mercy of the mob, although a couple of Italians did receive some rough treatment.

A month later, despite protestations from the Italians that the game should be moved because of the crowd trouble, Dougan watched from the Windsor Park stands as Northern Ireland earned their place in Sweden with a 2-1 victory in another bad-tempered encounter. McIlroy and Cush scored the goals, while Italy had Alcide Ghiggia sent off for one of the less excessive offences of the match.

Dougan was duly picked in the squad for the finals and teamed up with his colleagues in Belfast for two weeks of preparation, which included activities such as a ten-mile route march consisting of segments of walking and jogging – not exactly what the players would have needed at the end of a punishing season.

Meanwhile, the financial arrangement for the Northern Ireland team was to be a total of £150 for their three group games, reduced to £90 for anyone who didn't make an appearance. Such generosity, the Irish FA deemed, precluded them from paying an additional £2 per day spending allowance, despite a plea by the players to manager Peter Doherty on the day before they departed for Sweden.

The four home countries, who had all qualified for the finals, had agreed to offer the same compensation packages and the Irish FA were not prepared to break such a union of parsimony. There was a further distraction following the announcement that Ireland's opening game would be played on a Sunday, which led many in both football and religious circles to mount a vociferous protest.

Despite being lightly regarded by those previewing the tournament, McParland recalls that the Irish were confident about their potential: "The team was peaking at that time. We had been together since 1954, when some had been teenagers, and building up towards this World Cup from that time. We were a Cinderella team but we felt we were capable of performing well."

Optimism might have been even higher but for the shambolic nature of the travelling party. Goalkeeper Harry Gregg remembers: "One or two things happened. Billy McAdams was a good striker and was playing in the First Division at Manchester City but his club refused him permission to go to Sweden. He had to go on tour with them." The Munich air crash, which Gregg had survived, had also robbed the team of Manchester United half-back Jackie Blanchflower. "That type of thing honestly hurt us," Gregg adds.

When the squad departed for Sweden, the travelling party consisted of 14 players. The Irish FA had decided to take only 17 of their selected men to a tournament where no substitutes were allowed. Former *Belfast Telegraph* sports editor Malcolm Brodie recalls: "They simply didn't have more than 17 players good enough to take. We had never dreamt of reaching the finals, yet after beating Italy we were Sputniked into a situation ill-prepared and lacking in experience."

Gregg, understandably, was given permission to travel separately by train, while the Newcastle pair Alf McMichael and Dick Keith, who had missed the training camp, were due to meet up with the team in Sweden after a club tour of Romania. Fingers were being firmly crossed for their arrival because there had been no contact with the players since they "disappeared" behind the Iron Curtain.

Once manager Doherty, trainer Gerry Morgan and a medical advisor had taken their place on the Viscount turbo-prop plane that would fly to Stockholm via Copenhagen, there were still some spare seats, which were taken up by six Irish FA committee members.

From Stockholm, the party travelled to the resort town of Tylosand, the Irish FA priding themselves in having selected the most picturesque headquarters of any of the 16 competing teams. Curiously, the players, officials and travelling media were billeted in separate hotels but dined together.

Dougan, who had mistakenly been presented with two right boots by a sportswear manufacturer on the eve of departure, moved a step closer to making the team for the opening game when Rangers centre-forward Billy Simpson pulled a muscle on the first day of training.

Having neglected to have Czechoslovakia watched in any of their recent internationals, the Irish management relied on driving to watch them play Alliancen, a team comprising players from Denmark's top clubs. Ireland's own final warm-up game was against Ekilstuna, with Dougan named as centre-forward. When the selection committee informed the manager which players he would be fielding for the game against Czechoslovakia, to be played in the port town of Halmstad, it was Dougan, in his number 16 squad shirt, who was given the role of leading the attack.

Outside him on the right were winger Billy Bingham and Wilbur Cush, to his left Burnley's Jimmy McIlroy and Aston Villa's McParland – two legends of Irish football to whom even the cocky Dougan looked up. "The first time I'd met Derek was when he played for Portsmouth against us at Villa Park," McParland recalls. "We had maybe the best centre-half in the country, Jimmy Dugdale, and I was really impressed with how Derek did against him. As I was changing after the game I looked up and there was Derek coming to say hello to me. He was a young boy who had not long come over from Ireland and he just wanted to make himself known and have a chat with another of the Northern Ireland lads. I told him how well he had played."[5]

Dougan stated in one of his books that he was awe-struck by his famous teammates, who also included Danny Blanchflower, and never felt fully at ease in the national team until the era of such men had passed. He claimed it took a few years before he felt comfortable enough in a game against Scotland to ignore McIlroy's shout of "leave it" to take the ball on, beat defender Dave Mackay and cross the ball to set up a goal.

For once, it appears that Derek might have been guilty of a little false modesty. McIlroy certainly believes so: "Derek didn't lack confidence. I remember going to help him on his debut, calling for the ball, advising him, but he usually had a better idea."

And when I mention Dougan's comments to Gregg, he bursts out: "Oh, Jesus. In no way was Derek in awe of anyone," and proceeds to offer this story as evidence. "We had one or two in the party who were mickey takers, none more so than Wilbur Cush. And we had another complete and total extrovert in the team in Billy Bingham. All Wilbur had to say out loud when he was in their company was: 'Who do you think is the fastest? Bingham or Doog?' and they would both come back with: 'I am the f*****g fastest.' And they'd spent the next hour running up and down the beach trying to prove it. The next day it would be: 'Who is the best singer? Derek or Billy?' and they'd be off again. Derek was only a young lad, but he thought he could sing better, run faster, jump higher than anyone."

Bingham supports Gregg's recollection: "He was not in the least overawed. He was his own man and very confident about himself. He was strongly opinionated, but I honestly liked him and he

---

5   Belfast-born former Northern Ireland midfielder and manager Bryan Hamilton explains that it was common for the exiled players to band together in this way. "When I was at Ipswich and Everton, I would even have a look at the line-up for the reserve games and if there was someone from back home playing I would go and see them. If anybody came over from Northern Ireland you always followed their progress."

seemed to be very fond of me. I don't know why – maybe because we were both from east Belfast. We were room mates and I took him under my wing to a certain extent. He was always chatting to me and we had all kinds of competitions. I would challenge him, but only over 30 yards because I was small and quick off the mark."

Brodie explains: "Dougan was always extrovert, always leader of the pack – he was someone who felt that he could dominate the scene. When he came into the room his presence would always be felt. In many ways he was an Irish romantic and he had a great gift of blarney. It was said once of Danny Blanchflower that he not only kissed the blarney stone but swallowed it and Dougan was in that category."

But against the Czechs, Dougan struggled to put his performance where his mouth was. Cush's first-half header from a McParland cross was enough to earn a disciplined, hard-working Irish team a deserved victory, but the general consensus was that they had been lightweight up front, necessitating Bingham to play a more central role in the second half.

In the *Telegraph*, Brodie wrote of a "lack of thrust at centre forward" and said of Dougan: "He was right out of it in the first half, showed some flashes of skill in the second, but generally lacked drive… I am afraid big Derek is still not the answer." The next day, looking forward to the game against Argentina, he said it was "obvious a change will be made". Brodie recalls now: "He just wasn't up to it at the time."

Dougan had seen his last action of the tournament, his place going to Fay Coyle, only recently transferred from Coleraine to Nottingham Forest. Doherty's assurance that Derek had plenty of time and would soon have a permanent place did little to soften the blow. "I would have swapped all my other jerseys and all my other honours to put on the green jersey of my country," said Dougan later.

In one of his final interviews, he added: "Peter Doherty said: 'I don't think I am going to play you again because you are just here for the experience.' I said: 'I thought I was over here to play football.' The Derek Dougan of ten years later would have challenged and confronted Doherty. I would have said: 'I am going out there to play and you can do what you like about it'."

And he reiterated his belief that he had been the victim of the self-serving selection system. "I was really shocked because it is an unwritten word in football that you never change a winning side and they replaced me with Fay Coyle. He played one game and was on the losing side… I found out much later that the reason [he] made his international debut was that in those days the committee selected the team and Coleraine got another couple of thousand pounds [from Forest] if he became a full international. It was written into the deal. That was the reason they left me out."

Without recalling the specifics – in fact, Coyle had already been capped by Ireland – McParland adds: "That could have happened. There was one chap in particular who was going to England, so the selectors were pushing him. I wasn't fully aware of everything but my own opinion is that Derek should have been in the team. We were short of a man up front. I went in to play up front in the other games – moving in and out from the wings to cover as centre-forward – and I got a few goals because of it, but I thought Derek should have played. Whether Peter Doherty didn't have a real fancy for him I don't know."

Bingham says: "Peter Doherty never explained why he played some and not others but he had been a fantastic player and I think he could assess people. Many papers were pulling for Derek to get in, but you have to make your decision."

Gregg can see why Dougan was discarded at that time: "I would say that the World Cup came too soon for Derek. We took a lad from my home town, Fay Coyle, and on the day it was a bit too much for each of them. That period in Derek's life came too soon but the important thing is that many others, in the same circumstances, fell by the wayside. Derek was big enough to get over it and to come back."

The Irish had no answer to the skill of Argentina, going down 3-1, but a spirited performance against West Germany brought them a 2-2 draw. McParland scored twice and Gregg, despite injury, was outstanding in goal to earn a play-off against Czecholsolvakia for a quarter-final berth.

"I did my ankle in the first three minutes," Gregg explains. "I said to our old trainer Gerry Morgan: 'Don't take the boot off to bandage it, because it will blow up and I won't get the boot back on.' Norman Uprichard played against the Czechs with a broken bone in his hand so I had to play against France in the quarter-final even with a bad ankle."

Uprichard, who also remembers suffering a badly twisted right ankle against Czechoslovakia, says: "We were near enough classed as national heroes for reaching the quarter-finals. It was not expected for such a little country and it was nice to hear of us getting such a good press back home. It was heartwarming."

But Uprichard was not the only casualty as Ireland came from behind to win 2-1 in extra-time, courtesy of two more McParland goals. By the time they took the field against France in Nörkopping, just one day after an ill-advised 210-mile coach journey, three key players among the original 17 were on the sidelines while two more, Gregg and the versatile Tommy Casey, were playing while unfit.

After McIlroy, who described the team as "completely exhausted", failed to take advantage of an early chance, France scored just before half-time and ran out 4-0 winners.

My suggestion to Gregg that the 1958 team remains one of the best in Irish history brings instant correction. "No, it is *the* best. I'm not making excuses but, with the injuries we got, we just didn't have enough players out there. Looking at the players that played in most games, it was the best team we have ever had. In today's terms, every one of our best 11 or 12 was a Premier League player."

Brodie, who has covered 13 World Cups, concurs: "To achieve qualification for the quarter-final with a team of walking wounded was a remarkable achievement. It was the finest Northern Ireland team ever."

McParland adds: "We showed what we were capable of. In the end we were down and out with fatigue and injuries and that knocked us for the final game. I think Derek was a bit peeved with it all. He would have loved to have played a bigger part in our run.'"

Instead, hindered by an ankle injury, Dougan had to wait more than a year for his next international game, a 4-0 defeat in Belfast against Scotland in October 1959, when the Irish fielded the identical team to that in which he lined up in his first match. He played in a B match against France but, with only games against the other home countries on the full international schedule, it was another year before Dougan, now a Blackburn player, appeared again, wearing the number ten shirt in a 5-2 defeat by England. He had missed only three matches in the meantime, but three caps over almost two and a half years did not hint at much of a future in international football.

Gregg offers: "Derek was going through his Cheyenne Bodie period at the time and was still getting out of the high school. That 'I am Cheyenne' stuff was part of him growing up but that sort of thing didn't help him with the establishment. Also Billy McAdams came back, which didn't help Derek as far as the national team went."

Bingham believes that Dougan's unhappiness at club level detracted from his play in the early years of his career: "He never seemed to be settled; never happy with his lot. He was slightly controversial and argumentative towards his managers and tended to move around. He had ability but at that time was a bit of a rebel."

Terry Neill, who established himself in the Northern Ireland team in 1961 and remained there for more than a decade, says: "Peter Doherty, and guys like Danny Blanchflower, Billy Bingham and Jimmy McIlroy, used to tear their hair out because you never used to know when the Doog was going to turn up in a game. With Peter, everything was black and white. In his own way he expected everyone to have the same drive and enthusiasm as he had."

Incidentally, one of Neill's lasting impressions of his own early involvement with the Irish squad is Dougan's obvious determination to enjoy life to the full: "I didn't drink as a young player but I didn't want to appear to be stand-offish so I went along with them, feeling like the luckiest guy in the world to be in their company. Derek could get blotto on occasions, which is not a criticism, and I can remember a few occasions trying to get those long legs of his into a cab. There was a skill to it – you had to get the body in first!"

Having missed two more games, Dougan scored his first international goal in a 5-1 loss against Wales. He finally played back-to-back games for his country when he kept his place for the friendly in Italy, finding the net again in a 3-2 defeat, and was part of a losing effort in Greece in a disappointing World Cup qualifying campaign that ensured there would be no repeat of the heroics of 1958. "Danny Blanchflower was getting on in years and all the lads were going over the hill a wee bit," McParland comments.

Dougan had a rough ride throughout the contest, being elbowed and shoved all over the pitch. Eventually he made a gesture with his fist as a way of warning his assailant, only for the opponent to recoil as though hit. As the fans called for his blood and threw cushions on to the pitch, Dougan escaped with a warning from the referee but felt the incident contributed to him being dropped for the next game against West Germany in Berlin.

Injuries as an Aston Villa player helped to rule out further appearances until October 1962, when he scored in a winning Northern Ireland performance for the first time, a 2-0 European Championship qualifying win against Poland in Katowice. He played in the next two games, but the second of them, a return 2-0 win against the Poles, was his last game for his country for almost three years.

Dougan had not helped his cause by arguing in print that there was too much expectation placed upon him by the Irish fans when he played in Belfast and saying that he didn't want to play at Windsor Park.

Before his own selection for the national team he had heard tales of unsung players being transformed into heroes with the green jersey on their back, but up close he was surprised to see it working the other way, with accomplished players reduced to nervous wrecks by the pressure of representing their people. Yet he had quickly come to understand what they had been going through.

A few years later he would admit that his comments had been ill-judged but that "the build-up was too much for me" He explained that playing at Windsor Park was "a phobia that no psychiatrist could remove", adding: "You are in front of spectators who do not see you play each week and who expect you to perform wonders. Any mistake is magnified as an incipient weakness."

However, such a publicly-stated attitude angered many in the positions of power within the Irish FA and his transfer down the Football League would offer a convenient reason to ignore him. By the summer of 1965, as he completed his second season at Third Division Peterborough, Northern Ireland had played 43 internationals from the day Dougan had made his debut seven years earlier and he had been part of only nine of them. The captaincy of his country seemed a long way off.

Chapter 7

HERO AND VILLAIN

Bobby Thomson gives me a warning: "I am a bit grumpy," he says. "I am still getting over shingles." He is relieved to hear that I am not selling anything, but discussion of Derek Dougan can hardly be said to fill him full of joy. "Derek and I fell out. We were a pair of prats. But in the past five years I have forgiven more. A while ago I decided that next time I saw him I would offer my hand and say: 'Let's make up.' Four or five weeks later he died without us having the chance."

Thomson is a key figure in the two years Dougan spent at Aston Villa. Born in Dundee, he arrived in England via Albion Rovers and Airdrie to spend five years at Wolves, transferring to Villa in 1959 after playing only one first-team game in five years.

"The first time I met Derek was at the Trinity Road training ground," he recounts. "Our manager, Joe Mercer, was like a dad to me and I loved the ground he walked on. He called me over and introduced me to Derek. He said to him: 'This is Bobby Thomson. He can shoot with either foot, dribble, head the ball and score goals.' Derek said: 'What did you say his name was? Pelé?'"

§

It was his new colleague in the forward line to whom Dougan turned for lodgings after briefly occupying the spare bedroom at

99

the home of his manager after signing for Villa in the summer of 1961. Thomson continued: "He asked if he could stay a few weeks while he got organised. I said: 'Yes, of course you can stay.' He was the new centre-forward after all. But he took liberties. He lived at my house in Wolverhampton for nine months! I said to him: 'Isn't it about time you paid some rent?' My missus treated him like she treated me, and my seven-year-old son would say he had seen his bird dropping out of the window."

The relationship between the two teammates was a turbulent one from the start. "Derek wanted to be the cat's whiskers," Thomson continues. "He punched me in the nose in Italy. We were playing five-a-side before a game against Milan. I had my back to him and he kicked me in the back of the leg. When I turned round he punched me. I had a go back at him and was grabbing him and trying to bite his ear off!"

Our conversation jumps forward four decades and finds the two men falling out all over again: "If you wanted someone to fight your corner Derek was your man. He loved the spotlight and the fight. And he was very helpful. But I like to think I can do things by myself and one day, in about 1996, I was going to see Johnny Prescott, the old boxer. I had lost my driving licence at the time and when Derek called to see what I was doing he said he would pick me up. I said I would get a train and then walk but he insisted. But he never turned up. About three days later he called and I said: 'Derek, do me a favour. F**k off and don't phone me again.' After that he was a little bit frightened of me when we sat across the room at various functions."

Terry Conroy, the former Stoke and Republic of Ireland midfielder who became one of Dougan's closest friends, recognises the origins of such a situation: "It was a frustration to those around Derek that he couldn't turn anything down, couldn't say no. He worked on five or six things at once, going from one to another, and was a little bit disorganised."

And Dougan's niece, Josephine Long, adds: "Derek was the sort of person who would tell you he was going to Brighton for the day and you would get a phone call and find that he had gone to Scotland first. You never had any idea with him what he was going to do. He needed someone to be firm with him and organise him."

Dougan had been signed by Villa as a replacement for centre-forward Gerry Hitchens, scorer of 42 goals in all competitions during the previous season. Joining Jimmy Greaves, Denis Law and Joe Baker on their way to Italy in order to escape the constrained world of the British professional footballer, Hitchens had been sold for £85,000 to Inter Milan. Dougan was a relative bargain at £15,000.

"Derek's signing was really quick," says Villa forward Peter McParland. "All of a sudden one Sunday we heard about it and on Monday morning he appeared at the ground."

Mercer saw the arrival of Dougan as preventing him having to "make a new plan in the absence of Hitchens" and his new signing made his debut in the season opener at Everton, complete with re-shaved head. "We'll have to get him some billiard chalk," Mercer had joked when seeing Dougan's shiny bonce, while Bob McNab, then a young defender at Huddersfield, adds: "I remember Joe saying: 'If he scores goals every week he won't need to shave his head to get attention'."

Dougan admitted he did little to justify even his modest fee on his Villa debut. "It'll come," Mercer assured him. But in only one match he had established the pattern of inconsistency for which many teammates remember his days at Villa Park.

McParland, who played in the handful of games Dougan had by now achieved for Northern Ireland, remembers: "I could see he had terrific potential. He was one of the quickest players I had played with. But when Derek came to us at Aston Villa I think it was at a time when he was not taking the game particularly seriously. It was only when he went to Wolves several years later that he knuckled down to showing people how good he could be. Up to then the game was a bit of a joke to him. He was a jovial lad who didn't take anything seriously."

Thomson states: "Take nothing away from Derek, he was a great player, but not always in those days, especially away from home. I remember before an away game against [Sheffield Wednesday centre-half] Peter Swan he got a bad groin muscle. His arm went round me in the dressing room and I thought: 'Oh, I am centre-forward again.' I wasn't the only one who felt that he didn't always give it everything. There were days when Derek would lose the ball and just let the player go away with it. If you lose the ball you don't just stand there. But he was his own man."

And, according to Villa forward Ron Wylie, you simply had to accept that individuality as being part of the Dougan package: "He was a good centre-forward, with good skills, a nice first touch and was very quick. Of course he was very flamboyant but you take these things with the good bits. If you'd put him through the mincing machine you might have lost some of the things that made him such a good player. I played with one of great centre-forwards of all time, Tommy Lawton, and maybe Doog could have been in that category if he'd not had the kind of personality he had. Then again, if you'd changed him he might not have been so good."

Under the leadership of Mercer – a much-loved wing-half with England, Everton and Arsenal, whom he captained to two league championships and an FA Cup – a young Villa team had been promoted as Second Division winners two seasons previously. "Mercer's Minors", as they had been named by the media, finished a respectable ninth in their first season back in the top flight and also won through to the first final of a new competition, the Football League Cup.

With many of the top teams not entering, it was no substitute for the FA Cup, which the club had owned as recently as 1957, but it was an important stepping stone for the development of Mercer's side. "We had a good team," says Thomson. "We worked hard for each other and played it simple. Joe used to say: 'Anybody can have a bad game but you have got to put in the effort'."

§

McParland adds: We were a decent, hard-working team. We had young players coming through from the youth team and Derek was one of those Joe thought could be good for the club and had brought in to help move us forward."

The League Cup final, against Second Division Rotherham, was held over to the start of the 1961/62 season and the first leg, at Millmoor, resulted in a 2-0 defeat for Villa. Cup-tied from his involvement with Blackburn the previous season, Dougan watched in early September as his new colleagues scored two second-half goals in the second leg to take the tie into extra-time. With 11 minutes remaining, McParland found the net and Villa had secured the trophy, and their players a £90 win bonus.

Some time around midnight, Thomson and Dougan left Villa Park, giving a lift to 26-year-old *Wolverhampton Express and Star* reporter Malcolm Williams. According to Dougan, they stopped off for an hour at a private venue before continuing their journey home. As they travelled through Willenhall on their way back to Wolverhampton, the car left the road in Walsall Street. The subsequent inquest was told that the car travelled 273 feet from where Thomson had first applied the brakes, recording four impacts in that time: with a tree, two trolley bus poles and some hoardings.

Williams, married with two children, was killed when he was thrown forward, suffering a fractured spine and multiple other injuries. The inquest recorded a verdict of accidental death. Dougan, who was thrown out of the car, ended up with a broken arm and needed more than 50 stitches in his head, while Thomson suffered leg injuries. Dougan said that he remembered the impact and then: "I found myself lying on the ground." The coroner noted that the speed of the car was "very, very excessive".

Teammate Nigel Sims, who lived over the road from Thomson and Dougan, recalls: "First of all I had a phone call telling me there had been a crash and the next morning Bobby came over and told me what had happened. We rang the club and Joe Mercer said: 'Don't say a word to anybody, leave it to me'."

§

McParland recalls: "It was a terrible shock to everyone at the club. I had been chatting with the fellow who lost his life. Because I had scored the winning goal I said to him as he left: 'You have got your headlines for tomorrow's paper.' Next thing we heard there had been a crash."

With Villa having won a trophy earlier that evening, there was obvious speculation that an excess of drink had been involved, but both Thomson and Dougan always vehemently denied that had been the case. "I was not drinking," says Thomson. "I didn't drink when I had anybody in the car." Dougan concurred, stating that "it was a dreadful accident but had nothing to do with post-match drinking".

What exactly happened in the car remains a mystery almost half a century later. Thomson was charged at the time with careless driving, but magistrates found him not guilty because it could not even proved that he was at the wheel. But now Thomson claims: "Derek was always kidding and joking and had a habit of putting his leg across to make me go faster. I used to go through Willenhall every day and knew that bit of the road like the back of my hand. I was slowing down because we were coming to a Z bend. Derek said: 'Why are you slowing down?' and then his big leg came across and I lost control of the car."

There is, of course, no one left to support Thomson's version of the incident, a story he has gone public with only after Dougan's death and which can't be related without reference to the historically difficult relationship between the two men.[6]

Dougan commented on the crash many times throughout his life and, on the final occasion, a radio interview in 2006, he said it was caused by a blow-out. Whatever the cause, the crash jolted him, perhaps even hastened an awakening maturity. He knew that had the rear door on the passenger side been unlocked when he tried to get in the car, he would have sat in the seat that Williams had occupied. He also acknowledged in later years that the publicity around the crash had hastened his education about the place footballers held within the public's fascination.

Doctors warned Dougan to expect six months out of action, but with typical bloody-mindedness he was back in less than three. His response to the crash had a positive impact on a young forward from Scotland, George Graham, among whose first responsibilities on the Villa groundstaff was the cleanliness of Dougan's boots.

------

6   Thomson gave a slightly different version of events in his 2010 autobiography, claiming that a drunk Dougan had placed his deer-stalker hat on his (Thomson's) head and pulled it down over his eyes.

Showing an empathy with wide-eyed young players that would remain with him throughout his career, Dougan recognised the homesickness that Graham was feeling and filled the role of mentor to his young charge, on and off the field. "I could not have had a better tutor in how to enjoy life," Graham recorded.

Graham recalled the club being "numbed" by the events of the night of the League Cup victory. "I admired the way Doog lifted himself above a tragedy that would have knocked the heart out of lesser men," he said. "Doog had the strength of character to put [it] behind him."

Having scored three times in his first four Villa appearances, Dougan disappointed some of his new fans by scoring only seven more in the remainder of a league season in which his team finished in a promising seventh position, although he added two more as Villa reached the FA Cup quarter-finals.

A further rise up the table appeared a realistic prospect when Villa found themselves placed fifth in January 1963 after a run of seven games unbeaten. But momentum was lost under the blanket of snow and ice that covered the country for two months and kept footballers sitting at home waiting for a thaw. When it arrived, Villa's play went to slush, suffering 11 straight defeats that plunged them to a final position of 15th.

Dougan, who finished the season with nine league goals in 28 games, had suffered downfalls of his own. First, his fast start to the season had been halted by a sending off at Nottingham Forest, where he was mistakenly adjudged to have kicked goalkeeper Peter Grummitt. Then, as winter settled in, he slipped in the street and twisted his knee. During his absence he missed the club's two-legged League Cup final defeat against Birmingham and would say that he was troubled by the injury for the rest of his career.

Dougan felt like a stranger when he got back in the team, which was playing a different tactical game to that of earlier in the season. He wanted them to sign someone to partner him up front and believed that West Brom and England forward Derek Kevan, available for £30,000, would fit the bill. Instead it was Welsh inside-forward Phil Woosnam, bringing culture rather than aggression, who arrived at Villa Park. "Kevan and I would have made a formidable combination," Dougan complained. "If he had been put alongside me, I might have stayed at Villa Park for several years."

The problems of Villa's meltdown are credited by many observers to have caused the onset of the nervous illness that would force Mercer out of the club at the end of the following season. How much he was missed at Villa is the subject of differing opinions. While there is little doubting the affection that the football world continues to hold for "Uncle Joe", Dougan was heading for an inevitable fall-out.

Nigel Sims, a fierce Mercer critic, tells me: "Derek would not have got on with Joe because I can't think of one person who did. Joe had lost it – I think he was over the hill. Some of the things he did we did couldn't believe. We went to Blackpool and he said, 'I have had a word with Stan [Matthews] and he wants to get fit because they are playing [West Bromwich] Albion in the Cup next week. So don't touch him. He actually told our full-back Peter Aldis not to touch him. By half-time we were losing 3-1 so we told Peter to go out and get Stan. Joe did other daft things. One day we were playing Everton and he gave us our tickets and I said: 'I will pay for them when we get back.' He told me: 'You will pay for them now or you won't play.' Stupid things like that."

Dougan believed that "cardinal mistakes" were being made throughout the club, including the decision to sell the training ground for housing development. "Financial considerations took precedence over common sense," he said. "Such folly only confirmed my view that boards of directors know too little about football and understand the requirements of players even less."

While the issues of players' pay and contractual restraints had fired his interest in union matters, it was moments like this that planted the first seeds of his desire to run a club at executive level, which would continue to hold more appeal to him than the prospect of being a mere manager.

Matters with his own boss confused and distressed him. One minute it was being made known that the club was open to offers for Dougan and the next Mercer was telling him at training that he didn't mean to put him on transfer list. "Let's forget it," he suggested. But Dougan couldn't – he had lost faith in the club.

He also sensed that the tide was turning against him at Villa Park, that tales of his social life and his sometimes questionable attitude on the field might be undermining his future prospects there. The gossip, he felt, was unwarranted. One story had him knocking local heavyweight boxer Johnny Prescott, one of his regular running mates, down the stairs with a left hook. "I never hit my friend Prescott in my life," he said. "I never stayed out late with the players."

Certainly he liked to go out and party and his salary of £40 a week left him enough spare cash to do so, but he believed that stories of nightclub brawls, womanising and general hell-raising were "colourful and exaggerated". At the same time he accepted that they "contained an element of truth" and – especially after the headlines about the crash – he understood that footballers were entering an age of celebrity.

The end of post-war austerity meant that more and more homes could afford luxuries such as television sets and, although club football was not yet being broadcast nationally on a regular basis – *Match of the Day* was a year away – more well-known names from all walks of lives were being projected into people's homes.

Leading footballers, while not earning show-business wages, were becoming far enough removed from the salary plane of the average working man to fall into the category of the much-scrutinised rich and famous. "When you play for Portsmouth or Blackburn or Aston Villa, rumour goes round like wildfire and I had my moments," he said in 2006.

When Dougan discussed stories of his high life with Mercer he was assured by the manager that he knew they were not true – not completely anyway. Dougan also felt that he was maturing as a person. Not only had the car crash been something of a wake-up call, but he had by now met his future wife Jutta Fichtl[7], a 19-year-old German girl he pursued to the family home in Munich before marrying her in 1963 and with whom he became father to Alexander and Nicholas. "Marriage made me think seriously of the future," he

---

7   Notably, given Dougan's Protestant roots, Jutta was a Catholic – further evidence of his non-sectarian outlook.

said, turning his back on a "freewheeling, irresponsible life".

Yet Dougan's professional fears were confirmed when Villa told the press he was on the transfer list. He was then left out of the game against Liverpool so that Villa could give a debut to his young protégé, George Graham, who promptly scored in a 2-0 win. Dougan felt his club was scared of being made to look foolish by him performing well. Stuck with what he called his "bogus image", he said: "It was obvious I had no future at Villa Park. It was sad. I liked Joe Mercer. Perhaps I was too young and inexperienced to understand him."

In later years he would joke that Birmingham had not been big enough for both him and Mercer, and perhaps there is a grain of truth there in that his manager was evidently running out of patience with him, even though they had initially seemed well matched.

"Joe was the perfect chap to be Derek's manager," says Ron Wylie. "Joe could see he was a character and could understand that because Joe had been a bit of a personality himself as a player."

But McParland adds: "Derek was always a joker and Jack the Lad. He liked to mess around in the dressing room, although he always conducted himself as a well-mannered person and was very courteous, especially around the players' wives. I think Derek got on with Joe, but there was a time when Joe said, "Enough is enough." Joe had Derek down as the man he could build the team around had Derek put his mind to it, but he was not doing enough for him."

Dougan accepted that "whether I had misjudged Joe Mercer or he had pre-judged me no longer mattered. The situation had become complex". Two meetings with club chairman Chris Buckley brought no change in Dougan's situation, nor did letters of protest from fans who wanted him to remain at Villa Park. His self-esteem had taken a severe blow.

He had now suffered "three major setbacks" at three clubs in six years. Had a major club shown interest in him, maybe he would have been restored, but the only team that was serious about signing him was Third Division Peterborough United. Dougan described it as "a crushing experience".

The impact of Dougan dropping down the divisions should not be under-estimated. His profile was already among the highest in the game, his demotion being the equivalent of, say, Peter Crouch suddenly being shipped off to a League 1 team in the current era.

In an age where there were no celebrity TV reality shows to serve as a barometer of a player's status, it was significant that Dougan was the man selected as the featured centre-forward in the 1963 book *Soccer the British Way*, in which the game's biggest names, including Tom Finney, Denis Law and Billy Wright, discussed the techniques of their positions.

The book itself was mostly bland and obvious stuff, although Dougan – who was never a 25-goals-a-season kind of striker – makes it clear that he saw the centre-forward's role as much more than that of finisher. "When you are not actually scoring goals you have another responsibility – to lead the forward line and make opportunities for others. This means today you must be a ball player as well as a battering ram," he wrote. It is one of the aspects of his game that most of his teammates highlight when discussing his merits as a player.

For now, though, it was a quality that only lowly Peterborough were interested in acquiring. At least they impressed Dougan with their persistence in tracking him down while on holiday in Germany. Villa had agreed a fee of £21,000 and informed the prospective buyers they could speak with him if they found him. A series of telegrams unearthed him in Munich and Dougan was persuaded to cut short his vacation to meet with manager Jack Fairbrother. "Something told me he was a fair man so I agreed," he said.

Villa were about to lose a player who, according to George Graham "made an impact on the club and the city that gave him legendary status. Villa was a more exciting and vibrant place when he was around".

§

Friends advised him against accepting a deal with Peterborough as rumours had been growing in the meantime that a couple of First Division teams might be interested after all. At 25 years of age, Dougan had been around long enough to mistrust such newspaper talk. He took what was on offer: the highest salary in the Third Division. It didn't seem like much to boast about.

Chapter 8

THE POSH LIFE

If Derek Dougan feared that a transfer into the Third Division would cause his disappearance from public consciousness then the piece of football history I am holding in my hand is proof that nothing of the sort happened.

True, his time in the Third Division did at times seem to him like a 'wilderness', and the Northern Ireland management clearly failed to locate Peterborough on their scouting map. But the scrapbook that has arrived in the post tells a different story.

It is a history, lovingly compiled by an infatuated Peterborough United fan, of that club's 1964/65 campaign, a year in which Dougan helped them pull off the FA Cup upset of the season. Not surprisingly, the majority of the stories centre on Dougan himself.

Locally, he had his own newspaper column and enjoyed star status among less exalted players; nationally, his goals, character and talent for self-publicity made him the face and the voice of press coverage of the Posh's exploits. Few football fans anywhere in the country would have made it to the end of the season without a banner headline reminder that The Doog was still alive and kicking.

The book has arrived courtesy of former Peterborough forward Peter Deakin, an unexpected bonus from a letter sent in hope to an address on the electoral roll. "As soon as I heard from you I went to the post office to see about getting it sent safely," he has informed me, explaining that the scrapbook came to him via the late ex-Peterborough manager Noel Cantwell, who had been given it by a customer in his pub. "Noel said he thought of me when he saw what it was, a scrapbook of my first season there and Derek's second season, when we beat Arsenal in the FA Cup and got to the quarter-finals."

The book contains match previews and reports; news and features; wonderfully dated pictures and stories of Peterborough training for their games on the Blackpool seafront; and pictures of Posh fans holding up a banner saying "We Dig Doog", complete with a cartoon drawing of their hero. The affection and admiration in which Dougan was held in Peterborough jumps off every musty, faded page.

Delightfully, the original owner has left the stamp of his own personality in the book. A picture of Arsenal half-backs Ian Ure and Frank McLintock training for the game has been included, with the printed caption pointing out their combined transfer fees of more than £140,000. In red biro, the words "So Wot?" have been scrawled over the grinning superstars. A shot of a glum-looking Arsenal manager Billy Wright after his team's defeat has been given the home-made caption: "Smile please." A picture of Arsenal fans holding a quaint sign saying "May The Better Team Win" comes complete with the affirmation: "They Did!"

Peterborough fans could be excused their gloating after such a remarkable rise to prominence. This was not just any old Third Division club to which Dougan had been transferred from Aston Villa in the summer of 1963. As recently as three years earlier, while he was preparing for English football's biggest stage, the FA Cup final, Peterborough were still playing in the Midland League. They followed that year's championship success, their fifth in successive years, with election to the Football League and topped the Fourth Division at the first attempt. But a first glance at their London Road ground had been a stark reminder to Dougan that the journey he had made would have been unthinkable to him on that infamous day at Wembley in 1960.

He was now leaving behind the majestic setting of Villa Park, with its spectacular newly-covered mountain of terracing at the Holte End and a Trinity Road stand that had been opened by the future King Edward VI – a stadium that had housed more than 76,000 for an FA Cup match in 1946. Instead, his home was to be a ground that only a few years earlier had been able to boast only one small grandstand with seats for 400.

London Road had been much improved over the previous seven years, with identical covered terraces at each end and a new Main Stand across from the Glebe Terrace. Yet it still shouted lower division to a man who had never played a game in England outside the top flight. Even as a part-timer in Belfast he had played in bigger and better stadiums.

Behind the main stand was a council-owned car park that was used one day a week to house the local market. The club gymnasium was a small room under the main stand, the training ground a public park where the players had to pick their way around the dog mess. "I did not expect luxuries, but after the facilities of Villa Park I was unprepared for an almost entire lack of them," he wrote later in *Doog*, where he also recalled that his surroundings served as a stark warning of how he was in danger of squandering his career.

"It was apparent to most of my critics and the sports writers that I was on the way out. Decline and fall in a couple of seasons… I knew before my first season began there that I had made a mistake in going to the Third Division when I was a First Division player, rather like an Old Vic actor joining a provincial rep or a Westminster politician going into local politics. It was a jolt my senses needed. With the responsibility of marriage, I also realised the importance of getting back where I belonged and not letting my career peter out in obscurity. It was no consolation to know I was the highest paid player in the Third Division."

By the later years of his life, however, Dougan was able to look back at his London Road days with affection. "I was lucky to go to Peterborough for two reasons," he said. "I was the highest paid footballer in the Third Division at the time and then I was lucky that I injured my ankle very early and I am so grateful to a man called Albert Preston, the physiotherapist. He was ahead of his time and was superintendent of a special injury unit. Through a surgeon that he recommended they corrected the injury that I'd had for five years."

As he set up home in Peterborough, Dougan was given use of a club house previously occupied by former manager Jimmy Hagan, but described his arrival at the club as a "sobering experience". He sensed that the club was in over its head, still struggling to think of itself as a fully-fledged Football League organisation.

The one saving grace was the work of groundsman Ben Poole, who had produced an immaculate playing surface that he guarded like an angry Alsatian outside of match days. Dougan described the backward-looking administration of the club as "exasperating, especially when the incompetence was glaringly obvious. Small minded restrictions and pettiness abounded".

To Dougan's credit, his misgivings about his surroundings did not dampen the enthusiasm and professionalism with which he went about the job of scoring goals or his determination to enjoy the camaraderie of his new teammates

Winger Peter McNamee, who had been with the club throughout its Midland League triumphs, remembers: "Derek was brilliant, such a character. We were all excited about him coming and he was great to play with, great to be out with. He was always joking and teasing people, always up to tricks and seemed to really enjoy his time at Peterborough. I never heard him complaining about being in the Third Division. Everyone respected him and he was appreciated. We enjoyed having him with us and fans still talk about him even now."

Full-back Graham Birks, who joined Peterborough from Sheffield Wednesday a year after Dougan's transfer, adds: "I don't know anyone at Peterborough who doesn't think a lot of Derek. I never had any problems with him and he was very helpful. I think he had lost his way a little bit in his career and got a reputation for being a bit awkward, which was why he was at Peterborough, where they had never had any star players. But he never gave the impression that he thought he should not have been there. When we were out he mixed well. We all called him 'Duke' – I don't know how it came about, but he loved it."

McNamee continues: "He was on 50 or 60 quid a week at Peterborough and I saw only half of that. I said to him: 'All I should have to do is pass to you and the game should be finished.' He just laughed and said to me: 'Come on you little so-and-so. Get running.' I remember the games of cards on the bus. Because we were struggling with £25 we would be betting two shillings and then he would put in his ten shillings note and we had to run because we could not compete."

Such stories are related with undisguised affection, as is McNamee's memory of Dougan's debut for the Posh, a 5-2 home defeat of Wrexham: "Before the first game he said: 'If I don't score three today I am going to cut my hair off.' He scored two and when he came in on Monday morning he was bald. 'I never got the third,' he said. He did crazy things like that."

Shortly after his own signing, Dougan had been joined at Peterborough by former Cardiff City centre-half Frank Rankmore, who recalls the club's ambition on the field outstripping its tentative progress administratively: "There were efforts to try to get up a division and I think they had a bit of money at the time and tried to exploit that. The thinking was to have a strong spine, which is why they signed a goalkeeper called Willie Duff and had me at centre-half and Derek at centre-forward. Derek and I hit it off quite well but I think there might have been a bit of jealousy going on among the people who were already there. There was no out-and-out resentment, but the thinking was that his wages were a lot higher than most people's. I did question him once about why he had gone to Peterborough and his stock answer was that he was going to go round all the clubs in the League and then he would go back to the best one.

"Derek helped bring about an improvement in standards at the club. At the time that we signed the players had to take their own training gear home and wash it and bring it back. Derek refused to do it. He said: 'No way am I taking my own stuff home.' So everything changed."

Peterborough finished tenth in the Third Division in Dougan's first season, in which time he scored 20 goals in 38 games, more than any striker at the club. Birks says: "He had terrific pace and was deceptively skilful for a big man – all left foot, but very skilful. He could hold the ball up while we got forward and he told us that if we were ever in any trouble at the back just get the ball up there to him."

McNamee remembers a long-running side bet with Dougan: "He couldn't kick a ball powerfully. He could flick and glide. I said to him: 'If you ever score from outside the 18-yard box without getting a deflection I will give you a tenner'. He used to try, but he never managed it."

Towards the end of 1963/64, Fairbrother was replaced as manager by Gordon Clark, a former Manchester City full-back who had managed Distillery, Aldershot and West Bromwich Albion before coaching at Sheffield Wednesday. The arrival of Clark, whom Birks describes as "a hard man, but fair", was welcomed by Dougan. He said that Clark "renewed my sense of vocation, encouraged me when I was in low spirits and always reminded me that I was at heart a First Division player".

Just to prove, however, that very few managers can tick all the boxes for all of their players, Rankmore remembers: "I never rated Gordon as a manager. As a number two, I could see how he could be valuable, but not as the main man. For me, that impression was sealed when he gave us a b********g after the FA Cup quarter-final at Chelsea when he had played much of the game with ten men."

Clark was quick to use the presence of Dougan at the club as a means of strengthening the team. Peter Deakin, a forward signed from First Division Bolton Wanderers, recalls: "Gordon recruited quite a few players and said: 'This is a club that can go places.' I had played against Derek before and knew he was a good player and was flamboyant, an extrovert. It quite surprised me that he'd gone to Peterborough, although one of the temptations of playing here and one of the selling points from Gordon was the fact that Derek was at the club."

§

Clark impressed Dougan with his concern for his players' welfare and his willingness to grant them a certain freedom. Dougan was also allowed to lead the occasional training session, while McNamee adds: "Clark would give the team talk and Derek would take over and finish it off."

As well as discarding 14 players and spending £30,000 on experienced campaigners like Aston Villa's Vic Crowe, Clark won Dougan's approval through his attempt to improve things off the field, ensuring that players' wives got a dedicated tea bar instead of having to wait outside for their husbands, and bringing in the ground staff boys to look after the kit and help prepare the coach for away games. "He tried to run Peterborough like a First Division club," Dougan noted, but added: "The more he did for the club, the less he seemed to be appreciated by the board."

Birks has similar memories: "Gordon Clark was trying to get the club moving forward as a professional outfit but board was very part-time. I don't think Peterborough had the ambition to go much further at that time."

Clark was also approached by the players regarding an attendance-related bonus, as McNamee explains: "When Doog came, we went to the manager and said: 'Give us a pound for every thousand over 11,000.' Doog used to say: 'I bring them in, I should get the money.' I remember a week before a cup tie the manager dropped me and him into the reserves and 8,000 turned up at London Road because Doog was playing."

New strike partner Deakin recalls being impressed by more than just Dougan's pulling power: "His biggest strength was his ability in the air. If enough balls went into the areas he would be on end of 80 per cent of them. He could score goals and pick people out as well. He had this presence in the box and did the straightforward things well. His reputation helped as well. Some players in the Third Division were in awe of him and he was not slow in winding people up. He was very confident, although I thought he was a better player here at London Road than he was away from home. Away, you would not have said he would die for the cause."

Rankmore adds: "When we went to places like Mansfield and Oldham, I would imagine Derek felt he should have been playing in a higher level. When he first signed for Peterborough he would not have known what those games were going to be like. Maybe that is why he didn't perform so well in those places."

Such comments are supported by the fact that Dougan did not score an away goal in the 1964/65 Third Division season between the opening day and Good Friday. But if trips to football's more humble homes failed to fire up someone who had played in the World Cup finals, then the FA Cup was a more natural home. "No doubt about it," says Rankmore. "He was more up for it and he did give you that 'bring it on' attitude for those games. He was really looking to do something special."

Peterborough's famous run, during which Dougan helped himself to seven goals, began with a 5-1 win against non-league Salisbury, but then it needed an injury-time equaliser by Deakin to set up a 2-1 win at home to Third Division Queen's Park Rangers after a 3-3 draw at Loftus Road.

A visit to Fourth Division Chesterfield produced the expected victory, by a comfortable 3-0 margin. McNamee recalls: "Derek had scored two and I took a corner near the end. The keeper put it in his own net. Derek ran away with his hands up and I went over to him and said: 'You never scored that.' He said: 'Shut your little mouth up'." The record books show that Dougan was never found out.

Clark's belief that the club should think of itself as a fully-fledged professional outfit rather than a bunch of part-timers living out a transient dream was reflected in his insistence that the players should train for the Arsenal game in Blackpool, where the Norbreck Hydro Hotel was a regular destination for some of the north's leading teams, including Manchester United, Everton and the Sheffield clubs. It needed some additional funding by the Peterborough supporters' club to make it happen, but the trip was acknowledged by Dougan to have played a large part in creating a relaxed, yet professional, attitude among the 14 players who made the journey.

It was also a treat for the local pressmen, who justified their trip to the seaside by sending back pictures of players cavorting on the sand or in the hotel's much-revered heated swimming pool. And, despite Clark's reference to "plush living", cooperative reporters ensured there was no suspicion of high jinks by insisting that evenings were spent in the billiards room awaiting for the "early night" orders to be issued.

Birks remembers: "Before the Arsenal game was the first time we went away to Blackpool to prepare. We stayed for a few days at the Norbreck and Manchester United were there at the same time. We mixed quite a bit with them – there was not such a big gap between the top players and those in the Third Division in those days. With the side we had at Peterborough we felt we had a chance against anyone. We weren't one of those teams who just tried to pinch a win; we could score a lot of goals."

McNamee recalls the tactical discussions ahead of the big game: "Arsenal had a lot of great players – George Eastham, Joe Baker, George Armstrong, Frank McLintock, with Don Howe at right-back. I remember the manager saying to Doog: 'Ian Ure will follow you, so don't stay in the middle. Go left, go right and take him for a ride.' Doog took him for a ride all right."

Deakin describes Dougan that day as "the scourge of the Arsenal defence", adding that he "ran Ure ragged". So much so that one journalist would write: "Dougan was the master of Ian Ure and no one who saw the game can have any doubt that in this form there can be few, if any, better centre-forwards in the game."

After the teams and the 30,000 crowd had observed a minute's silence to mark the death of former Prime Minister Winston Churchill, the underdogs had the better of most of the first half, with Rankmore commanding at the back and only Eastham and Armstrong showing glimpses of First Division quality. "We played well that day," says Birks. "They had two good wingers but we stopped the supply."

§

Yet it was Arsenal who went into the interval in the lead when young striker John Radford shot high into the net following a corner. "They expected the second half to confirm their side's superiority," Dougan would write and, indeed, for 20 minutes it seemed only a matter of time before the favourites extended their lead during wave after wave of attack. But the second goal never arrived, and it was Dougan who struck an equalising goal with 18 minutes remaining. "Vic Crowe started a move down the right and Ron Barnes, the right winger, took the ball on. I dummied to go to the right of Ian

Ure, dummied back again before taking a pass from Oliver Conmy to steer the ball past Tony Burns."

Five minutes from time came what proved to be the winner, a move started by Deakin and finished by McNamee, who recalls: "I picked ball up just over the halfway line and I remember McLintock and someone else laid off me and I just got between them. I drew Howe towards me and I slipped it to Ronnie Barnes and he cut it back for me to run on and score."

After a couple of expert saves by Duff, the whistle sounded on an upset victory that, although it took another season, helped seal the fate of Billy Wright as Arsenal manager. Rankmore recalls: "Billy Wright had brought champagne with him for some reason or other, but he took it back unopened. He never gave any to us."

Birks adds: "One of the things Duke said after the game, in a kind of sorrowful way, was that it might be the end of Billy Wright. He was quite matter of fact about it."

Such concerns, of course, weren't about to get in the way of Peterborough's celebrations. According to McNamee: "We had a great night out and we never had to buy a drink wherever we went. I can't remember much about it and I don't know how we got home!"

While the people of Peterborough recovered from their collective hangovers, Gordon Clark endeavoured to introduce some harsh reality by warning that it would take three or four years for the club to establish itself in the professional way he felt was required.

In the meantime, his team prepared to face Second Division Swansea in the fifth round. Inevitably, it was Dougan upon whom much of the spotlight fell. He used it to project his claim for a recall to the Northern Irish side, saying: "My biggest heartache is that Ireland don't pick me any more. It grieves my father too."

§

Having been 'rewarded' for their efforts by the presentation of a new shirt each by a local outfitters, McNamee recalls thinking that a far more treasured prize had been squandered when Peterborough could only manage a goalless draw at London Road.

"Although we trained hard at Blackpool we enjoyed ourselves as well and we were keen to go back there if we beat Swansea. There were no goals in the first game and near the end I chipped on to Derek's head and he put it over the bar. A couple of minutes later someone set him up with another chance and he missed it. All the way down to Swansea on the coach for the replay we were having a go at him for missing those chances and messing up our trip to Blackpool. He was very quiet and thoughtful. At that time, there were no extra bonuses paid by the club in the cup, we just got the usual £4 for winning. The draw for the quarter-finals had been made on the Monday and we got Chelsea at Stamford Bridge, so just before we went out the chairman came in and said: 'There is a big bonus if you win. It will be in your pay packet on Thursday. It will be a lot more than your wages – a few hundred pounds.' Well, we beat them and as we came off I didn't know Derek was behind me. 'You silly little sod,' he said to me. 'If I had headed in that one on Saturday all you would have got was the £4. I used my brain and you got the big bonus'."

Deakin, who blames "a bit of showboating" for Dougan's miss in the first game, scored both goals in a 2-0 replay victory. "Derek pushed through an absolutely glorious pass to me and I was brought down in the box," he recounts. "I remember him asking some of the opposition if they cared to have bet on whether I would score the penalty or not."

The *Peterborough Evening Telegraph* cited the contribution of Dougan, who had by now shared 13 cup goals with Deakin, as a vital component of the victory. Reporter Alan Curling wrote: "When Derek Dougan really turns on the heat Posh are almost unstoppable. It would have taken more than a double centre-half to hold him last night. He fought for every ball and chased every possible opening."

§

Seaside preparations for the quarter-final were given an interesting twist when it was discovered that they would be sharing the Norbreck with opponents Chelsea, but in front of 63,000 at Stamford Bridge the teams were never in the same neighbourhood. Peterborough's hopes of a further upset lasted only the 90 seconds it took for Crowe to tear a groin muscle and leave the field for treatment. By the time he limped back on after 20 minutes, Tommy Docherty's exciting young Chelsea charges had scored three goals on their way to a 5-1 win.

Deakin says: "It was always going to be a hell of a job to beat them at Stamford Bridge. Maybe at London Road we might have done something, but there was a massive crowd and they were jumping. Chelsea were a pretty hot young team and it was over in quarter of an hour."

In the aftermath of Peterborough's cup heroics, Dougan was the spokesman when the players refused to attend a civic reception thrown on their behalf by the local council because an invitation had not been extended to their wives. A council member had even spoken to the players at London Road for 20 minutes in the hope of achieving conciliation, although Dougan gained the impression that some councillors were asking: "Who do these players think they are?"

Dougan used his column in the *Peterborough Standard* to point out: "A less expensive affair would have pleased us if our wives had been included." He wrote: "There was no question of us attempting to be bad mannered over these invitations. We really felt that after so many days away from our families during the cup run we honestly could not attend this kind of function on our own. Indeed, I myself have declined several invitations in the past weeks because I thought that the position was similar to the one which has arisen with the city council."

Without FA Cup thrills to sustain him any longer, Dougan once more felt the starvation of top-level football. To him and his teammates it was obvious that his departure from Peterborough was not too far in the distance. "The excitement of our Cup run did not make me forget my determination to get back to First Division football and perhaps regain my place in the Northern Ireland side," he said. He had found it too painful to watch any First Division football while at London Road, preferring to wait until he was back where he felt he belonged – with a chance to prove that, at the age of 27: "I was not a has-been".

Peterborough's push for promotion faded in the wake of their cup run, as is so often the case. Deakin explains: "The team here was almost as good as the one I had come from in the First Division and it looked as though we had a hell of a chance to get promotion. But after reaching the sixth round of the cup it was not easy to make up the backlog of games. And after playing at Stamford Bridge it was not easy to go to places like Gillingham on a cold Tuesday evening, where they are waiting for you with their sleeves rolled up."

At the end of a season in which he added 18 league goals in 39 games to his FA Cup tally and the club had finished eight points adrift of promotion in eighth place, Dougan was on his way. Following newspaper talk of a move to Blackpool, it was Leicester City boss Matt Gillies with whom a £26,000 deal was negotiated.

According to Peterborough manager Clark, a transfer was unavoidable once the club decided they could no longer afford his wages. "I did not want him to go, but it was not possible to have a player here on unsatisfactory terms," he said.

Dougan made a respectful exit, expressing regret and predicting big things for the club, but inside he was elated. "There was nothing to keep me at Peterborough," he recorded later. "I had a sense of being stranded in the wilderness. When I signed for Leicester I knew how Floyd Patterson felt when he regained the [world heavyweight] title."

Birks says: "Duke was far too good for the Third Division and it was inevitable he would move. He had a great record with us. We had played Leicester in the League Cup and I think they had watched him for a while."

Deakin adds: "He had done the business at Peterborough and I was just sorry I couldn't go with him, having been his partner in crime. Between us we had scored about 50 goals and had plenty of banter about who would get more. Many of my goals were as result of balls put in the box and Derek putting them down for me. We did have a very good link-up, which didn't surprise me."

Dougan's Posh teammates sent him on his way with their best wishes, while he left them with many cherished memories. Despite his frustration at being removed from the highest level of English football, he had been a happy and popular colleague. There is a suggestion that perhaps he actually thrived in a situation where he was undisputedly the number one player, his face and red Jaguar known all over town, part of his ego content at being by far the biggest fish in a much smaller pond.

"Everyone knew each other in Peterborough in those days," says Deakin. "He was quite a revered character in the town. He had quite forthright views and he got the club a lot of notice because he always had something to say and if anyone wanted a headline he quickly provided one."

Rankmore adds: "He was so well known, although that also went for a lot of the players because Peterborough was not a big place and everyone focused on the football club. He liked doing his column and the local reporter took him under his wing a bit and gave him advice about writing for the newspaper. Derek always thought he could make a living out of it."

McNamee concludes: "Derek liked Peterborough and he was fun. He was always up to something. We had one lad who was a bit of a pig, couldn't say no to any food. Up at Blackpool, Derek had some broken biscuits made into parcel and had this chap's name called out to go and collect it at reception. He was all excited and then found out it was broken biscuits! Another time, I got a call at about 10pm. 'Peter, I am in a ditch. I can't get the Jag out.' About four of us had to go and pull him out of this field. After he went to Leicester some of us used to go and see him for a chat. We missed him."

Chapter 9

BACK IN THE BIG TIME

Tom Sweenie, a young Leicester City inside-forward at the time of Derek Dougan's signing for the club, was one of the first of the club's former players to respond to the *Leicester Mercury* when it asked for volunteers to fill in a questionnaire about their time at Filbert Street. Asked which teammates he had roomed with, Sweenie's response was: "Derek Dougan – he was educational."

When I ask Sweenie about that comment he recalls Dougan joining his new colleagues while on tour in Germany: "He was a very intelligent guy. He became my hero of all the people I played with. Derek flew over to Germany and arrived while we were having a meal after a game. He was introduced to the players and then started talking to all the waiters in German. Everyone was impressed. He was a real smoothie and we found out that he was quite fussy. I remember that we had a big Christmas party. I had only just started to drink beer and Derek went to the bar at this night club and stipulated exactly what he wanted – whisky with Canada dry. I thought a dry ginger ale was a dry ginger ale, but American wasn't good enough for him."

The excitement in Leicester over Dougan's arrival extended well beyond the city's bar staff. Record season ticket sales were reported in the wake of his transfer from Peterborough. "The Leicester manager [Matt Gillies] was clever," says Sweenie. "During the summer he always signed a big name so that all the fans would buy season tickets."

There was also satisfaction in the dressing room that Dougan would now be bringing his tricks to bear on Leicester's behalf. Full-back Richie Norman explains: "He had always been a real handful for Ian King, our centre-half – and all of us, actually – with his height and ability. He was quite a lad in chatting away to the opposition to try to break concentration and then he would shoot off and get the ball."

Having spent two years believing that he was a First Division player forced by circumstance to play two flights lower, it was now time for Dougan to justify his self-image. Leicester teammates recall that it was a challenge that excited, rather than daunted, him.

England goalkeeper Gordon Banks explains: "There is nothing like a new club to give you a lift and give you a presence of mind to say: 'I will show these supporters. I will show I am worth the money and that I am worth my place.' But Derek also had the confidence along with that to believe in himself and believe he belonged back in the First Division."

Midfielder Bobby Roberts adds: "Derek was very confident guy. There was never any doubt in his mind that he would be a success and he had two terrific seasons with us."

According to Norman: "We had a good side but we were struggling to score goals. We knew he had been a good player and would still be. Signing him was good prestige for our team."

Norman, incidentally, had been in the Wembley crowd when Dougan made his infamous appearance for Blackburn in the 1960 FA Cup Final. "Me and Gordon Banks went down to the final in Gordon's little Standard 8. We had a couple of tickets standing up behind the goal. Derek played, but then we heard he had asked for a transfer. I thought he was a bit of a character – things like that didn't happen in those days. I ended up becoming good friends with him."

Dougan believed his transfer to Leicester had owed something to a game in 1962 when he and Bobby Thomson had shared six goals in an 8-3 Aston Villa victory. Chairman Len Shipman had remembered the performance and recommended him to Gillies, who was attempting to build a team to match the 1963 side that had challenged for the Double before finishing fourth in the league and losing to Manchester United in the FA Cup Final.

Dougan felt he had evidence that Gillies, a Scot who had been in charge for six years, had not been the one to initiate the transfer, claiming that "his attitude towards me was curious indeed". He wrote: "Almost from the day I arrived there was an undercurrent which made me feel I was not welcome as far as he was concerned."

Yet Eddie Plumley, club secretary at the time, recalls: "It was the foresight of Matt Gillies and the coach, Bert Johnson, that took Derek from Peterborough. They saw something in him and he was an absolute revelation."

Further dissatisfaction was caused when Dougan, whose claim to have taken a £1,000 pay cut to get back to First Division football is supported by Plumley's memory, said that he had been misled about the salaries of his new teammates: "When I found out that the players were not being paid the same wages and that there appeared to be discrimination I was very disappointed."

Future Wolves teammate John Holsgrove relates the story of Dougan's attempt to improve his finances: "Derek told me that he went in to ask for a £2 rise and Matt Gillies wouldn't give it to him. It got to a point where they agreed on £1 and Matt got out his packet of cigarettes and wrote '£1 a week for Dougan' on the back of it. That was how they dealt with the players."

Such an exchange, however, was a symptom of something of greater concern to Dougan than money, which was – and stop me if you've heard this one before – the lack of rapport with his new manager, a former Leicester player who had been in charge of the team for six years. Dougan could easily have been talking about Freddie Cox, Dally Duncan, Joe Mercer or his future Wolves boss Bill McGarry when he commented: "I found him remote and uncommunicative, while he in turn found me wayward and too self-determined… he thought I had too much to say for myself and this made him suspect me of being potentially troublesome."

Sweenie says: "Derek was definitely a man of strong views. At Leicester there were a lot of us Scottish players and we had a lot of banter in the dressing room. He was outnumbered but he always came out on top because he was so clever in his arguments. I think the management at Leicester realised they couldn't handle him."

Norman has a similar view: "Derek had strong opinions that did not always coincide with the management side of things. If ever we had a meeting it would go on a bit, and when it got to 'anyone else have anything to say?' it would always be Derek, whether about football or something administrative."

Gillies, it should be noted, was not a Freddie Cox type who was generally unpopular with his players. Many of Dougan's teammates had been led by Gillies to within touching distance of the pinnacle of English football, so even if they acknowledge that he could be distant from the team, they did not all see it as a fault in the way Dougan clearly did.

Peter Rodrigues, a promising right-back bought from Cardiff, says: "Matt signed me so I thought he was a gent. You knew where the line was and what would happen if you broke the rules. I was just a young player keeping my head down and doing the business. Doog and the other senior players were very welcoming and I looked up to him. He and Matt were just different characters."

Roberts adds: "Matt was a terrific manager. Managers then were different to now, not as high profile. They didn't say as much or get the press coverage. We didn't see Matt coaching every day, but we saw him on a Saturday and you knew how he wanted you to play. Other than that, the only time you saw him was when you wanted to negotiate new wages!"

Banks, who won the World Cup with England at the end of Dougan's first season at Leicester, adds: "I don't think any of us had a rapport with the manager because he didn't mix with the players. We saw hardly anything of him. We had jokes and laughed about him."

Inside-forward Davie Gibson admits to being unsure why Dougan and Gillies "just didn't gel". He says: "Matt didn't drop him so I can't understand why Derek didn't like him. Usually, as long as they pick you, players will be happy with the manager. But Derek could find an argument in an empty house if he wanted to."

Gibson can also see how his teammate could get Gillies's back up on the field: "I always said he was a Jekyll and Hyde character. He must have been a manager's nightmare. He was a free spirit and, for better or worse, you never knew on the day what you would get. I felt the game was too easy for him. Sometimes he would go out and float around and have players at swearing him, asking if he was going to try. Then he could have a brilliant five-minute burst, score you a goal and win you the game."

Roberts continues: "There were a couple of days when you wondered what had happened with him. Strikers do have that sort of thing where they go missing. Over the piece, though, he was terrific and you could always rely on him to get you goals and make goals."

Sweenie also has mixed memories: "Derek was international class but the big minus was his work rate. I would sometimes be running all over the place because I was the baby in the team and he would go over and talk to the crowd. But sometimes he would have me in state of shock with the things he could so. He was three or four moves ahead of anyone."

Plumley adds: "I always remember sitting with the coaches on the sideline and them saying 'just watch this'. He would sometimes arrive just a second too late to make the tackle. He looked to be chasing people down when in fact he never really got there and people would think he was unlucky. But he had such skill, enough to have been successful in today's game."

Norman believes part of the problem was that "Matt liked a family type of team, everybody in it together", adding: "Discipline was a lot tighter. Matt wasn't rigidly strict but he liked smart people and manners about the place. He would even insist on collar and tie to come to training. Obviously on the field it had to be the same."

Whatever the state of his relationship with the manager, there was no doubting the affection and admiration Dougan inspired among many of his new colleagues, even if it was mixed with those moments of frustration. In his first season at Filbert Street he scored 19 goals in 37 league games as Leicester finished seventh in the table and were among the division's three top-scoring teams with 80 goals.

Gibson says: "I would say we had a better team when we nearly won the Double, but we had a good team and had signed Derek and [winger] Jackie Sinclair. Big Derek used to moan about Jackie: 'The miserable wee bastard won't cross.' Jackie was a goalscorer, but I used to say to Derek: 'Mike Stringfellow crosses enough for you to score your share.' Derek had a magic touch for a big guy and when he put his mind to it he was a good, honest pro."

Norman recalls the outlet Dougan provided for his defenders: "He was a good target man, great at control and collecting the ball from the back. If you were really in trouble you could knock a high ball in and he would deal with it. He was aggressive with it – he didn't let you stand in the way too long. At end of it he got goals. He was deceivingly quick and at training he used to beat anybody over 20 yards."

Banks supports his teammates' memory of Dougan's speed and fitness: "I will never forget training sessions where we used to do a seven-lapper. There were seven points on a running track round the pitch and we had to sprint to the first one and then jog round. Next time, you sprinted to the second then jogged round. The sprinting became longer and towards the end you were really tired. We got to the sixth one and were sprinting over the far side of the pitch and everybody was blowing like mad. I am in the middle of the group, pounding away down the back straight, and Derek comes from the behind and starts talking to me. 'Come on, Banksy,' he is saying. I couldn't believe he had breath to speak – and then he pushed on to the front. He was a very, very fit guy."

Rodrigues recalls Dougan's competitive nature being evident in training: "As an opponent in matches, he would annoy you. He would do the same in practice matches, get a little niggly. But if you are that character, then that's how you are. You can't be something Monday to Friday and then something else on Saturday."

Dougan, as usual, made his mark off the field, and not just with impressionable youngsters like Sweenie. "He was one of main characters in the dressing room," says Norman. "Nothing fazed him. He had little routines like stretching himself out on the dressing room floor – because this was before all the stretching they do now. He always used to complain about his back. That was quite a body there to stretch out, so we couldn't move until he had done all this.

I used to travel a lot with him and we used to chat away. He was always happy and loved days at the golf club. He was not keen on golf at that stage and while we used to go out and play golf he played cards. He was always his own man and knew where he was heading. He was smart; immaculate in fact. He wore shirts with collars three or four inches wide, separate to the shirt itself. He had them specially made in Blackburn."

Gibson recalls: "Derek was a big fun guy; he had a lovely personality. He was a match-winner and you want someone like that with you on a Saturday. I enjoyed playing with him and he put smile back on supporters' faces. He was a showman, no two ways about that, but he produced the goods."

Banks adds: "We used to have a laugh in the dressing room. He was good fun, cracking jokes and messing about. But he had a serious side. I remember the manager put me up for sale and he stormed into see him and said, "Have you gone crazy?" He gave Matt a piece of his mind."

Personal fitness was another issue Dougan took seriously, an apparent result of his Wembley experience with Blackburn. Plumley recalls: "He was one of the first guys who, if he got injured, never did anything until he felt he was perfect. I also remember him coming into the office one day and saying he needed some money for his travel allowance. I asked him what it was for and he said he had been to see some magical specialist in Germany for treatment. He said he hadn't spoken to Matt but it would be OK because he was now fit again. I said: 'Well, you'd better check it with the boss first.' He never came back about it."

Back in the spotlight of the First Division, Dougan's public profile was heightened a little more by his appearance in the first season of *Quizball*, a BBC show that ran from 1966 to 1971. Football teams, represented by players, coaches and a celebrity fan, competed in a general knowledge contest in which they could select four easy questions in an attempt to score or opt for fewer tougher questions, bringing the phrase 'Route One' into the football lexicon as indicating the most direct passage to goal.

Dougan relished the opportunity to show that his brains were not kept in his boots, lining up with Plumley, centre-half John

Sjoberg and TV personality Lady Isobel Barnett, who had scored five 'goals' in a quarter-final victory. Plumley recalls: "We did all right but then got stuffed in the semi-finals by Arsenal. Lady Isobel was a big quiz star at the time but it was ironic that all the sports questions seemed to fall to her that day."

Back on the real football field, Dougan's career at Leicester was nearing its conclusion, maintaining his habitual two-year cycle. After playing 31 league games in 1966/67, during which he scored 16 goals – plus another five in the League Cup – he was sold to Wolverhampton Wanderers. "There was certainly no reason for it form-wise," says Richie Norman. "He was banging in the goals."

Bobby Roberts admits: "It was a bit of a shock, but Leicester had a name at that time of selling players, like McLintock and Banks. We always seemed to sell one to bring one in. Derek had done well but you were aware of something in the background; that he and Matt were not getting on that well."

It transpires that Dougan had finally given Gillies the opportunity to get rid of him. Room mate Davie Gibson takes up the story: "We played down in London and the team went to Brighton for a long weekend afterwards. We had a couple of beers and on Sunday Derek went to Portsmouth to see Sammy Chapman. He stayed there overnight but arrived back in time for training the next morning. Our old trainer, Davey Jones, came in that morning to make sure he was up for breakfast and Derek wasn't there."

Norman adds: "We were given Saturday night and Sunday free and on the Monday we hadn't seen Derek since we booked in. On Monday morning, Gordon [Banks] and I saw him coming in. The management didn't like Derek going away on his own. Even though it was a free weekend you weren't mean to disappear."

Gibson continues: "At that moment his past caught up with him. Matt thought he had been out on the town. Derek came back up to the room after seeing the trainer and told me: 'They have sent me home.' When we got back on the Wednesday I saw him and asked if he'd been fined. 'The bastards have transferred me to Wolves,' he said. It seemed like the club had decided 'we have had enough of this guy'. We could all have been up all night in Brighton; thousands of players have done it and not got caught. When Derek was rooming with me we had a couple of pints but were always back when we were supposed to be. This time destiny took a hand and it turned out to be the best thing that happened to him."

Dougan might have been angered by the manner of his summary removal from Filbert Street, but overall he was relieved to be free of the Gillies regime, which he felt was threatening to stagnate his career. On his return from Brighton, he had been called into the manager's office and told that Wolves manager Ronnie Allen wanted to buy him. He had ten minutes to make a decision, barely time to call his wife. When he later asked Allen what the rush had been he was informed that he had been attempting to sign him for the previous six weeks.

Many fans wrote to Filbert Street expressing their anger at the deal and threatening to cancel season tickets. Several teammates were equally disappointed. "He was a breath of fresh air when he came to Leicester," says Gibson. "It was a sad day when he left, but being transferred to Wolves turned out to be the best thing that ever happened to him. He finally grew up when he left Leicester and went on play the best football of his career. It took him all that time to mature."

Chapter 10

HAPPY WANDERER?

If anything encapsulates perfectly the enigma of Derek Dougan, then it is the eight years he spent at Wolverhampton Wanders, the club with whom he is most instantly identified and in whose colours he was born aloft at his funeral.

It was in the shadows of the distinctively gabled Molineux Street Stand that he finally settled at a club for more than his habitual two years; in the gold and black that he at last won a major honour in English football.

And it was during the period between 1967 and 1975 that he grew from a quirky and sometimes controversial footnote to the big stories of the day into a genuine headline-maker, an icon of the first media-driven age of football superstars, his grin, lengthening hair and soon-to-be-cultivated Zapata moustache a staple of the glossy youth-orientated football magazines and technicolor televised highlights. And yet...

Dougan had arrived at the club full of naïve optimism, which he maintained at least until publishing his book *Attack!* in 1969. In it, he wrote: "Only with Wolverhampton Wanderers have I found what I expected to find on the English shores when I arrived at Portsmouth at the age of 18."

Contrast that with this statement from 1980's *Doog*, where he summed up the complexities of his Molineux career thus: "It was a wretched environment, which I compare to an open prison at least as far as I was concerned. And yet my years with Wolves were the most satisfying of my career. This is no contradiction. I loved the club, but not the managerial dictates and the petty forms of discipline."

So what caused such a change of outlook – apart from the obvious need to watch his words in his first book, written while he was still an active player? It might appear simplistic to blame it all on a change of manager, but that is the biggest single contributory factor. When Ronnie Allen, the man who took him to Wolves, was replaced the following year by Bill McGarry it was, in Dougan's mind, like the move from Eddie Lever to Freddie Cox at Portsmouth all over again.

"Derek was too big for Bill McGarry," ventures Wolves defender John Holsgrove. "People don't understand that players nowadays run the show and the big names can say things and do things and get way with it. In general, at most clubs the players are far bigger than the managers. But in our day it was the other way round and Derek was a challenge to that."

It didn't take long for McGarry to establish himself on the list of managers with whom Dougan had spectacularly failed to get along. In *Doog*, he described his seven years under McGarry as "the most traumatic of my career" and spoke of "torment, frustration" and a frequent desire to walk out of the club. That he stayed was, he said, down to his affection for chairman John Ireland and the "aura" that remained from the club's greatest days.

Dougan was hardly the first player to find himself suddenly forced to play under someone other than the manager who had signed him, but his empathy with Allen had been powerful, and appeared even more so when set alongside his detachment from McGarry.

His ego had been stroked by the knowledge that Allen had been pursuing him for some time and he was relishing the challenge ahead of him at Wolves. The fact that he had once again stepped out of the First Division was mitigated by joining a club that was challenging strongly to regain a place in the top flight of English football, a division they had won three times in the 1950s.

Allen, a former England forward, had become Wolves manager in 1965 in place of Andy Beattie, whose year in the thankless role of successor to the legendary Stan Cullis had resulted in relegation.

"Ron knew he would be a manager eventually," says Holsgrove, a former Allen teammate at Crystal Palace who was signed for Wolves by Beattie. "Andy was fire-fighting and I knew he would be on his way."

Allen's rebuilding included the signing of wing-half Mike Bailey from Charlton and forward Ernie Hunt from Swindon. Crystal Palace striker Dave Burnside was added in 1966/67 and, with the team sitting in second position in March, the final piece of the promotion jigsaw arrived in the very individual shape of Dougan.

"We knew of his reputation," says Bailey. "Our first thoughts were: 'We are picking up some big players here.' It gave us a hell of a lift, not only from what he brought on the field but the intent it showed at the club. Derek was such a brilliant buy because he came to us at the right time. We were top of the league with Coventry, going for promotion, and without a shadow of doubt he pushed us all the way into the First Division and it was the start of something big."

Holsgrove recalls: "The discussion around the club was that this fellow was a bit this and a bit that, but I decided to take him as he is. He was a larger-than-life fellow and we became friends. Some people in the club didn't get on with him but he was a great signing from a football point of view. I always tell people he was one of the best signings I have ever been involved with. No one can play on his own and it was a very strong team with some fantastic players, but you could see we needed something in the last couple of months. It was a long season and we needed a bit of a fillip. Maybe it was just psychological but he was colossal. He walked into the club and made a difference."

Not before he had needed some help in actually getting inside Molineux. Wolves fan Peter Bartlett recalls: "I was co-editing the local college newspaper and a couple of the guys who fancied themselves as reporters went down there to the ground in the hope of finding somebody. They found this tall, lanky chap and he had to ask them the way in. They quickly worked out who he was and he gave them a full interview. The *Express and Star* liked it so much they ran it as well."

After playing his first game for Wolves in a 1-0 victory at Plymouth, Dougan made a home debut that has gone down in the folklore of the club. The stage could not have been better set for someone who so craved the big occasion – an expectant crowd of 30,000 and the BBC's *Match of the Day* cameras – and Dougan responded in magnificent style.

He scored his first Wolves goal after a cross from left-winger David Wagstaffe fell to Bobby Thomson[8], whose side-footed effort deflected into the path of Dougan and gave him a simple chance from three yards. His triumphant leap demonstrated his delight, which was doubled in the second half when he ran on to a through ball in the inside-right channel and saw his scuffed right-foot shot bounce into the net. The hat-trick arrived following good work on the right by Wagstaffe and a header across goal by Terry Wharton. With the ball dropping behind him, Dougan connected with a flick of his left heel and met the descending ball with a fierce volley from just inside six-yard box.

Holsgrove says that Dougan's performance was "just unbelievable and summed up what he meant to the team", while Wagstaffe recalls: "He arrived in a fairytale manner. That first home game was something special and I will never forget it. Whoever wrote the script must have been the same person who wrote the Roy of the Rovers cartoons. You couldn't have dreamt it up."

On the Molineux terraces, the reaction was no less effusive. "It was breathtaking," Bartlett remembers. "You could see he was a class apart even from someone like Peter Knowles. You could see what he was trying to do and, of course, he played to the gallery. Before long all the songs were about the Doog."

London-based fan Robert Goddard adds: "I was talked into going up to Wolverhampton and my first game was Derek's home

---

8   Not to be confused with the former Aston Villa teammate of the same name.

debut. He came out with his first clenched to the sky. I was on the North Bank and when the third goal went in I fell forward with the others and cried my eyes out. Everybody loved him."

Dougan failed to score in single-goal victories on consecutive days against Huddersfield but then had a run of six goals in six games, including two each in a pair of 4-1 wins at home to Bury and Norwich. The first of those victories secured promotion with three games still remaining, but defeats at Coventry and, on the final day of the season, at Crystal Palace left Wolves one point behind Coventry in the battle for the division championship – although a comfortable six points clear of Carlisle, who missed out in third place.

Wolves' success was a reward for the adventurous approach of their manager, who fielded an old-fashioned forward line of two wingers, with two advanced inside-forwards up in support of Dougan at centre-forward.

Nine goals in 11 games had made Dougan an instant cult hero with the Wolves fans, although his late equaliser in the 1-1 draw against Millwall at The Den had clearly incensed one home supporter. Dougan, typically, had had the crowd on his back throughout the game and one fan could contain himself no longer, charging at the object of his anger and aiming a kick. Dougan stood his ground, fearing that turning away would have allowed his assailant, one Albert Yates, to bring him down from behind, and four policemen were quickly on hand to drag the man away.

Wolves spent the summer of 1967 in North America, posing as the Los Angeles Wolves of the newly-formed United Soccer Association. A rival to the equally new National Professional Soccer League[9], the USA had decided that instead of scrambling to sign players it would simply import entire teams and disguise them as their own.

By this bizarre notion did Stoke City become the Cleveland Stokers, Aberdeen the Washington Whips and Sunderland the Vancouver Royal Canadians – among other bizarre transplantations

---

9   The two organisations merged after the 1967 under the title of the North American Soccer League, which was to run until 1984.

that also included Dundee United (Dallas Tornado), Hibernian (Toronto City), Glentoran (Detroit Cougars), Shamrock Rovers (Boston Rovers) and teams from Brazil, Holland, Italy and Uruguay.

Instead of a couple of weeks at the seaside with Jutta and the boys, Dougan was to spend his summer locked in a competitive 12-game schedule that spanned almost two months and all four compass points of America. In modern times, such a proposal would cause uproar among well-travelled players, but to the less privileged men of the 1960s – whose experience of overseas depended mostly on their selection for national teams – it was the opportunity of a lifetime.

Aberdeen goalkeeper Bobby Clark, whose 'Washington' team contested a memorable final against Wolves, recalls: "Players weren't spoiled back in those days. We were a lot happier about things like that. America was an exciting, far-away place, somewhere we had never had the chance to play before. To go there and live in the Hilton for a couple of months, to play in an indoor stadium like the Houston Astrodome, to be flying to every game, to go to Disneyland and see Andy Williams in concert – it was all so different to anything we had known before."

Dougan, however, did not exactly board the plane wearing Mickey Mouse ears and clutching his suntan oil, as Bailey explains: "Derek had strong opinions and the one occasion I really remember there being a bit of a confrontation with the management was when we were going to America for about seven weeks. Derek didn't think we were getting enough money for it and made his feelings known."

Wolves began their campaign in front of 35,000 at the Houston Astrodome and after four wins in their first six games were always on course to win the Western Division title, Dougan scoring in three consecutive victories. He was also sent off, harshly, for questioning the referee during a game against Dutch team Den Haag, posing as the San Francisco Golden Gate Gales.

Eventually, division winners Wolves and the Whips (Aberdeen) tossed a coin to see who would host the one-off final, with the Los Angeles Coliseum emerging as the venue a few months after it had hosted the first-ever Super Bowl. The game concluded a tournament that had been marred by many ugly incidents, which at least dispelled the notion of teams not taking it seriously. Wolves and Aberdeen had themselves brawled their way to a 1-1 draw during the 'regular season' – a game which had to be replayed when Aberdeen complained Ronnie Allen had used three outfield substitutes instead of two plus a goalkeeper

§

The final, however, was a remarkably thrilling 126-minute affair, eventually won 6-5 by Wolves courtesy of an own goal by Ally Sherwan in sudden-death additional extra-time. Clark recalls: "There were penalties saved and scored, good goals and bad goals. It was a bizarre situation in a way. It was like a basketball game with all that scoring. But it was one of those games you desperately wanted to win."

Dougan, skippering the team in the place of the injured Mike Bailey, scored the first goal in extra time to give Wolves a 5-4 lead, while Aberdeen defender Frank Munro grabbed last-gasp equalisers in normal time and again in the main period of extra time as part of a hat-trick, helping to secure himself a £45,000 transfer to Molineux that resulted in a lifelong friendship with the man he had been marking in Los Angeles.

"I had played against Derek before for the Scottish League but didn't know him until I joined Wolves," recalls Munro, left disabled in his later years by a stroke. "We remained great friends and he used to come and see me every day when I was ill. I am still stunned by his death and keep going to pick up the phone to dial his number."

For his part, Dougan always claimed that it was his glowing report on Munro that persuaded Allen to make the signing: "I had no hesitation is saying that he was a player of immense talent and he would do well to get him. I am not sure he counselled with anyone else. He backed my judgement and his own and went ahead."

Preparing his weary men for their return to First Division football, Allen predicted: "We will be a very hard side to beat. During our two seasons in the Second Division every opposing side has been more than usually keen to beat the once-mighty Wolves. Now we are keen to show the so-called top dogs that once again we've got what it takes."

He described his young team as one "without any individual stars", and added: "We have a number of experienced players in the side and many promising youngsters who could become big names if they continue to progress."

The club's first season back was a struggle, however, with 17th place in the table being accompanied by first-hurdle defeats against lower-division opposition in both cup competitions. Dougan was surprised early in the season when Allen sold striking partner Hunt to Everton for £80,000, doubling the money he had paid for the west-countryman, and felt he lacked support for much of the season. Nevertheless, he confirmed his status as a First Division forward of note by top-scoring with 17 goals in his 38 league appearances. His ability, often hidden by past controversies and inconsistencies, was becoming ever more apparent.

Terry Neill, Arsenal centre-half throughout the 1960s and Northern Ireland teammate, remembers: "There was a little bit of an edge when we faced each other and I came out on the losing side most of the time. He ran me ragged. He was a good athlete, had a good touch and was good in the air. He had these patches where he seemed to drift out of game with an air of disdain, almost reminiscent of Thierry Henry. Playing against someone like that can be more difficult than someone who is up for it from the start. Then, you can set your mind for 90 minutes of hard labour. With Dougan you'd be thinking: 'I haven't seen him for ten minutes' because he would be laying the ball off on the wing and floating about out there and suddenly, bang, and he'd be back."

John Holsgrove states: "Derek was not a great passer and didn't seem to me to have great control, but he had that fantastic streetwise ability, which was head and shoulders above the rest of us. He would go out and rattle opposing centre-halves. I remember him playing against Alan Stephenson at West Ham and all through the game he would be saying: 'You are not half the player of Holsie'. He had pace, a very good left foot and had that intuition about where the ball was going to land. He was not manufactured, he learned to dribble on the streets of Belfast and he had the hunger."

Bailey adds: "What he really brought us was experience. We had two very good wingers and we needed someone who was excellent in the air and very enthusiastic. He had a crafty way of backing into defenders and could win you the odd free-kick that could make all the difference in a tight game. He was a very good athlete as well. You knew you could knock the ball into spaces for him."

Long-serving left-back Derek Parkin says: "He was a tremendous runner off the ball and was so easy to find. He used to tell you to hit the space and would guarantee that nine times out of ten he would get it. He was so awkward to play against because he did what you thought he wouldn't do. He made brilliant runs and when he was pushed or kicked he just got on with the game."

Midfielder Kenny Hibbitt, who signed for Wolves during the 1967/68 season and was one of Dougan's suppliers for the next seven years, says: "I thought he did great and I loved the guy. He was crafty, very crafty. He had pace – not electric, but he used to knock the ball past defenders and run into them and get free-kicks. Then he would jog into the box and get on the end of them. He had some right battles with defenders. They didn't like to play against him."

Peter Simpson, a stylish defender in Arsenal's accomplished team of the late 1960s and early 1970s, names Dougan as his toughest opponent, describing him to me as "big and gangly and [he] could knock you about. You had to use your arms and bodies to make sure he didn't get the ball."

Gunners teammate Frank McLintock adds: "Derek would come and see us before the game and he always looked 7ft tall because he was so skinny and angular. As soon as he had gone Peter would say: 'You pick him up at corner kicks.' I said: "B*****s. You pick him up if he is on your side'."

Alongside that pairing was full-back Bob McNab who explains: "Dougan was quick, brave and strong and he hit you and wasn't going to be shoved around. He challenged and chased for the ball in the channels and caused you all sorts of bloody problems. He was difficult to mark because he would be all over you, a bit like Emmanuel Adebayor now. He played on your shoulder and attacked the space behind you and no defender likes players who do that. Bobby Moore told me that he didn't like playing against him. With Waggy on one side and Kenny Hibbitt on the other, that made him very effective and John Richards ended up living off him."

Stoke City's Terry Conroy says: "Derek was awkward, argumentative and played to the crowd, particularly at home. He would go down when he had been hit hard and he would milk it to get referee to give him the decision. He was a towering figure. Our centre-half Denis Smith was rock, he was like granite. They were great battles, unbelievable tussles. It was two giants meeting – no holds barred and no quarter given, 90 minutes of toe-to-toe slugging.

"He was like that with every centre-half and almost every centre-half was like that in those days. It seemed to me that every club had a Denis Smith and there were centre-forwards like Andy Lochhead, who was an absolute brute, and Ron and Wyn Davies. Guys like them and Derek could all handle themselves – they were all six-footers who could dish it out and take it. In those days everything went and defenders had a license to kill for first 20 minutes because the referees did nothing."

§

Former West Bromwich Albion defender Alan Merrick remembers: "If you played up front back then you had to be tough as nails. Doog's forte was that he had such an incredible touch to go with it, wonderful qualities that you see from the best modern players. I basically took the nose off his face in one game. In those days you could throw elbows and I thumped him good and proper when we went up for a header. I was petrified for the rest of the game about what he might do back."

Teammate and Scotland centre-half Munro recalls Dougan's combativeness showing itself when the two friends lined up against each other in an international: "Derek was very quick and I remember a game against him at Hampden Park when the ball broke to me around the edge of our box. I went past him and carried it out and he chased me for 20 yards and hacked me down from behind. I said to him: 'What are you doing, you bloody idiot? We have got a big game against Arsenal coming up.' He looked at me and said: 'Frank, I have no friends in this game'."

Holsgrove has similar memories: "Derek gave it back a lot and I only once saw him come off second best. The ball was knocked across, Norman Hunter saw him coming and slowed to let him get there first and then 'wallop' – and they had to carry him off. That was so unusual. He would talk to defenders and have a go at them in his typical way. After I went to Sheffield Wednesday I came back in the League Cup. It was good to see some old mates but when I went to shake his hand he crossed his hands in front of me and said: 'No friends'."

Gordon Banks, however, remembers Dougan's speed of thought as vividly as others recall his love of confrontation: "I thought he was a great player and he probably scored the best goal from a header that was ever scored against me. He always used to be at the far post and one time the ball came over and I had two full-backs on the line. I came to cover the far post as Derek was about to head it. He didn't power it because he knew I had that covered, but as he hung in the air he cushioned the ball and floated it over me. The full-back jumped and it went just between him and the bar – the only place he could have put it. Not only did he execute it so well, but to have been thinking how he could do it as the ball came over was marvellous."

Dougan's contribution to the team was only part of the reason that the Molineux fans took him to their hearts. His histrionics, theatrics and obvious passion for the game meant as much to those on the terraces as his goals. Holsgrove explains: "Derek put on a good performance for the supporters. He knew where his bread was buttered and didn't want to lose his reputation in the game."

Hibbitt adds: "He loved the fans and the way he waved and approached them when he scored was typical of him. He didn't run off with his shirt over his head like they do now. He went to the fans and said: 'How about that?'"

Defender John McAlle cites another example of what he calls Dougan's "charisma": "I still smile about when he used to miss the occasional sitter. He would look directly at the supporters and they would all shout back 'unlucky, Derek'. Then he'd turn to us and we'd do the same."

And Parkin adds: "He had what football lacks now, that rapport with the crowd. He was a legend at Wolves, a bloody God."

Dougan was shameless in admitting that he was a showman, but insisted: "I know when to be serious and when to give the impression of having fun out there. There's a greater pressure today not to lose and obviously your manager isn't too happy if he thinks you are being rather flippant and light-hearted with your game."

He continued: "I do try to react an awful lot to crowds, the bigger the better... I've always felt that a footballer is an entertainer. If I scored in a crucial match, I think it would be a good job that the gates were locked. Otherwise I'd be out into the road."

He also acknowledged that his popularity carried certain responsibilities. Parkin recalls Dougan, freshly showered and changed, standing in the rain signing autographs after games until the last fan had been satisfied. "He always told me: 'You must sign autographs.' That's why he was so popular."

As had been the case at Leicester, there was a practical application of Dougan's larger-than-life character. Hibbitt explains: "I had watched a lot of Wolves game on TV before I joined in 1968. I was only 17 and I was a scared rabbit going from Bradford Park Avenue into this big arena with about 35 or 40 professional players. I was in the bottom dressing room, where the reserves start before moving in to the first team, and I remember that as I came out this big tall figure standing outside was the first one to come up and welcome me and wish me all the best.

"He took me under his wing and did the same with young players like John Richards, John McAlle and Derek Parkin. Doog was the man for me. I respected him and I know he appreciated the goals I set up for him. When he walked through the changing room door in the morning you took note. He had presence and charisma, something you don't get so much these days."

Parkin, signed in 1968 from Huddersfield, recalls Dougan giving him "the best piece of advice I ever had". He explains: "I wanted to play First Division football but in those days you had no agents so you went where the club told you to go. One day Huddersfield told me that Wolves wanted to talk to me. You are frightened of missing out on an opportunity like that so you sign straight away.

"Anyway, we used to go to games by train and I remember some time later the Doog sitting in the same compartment and I said to him: 'If you were me, what would you do?' He had a nice big car and house so he seemed like the guy to ask. He said: 'Put your money in a pension scheme and buy the biggest house you can afford.' That's exactly what I did."

Geoff Palmer, who went from apprentice to long-serving full-back, describes Dougan as a "father figure". He continues: "When I joined I had the task of cleaning his boots. He wanted all his stuff laid out nice and clean before training – and he was a good tipper at Christmas. I was an impressionable 19-year-old and he would give you a gee-up when you were down. It was not only the youngsters in the first team he took an interest in; it was all the young lads at the club – particularly when he became PFA chairman. He talked to them and spent time with them and let them know they could go to him with problems.

'When Bill McGarry became manager he was a real stickler and there were times when he would have a go at you. Doog would have quick word in your ear, something like: 'Put it behind you and get on with the game.' He was always listening to what was going on around him and he could tell when you were down and would give you a pat on the back. To be fair, all the senior players at that time, people like Mike Bailey, Dave Wagstaffe and Frank Munro, looked after the young ones.

"If a team like the Leeds side of that era, with guys like Billy Bremner, Norman Hunter and Jack Charlton, had a go at you on the pitch it was nice to know that the senior players were there to look after you. Going to places like Old Trafford and Anfield was a big experience and players like Doog would put an arm on your shoulder and tell you to forget what was going on around you."

Dougan was finally applying the maturity had been missing from his game at previous clubs, even impressing players with his approach to preparation for games. "There is no fitter player at Molineux," Wagstaffe told *Shoot!* magazine. "Derek is the first at the ground every morning raring to go. He takes training very seriously and even after all his years in the game still gets a kick out of the more tedious side of preparing for a match."

Parkin recalls: "The Doog was a great trainer. I am coming into the club as young boy and looking at him and thinking: 'This guy is ten years older than me and he is out at the front in training. I will stick with him'."

Bailey remembers Dougan as being "very enthusiastic", although Hibbitt does temper his memory of his colleague's training habits with "he didn't like the weights".

Life at Molineux changed in November 1968 when Bill McGarry entered the building. The team had started the season with only two wins in their first ten league games by the time Liverpool came visiting. A 6-0 defeat, watched by almost 40,000, would have been humiliating enough on its own but to compound matters two of the goals were scored by the blond forward Alun Evans, whom Ronnie Allen had just sold to the Anfield club for £100,000, making him the most expensive teenager in British football history.

Dougan felt that the thrashing "gave [the board] the excuse they needed to get rid of Ron". Dougan's winning goal at Coventry a week later was not enough to save his manager. In fact, it was suggested later that that the Wolves directors had been trying for several months to entice McGarry from his position at Ipswich, where he had won the Second Division title the previous season.

Dougan, never slow to believe he had the solution for everything, felt that his advice could have saved Allen from his fate. He had tried to get Allen to sign Gordon Banks from Leicester, believing he could have provided a stabilising influence at a time when Phil Parkes, who would go on to make more than 300 Wolves appearances, was still maturing.

In the end, Dougan felt that some factions within the club had been unable to forgive Allen his connections with rivals West Bromwich Albion, for whom he played for more than a decade, and he also identified the need for Allen to have had a strong assistant to work with the players. "If he had concentrated more on the essentials of management and a little less on the coaching, he would have made his position more secure."

Holsgrove has a vivid memory of Allen's departure: "He came in and said: 'You will regret me leaving.' The way he said it was a bit stark." Whether or not it was intended to be a hint about the new manager, it turned out – as far as Dougan was concerned at least – to be a moment of prescience.

McGarry had won four England caps and played in the 1954 World Cup finals in Switzerland before beginning his managerial career at Bournemouth and moving on to Watford and then Ipswich.

According to Holsgrove: "Ron and Bill were chalk and cheese, they would not have got on as managers and they were opposites as players. Ron was one of the best two-footed players I have seen while Bill was a bit dour as a player. They were both England internationals but they were at other ends of the spectrum. Allen knew he could only go so far with Derek in terms of what he could do, but McGarry would say what he thought and you had to take it on the chin as a player. But McGarry had no personality and from the day he came in he saw Derek as a threat. Derek always felt that McGarry would do what he could behind the scenes to reduce his influence on the club."

Dougan claimed that McGarry was so uncomfortable around him that he would never call him by his first name, preferring "Dougan" or "Big Man", and struggled to look him in the eye when they spoke. By way of illustrating the often contrary nature of Dougan, it is worth noting that in one of his books he talks with affection about the way Wolves chairman John Ireland always addressed him as "Big Fella" instead of using his name. It clearly didn't bother him when coming from someone he admired and got along with famously.

Frank Munro says he was well aware of his friend's impossible relationship with the new manager: "Bill's problem was that Derek was such a big name among the fans at Wolverhampton. At every game there were about seven or eight guys in front of the directors' box, and the manager used to watch the game from there in the first half. The fans turned round and used to shout that they wanted Derek as manager. I think Bill eventually believed that Derek wanted to be the boss."

Hibbitt recalls that problems stemmed from "the way Bill used to run the place with his training methods". He continues: "Jim McCalliog didn't get on with him either. He was a sergeant major-type who worked the players hard. We were all decent players and experienced guys like Dougan and McCalliog didn't want to be running round the pitch like slaves. They looked on him as a bit of a bully. In the seven years I was with him he only said 'well done' to me once, but I did have respect for him and he had a great influence on my own career."

McGarry's methods made far less use of ball work than Allen's had done. Rather than strike a balance in the manner of Malcolm Allison at Manchester City, McGarry – who himself maintained an impressive level of personal fitness – became preoccupied with physical preparation, which at least turned Wolves into one of the best-conditioned teams in the league.

But, according to Dougan: "He was going to brow beat us into success and did not mind being seen as a hard taskmaster." He also recalled McGarry screaming at him: "I'm the manager. I don't want you to like me." Dougan would end up saying: "Seven years later I was still taking him at his word."

Odd rules that McGarry either introduced over time, or made up on the spot, would infuriate Dougan, including his refusal to allow Holsgrove to order a prawn cocktail with his Friday evening dinner and restricting his men to one bread roll. "What do you think this is – Butlin's holiday camp?" McGarry would bark.

Cups of tea in hotel rooms were also outlawed, as were telephone calls home at the club's expense, perks that had been accepted under the previous regime. No sweets were allowed except barley sugar, while apple pie and trifle were the only desserts to escape the banned list. Rules were imposed randomly without explanation and Dougan's preference for pasteurised milk instead of sterilised in his dressing-room tea was the cause of further conflict.

On one occasion, after a defeat against Burnley, McGarry directed his anger at the elderly gentleman who delivered Dougan's tea – one of the rare occasions Dougan recalled eliciting an apology from his boss. "I found that if I challenged Bill McGarry there was always a good chance of him backing down," he said. "But it wasn't always possible or advisable to do this."

Dougan's view was that players should not be disciplined by their manager but, like members of any other profession, encouraged to be self-disciplined. He felt that the McGarry approach sent a message that the players were nothing more than children who could not be trusted. In the end, he likened the blockade between him and his boss to an electrified barrier.

What mystified him was that he didn't believe he'd given McGarry cause for such a reaction. He was on time for training, never missed the team bus and, in his increasing media work, was careful never to say anything detrimental to the club. The conclusion was that Dougan's previous, well publicised, difficulties with managers had led McGarry to adopt a confrontational stance from the start – a case of getting the retaliation in first. McGarry's approach was to make endurance as much a feature of Dougan's remaining years at Molineux as enjoyment.

Under their new management, Wolves stumbled along for the rest of 1968/69 to finish in 16th position. Dougan's personal return from 39 league games was 11 goals and he added three more in cup competitions, with Wolves remaining unbeaten in all of the games in which he scored.

After playing for Northern Ireland in the British Championship[10], Dougan flew, this time reluctantly, to the United States, where imported teams were again being used to bolster the first part of the North American Soccer League season.

Dougan's former Aston Villa teammate Phil Woosnam, now league commissioner, had recruited six British teams to represent the remaining NASL clubs, which meant that Wolves temporarily became the Kansas City Spurs. In front of small crowds barely scraping into the few thousands, Wolves repeated their success

---

10   This was the first year in which the tournament, also known as the Home International Championship, was condensed into one week at the end of the season rather than being spread throughout the season. The organisers attracted much criticism for allowing live television coverage of the games, which was held responsible for the turnout of only 7,483 to see Northern Ireland's midweek visit to Scotland. Dougan, a firm believer in the benefits for the game of increased TV exposure, preferred to blame the torrential downpour that left Hampden Park awash.

of two years earlier, winning six of their eight games and being made honorary citizens of Kansas City for their efforts.

An old friend, Gordon Clark, came calling on Wolverhampton as the new season approached. Now chief scout at Arsenal, Clark was assisting Gunners manager Bertie Mee in an exhaustive, and ultimately futile, search for an international calibre centre-forward. Dougan was among several high-profile names the London club enquired about, but despite the ongoing relationship problems McGarry insisted that his striker was to remain at the club.

According to Dougan, Ronnie Allen had adopted a different approach a couple of years earlier when he had been prevented from accepting an £80,000 offer from Coventry by the intervention of chairman John Ireland, while McGarry would also reject subsequent enquiries for his striker from Leeds, Manchester United and Liverpool. Dougan wondered whether his possible transfer to Arsenal was blocked because of the antipathy between him and his boss and a reluctance to allow him to go to a higher-placed team.

Perhaps it was simpler than that. Whatever personal discomfort McGarry might have felt around and towards Dougan, he was fully aware of his value to the team. Several forwards were brought to the club during Dougan's time there – men such as Frank Wignall, Hugh Curran, Bobby Gould and Steve Kindon. Dougan felt that McGarry was trying to find someone to replace him. None of them did. Maybe they were never intended to.

Kenny Hibbitt certainly recognised the faith McGarry had in Dougan to deliver on the field: "He still picked Doog every week," he points out. "I remember the year we were playing Coventry in the quarter-final of the FA Cup. During the warm-up, Doog goes over and puts his hands up to the crowd and next thing he is laid flat-out cold. Steve Kindon had been warming up Phil Parkes and whacked this volley into the back of his head and knocked him out. McGarry was really concerned and called Kindo some right names."

Wolves might not have lost Dougan in the summer of 1969 but they were about to be denied the services of one of their best and most-revered players. It was an event that stunned the football world and added a permanent "what if" to the story of Dougan's career.

Born in Geoff Boycott's home town of Fitzwilliam, Yorkshire, Peter Knowles had made his Football League debut for Wolves at the age of 18 and quickly established himself as one of the club's prime assets with his balance, vision and skilful right foot.

As is so often the case in English football, with sublime talent went a questionable temperament, an impression of each game being played on the very edge of emotional control. Knowles's indiscretions were of the verbal, rather than violent, variety, with many a referee subjected to the edge of his tongue and opponents keen to see him niggled and knocked out of his stride. In English football in the late 1960s there were plenty of volunteers for such a role.

With Wolves up in the First Division, where Knowles had more space in which to flourish, his career appeared to be progressing on an inexorable path towards full England selection and a place in the World Cup squad of 1970. But by the start of the 1969/70 season, another influence had entered his life.

A newly-converted Jehovah's Witness called Ken Fletcher had been nervous about knocking at the door of a house he knew to be occupied by a professional footballer and was pleasantly surprised when he was invited to call back the following week to discuss the bible. Fletcher described Knowles as his first successful convert and teammates noticed that Knowles had taken to reading the bible on the coach to away games.

Wolves opened the season at home to Stoke, with Jim McCalliog, a £70,000 signing from Sheffield Wednesday, lining up in midfield. A couple of Dougan goals and several town-centre arrests later, Wolves were comfortable winners, repeating the achievement under their new £200,000 floodlights against Southampton four days later. Wins at Sheffield Wednesday – where Dougan was sent off for allegedly striking opponent Peter Eustace – and Southampton saw Wolves placed on top of the league, with two more draws maintaining their unbeaten record.

But on the front page of the *Wolverhampton Express and Star* on Thursday 29th August came a story that pointed powerfully to the bombshell that was on its way. "Is Knowles near a career crisis?" asked the headline, with the story saying that the player was "facing a moral crisis" because of the increasing demands of his religion.

On the following Monday, after Wolves' first defeat of the season, the retirement of Knowles from professional football was confirmed by the player himself: "There is nothing to stop me playing professional football and being a Witness, but I know the longer I play football the more I will drift away from being a Witness. Five days a week I am a Christian but when Saturday comes and I put the football shirt on I am not a Christian. You have to be a Christian every day of your life."

Knowles, the story explained, would play two more games before turning his back on a £100-a-week wage for a life of door-to-door voluntary work. Bill McGarry wondered if he had been ill-advised by his new acquaintances, while many of the supporting stories reacted as though Knowles had been abducted by a sinister cult.

Knowles offered further explanation in a BBC interview: "No matter how long I play football and no matter how near to perfection I come, I know... that I could break somebody's leg," he said. "And I'd hate this on my mind. It is not just the thought of breaking somebody's leg; it is the thought that that person could be out of work, that person could be crippled for the rest of his life."

Such convictions in a football dressing room leave the bearer open to much abuse from teammates and Dougan was among the most vociferous in trying to goad Knowles out of his intended course of action. "The fact that he was taking himself so seriously only encouraged a great deal of mickey-taking," he said.

Dougan also saw a good deal of irony in his teammate's fears about being over-competitive on the pitch, where he felt he "lacked moral courage" and his aggression was of the temperamental rather than physical nature. "Time and again I saw him pull out of tackles against rugged defenders," he said.

Knowles played in a League Cup win against Tottenham and, on Saturday 6th September, the day that ITV sent out its first test colour transmission, the player who was seemingly born for football's conversion from monochrome broadcasts appeared in

The Doog, RIP. Derek Dougan's coffin is carried into his funeral service at St Peter's Collegiate Church in Wolverhampton. The bearers pictured are sons Nicholas and Alexander and friend Doug Hope (Press Association).

Mersey Street School in Belfast, where Dougan took his first steps as a footballer. The closed doors reflect the changing landscape of his home town (Author).

The biggest moment of Dougan's early career in England, celebrating with Blackburn Rovers fans after scoring the second goal in his team's 2-1 FA Cup semi-final victory against Sheffield Wednesday at Maine Road in 1960. The final was to prove a less happy occasion (Press Association).

By the time Dougan signed for Aston Villa his reputation was growing and he was featured in the local newspaper's promotional campaign, his caricature appearing on beer mats (Author).

The growth in glossy football magazines in the late-1960s and early-1970s meant more exposure for the Doog. Here *Soccer Star* features him in action for his country against Scotland's Ian Ure.

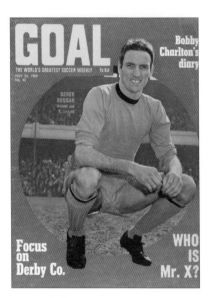

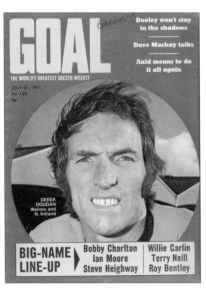

Dougan's face guaranteed instant recognition on the newsstands and *Goal* was one of those publications who regularly made him their cover star, these two issues dating from 1969 and 1971 as Wolves were entering their finest years of the Bill McGarry era.

Dougan was also good value for a story, although when *Shoot!* featured extracts from his first autobiographical volume, *Attack!*, it ignored the often dark tone of much of what he had written about his career as a professional footballer.

Being named as captain of Northern Ireland was a proud moment for Dougan. Here he walks out at Windsor Park alongside England skipper Bobby Moore before their 1971 game in the Home International Championship (Press Association).

Dougan's sister, Coreen Long, and niece, Josephine Long, at their home in Belfast (Author).

Broadcasting was a natural home for Dougan. As well as his television work for ITV, he hosted his own radio show in Birmingham (Press Association).

Dougan attempts to escape the attention of Arsenal defender Peter Simpson, who described the Wolves man as his most difficult opponent. On the right of the shot is Brendon Batson, whose future role at the PFA would keep him in close contact with Dougan in his later life (Press Association).

The crowning moment of Dougan's playing career. The memories of Wembley 1960 are erased by Wolves' 2-1 win against Manchester City in the 1974 League Cup final (Press Association).

Dougan prepares for a Professional Footballers' Association meeting with secretary Cliff Lloyd and committee members Terry Venables and Bruce Bannister. Dougan's eight years as PFA Chairman culminated in achieving an important step towards greater freedom of contract for players (Press Association).

Ex-Stoke players Terry Conroy and Gordon Banks join Dougan and Merlyn Humphreys at one of the many fund-raising events he attended in his latter years (Merlyn Humphreys).

Among Dougan's more ill-advised activities were his political ventures. Having stood unsuccessfully for Parliament in East Belfast he teamed up with Doug Hope as a representative of the UK Independent Party, even representing them on BBC's *Question Time* (Merlyn Humphreys).

Dougan's face, and those of three other players, was removed from the famous Belfast mural of George Best after his support of a united Ireland football team again attracted the attention of vandals opposed to his views (Author).

Merlyn Humphreys, who shared the last few years of Dougan's life, at home with her memories of an 'unforgettable' man (Author).

his final professional game, a 3-3 draw against Nottingham Forest. Throughout the match, the Wolves crowd mixed humour with pathos by singing his name to the tune of various hymns.

In one picture from that day, Knowles looks so happy in celebrating a goal with the scorer, Dougan, that is impossible to believe that he is about to walk away from a game he evidently still cares about. Yet there was no last-minute change of heart.

Discarding his kit on the floor of the changing room and shaking hands with his teammates, he took one last walk across the Molineux pitch and exited through a door in the stand opposite the players' tunnel. Waiting for his wife, Jean, to meet him in their yellow sports car, he was surrounded by fans, some in tears. Two teenage girls handed him a bible in wrapping paper. "I have had enough of football," he said. "There will be no comeback, now or any other day."

§

And there never was. A player whose creativity could have added so much to Dougan's own game had gone. He might have questioned his moral fibre but Dougan was well aware of Knowles's talent, citing his ability to strike an accurate ball more than 50 yards with either foot without a run-up.

Frank Munro ventures: "If Peter Broadbent was the best who ever played for Wolves then Peter Knowles was not far behind. If Knowles had carried on I think we could have reached the next level as a team, and I think Doog would have had even more success with Peter playing just behind him."

According to Holsgrove, the retirement of Knowles was, in football terms, "a tragedy". He says: "I remember him telling Waggy the world was going to end in 1971. Doog had his opinion of Knowlesy but in a way he might have respected him. Not many people have a strong view and stick to it. It was a massive blow to the club but John Richards eventually got his opportunity because of it and he went on to make a great partnership with Doog."

With Knowles having swapped the sports pages for the bible, Wolves were unable to maintain their early-season form, drifting towards 13th place in the First Division and disappointment in the cup competitions. Dougan finished with eight League goals but his season became a tale of insult and injury. The former was the string of abuse Dougan was said to have delivered to a linesman during a home defeat against Everton, for which referee Keith Walker sent him off.

When the FA's six-man disciplinary committee pondered Dougan's punishment they took into consideration the suspended 14-day ban they had issued for the previous dismissal against Wednesday and inflicted upon him an eight-week suspension, equalling the longest for any player since the Second World War.

The words of Mike Bailey and opponents Sandy Brown and Colin Harvey in speaking up for him had been insufficient to avoid a ban that would rule him out of eight games and cost him around £800 in wages. Wolves chairman John Ireland claimed it was "poor justice" for a non-violent offence, although threats of Dougan taking action against the FA for restraint of trade never materialised.

Everton were to prove Dougan's unlucky team and when he met them again in January at Goodison Park he suffered an ugly clash of heads with England full-back Keith Newton. Surveying the damage caused by Dougan's attempt to get to a high clearance by Phil Parkes, the Everton club doctor suggested an immediate visit to hospital, but Dougan insisted on waiting until he had returned to Wolverhampton.

Dougan was stunned by the lack of concern shown by McGarry, who he said never once spoke to him on the coach journey home or visited him in hospital after he had been admitted for major reconstructive surgery. The bone under Dougan's left eye had been broken in four places and 30 stitches were needed in his mouth after the surgeons had wired the pieces back together.

Dougan was in a sorry state, worsened by McGarry's "apparent indifference" and the doctors' prognosis that he would not play again during the season. After ten days, during which teammates had been to see him but conveyed no kind of message from their manager, Dougan discharged himself and set about proving the medical experts wrong, as he done when making an early return following his car crash at Aston Villa. Part of his motivation was a desire to make McGarry to take notice of him.

After two months training and convalescing away from

Molineux he had still not heard from McGarry. But when he took Jutta out for lunch one day, the manager himself happened to be leaving the same pub at that precise moment. "I'll never know how I restrained myself from striking him," Dougan said. After a polite enquiry about Dougan's general health, an embarrassed McGarry departed, leaving his player fuming that he had not asked when he might be returning to the club or for the latest doctors' report.

Dougan was tempted to submit one of his infamous transfer requests there and then, but was resolved to stick it out at Wolves. He felt he was constantly fighting a battle with his reputation for being nomadic by nature, even though he insisted that his constant transfers had been a result of a "refusal to be submerged by systems and pre-determined styles that would have stifled me".

His perseverance was about to be rewarded. They might not have been returning to the glory days of the 1950s, but the on-field fortunes of Wolverhampton Wanderers were about to take an upward turn.

Chapter 11

MEDIA DARLING

It is early in February 2008 and another new era is beginning. A home friendly against Switzerland would not, under normal circumstances, be a game to quicken the step of spectators fighting their way from Wembley Park tube station or, in these days of wall-to-wall live televised football, induce much more than a yawn from those tuning, by force of habit, into BBC1.

This particular England match, however, is the first game under the guidance of the new head coach, Fabio Capello. He is Italian, with stylish glasses, and he is not Steve McClaren. Therefore the evening is imbued with a sense of the unknown and the unexpected, a promise that anything could happen.

Such a statement can not be extended to the nature of the BBC's coverage of the event. You know what you are going to get. It will be professional and polished from start to finish, with not a hair or autocue prompt out of place. Gary Lineker will be so smooth as to utterly belie the pressure of live television; Alan Shearer will wear a serious frown; Alan Hansen will mix insight with cynicism; Ian Wright will play his role as the unscripted wild-card with word-perfect precision. The clothes will look as though they have been imported straight from the local discotheque and will sometimes be barely visible through a haze of cigar smoke.

OK, I made up that last bit. For that you have to go back to 1970, when ITV showed the way forward by presenting football analysis in the style of four blokes enjoying a pint at the local. The "World Cup panel", which added studio-base vibrancy to a tournament already made unthinkingly exotic by colour television and the wonderful Brazilians, is acknowledged as having revolutionised TV punditry.

It is true to the extent that the panel format henceforward became the standard for televised football, but it is also true that to watch the presenting team on the latest Sky Sports *Super Sunday* bears little resemblance to the chaos over which Brian Moore attempted to preside in the summer of '70. It was more *Tiswas* than *Match of the Day*.

The man responsible was John Bromley, then the head of ITV sport, who asked Moore, the network's leading commentator, to stay at home rather than travelling to Mexico, teaming him as usual with Jimmy Hill. What followed was an inspired piece of alchemy as Derek Dougan, Manchester City coach Malcolm Allison, Manchester United midfielder Pat Crerand and Arsenal and England full-back Bob McNab were thrown into the mix, wearing colours so bright and collars so wide that Moore looked like the John Alderton character Bernard Hedges, trying to control his rowdy and fashion-conscious Class 5c in *Please, Sir!*

The result was a month of television that was loud, brash, often controversial, sometimes downright insulting and always hugely watchable. For the first time in the broadcasting of sports events, ITV's figures regularly matched the BBC, which managed to look safe and staid even with Brian Clough as part of its team.

Allison, in the process of evolving into "Big Mal", was the star of the show, irreverent and dashing but with the mind of a brilliant coach to add substance to his style. Dougan played the role of his nemesis, sitting to his right, often choking on the fumes from a Cuban cigar, and mixing Irish charm and humour with a hard critical edge. Scotland international Crerand, in the manner of his play, was abrasive and energetic, while McNab offered the insight of a player who had been in the England squad until a few days earlier, when Sir Alf Ramsey had trimmed his squad from the provisional 28.

It is a sign of the strength of personality on view that McNab, who has forceful and eloquently-stated opinions, was considered the quiet man of the crew, often struggling to get a word in as the others delighted in winding up Jimmy Hill.

"We need some people who can actually talk lucidly about football," had been the guiding principle of Bromley, who changed his mind about using his panellists individually and opted instead to throw them all on screen at once and see what happened. "Crerand and Allison were the baddies," he added, "and the charming Dougan with the lovely McNab were the goodies. The whole mix was absolutely right and it took off and they became folk heroes in four weeks."

Moore recalled that "they gave football punditry a fresh intoxicating sparkle that has never quite been matched since", and said it was down to individuals who were "attractive men with a knowledgeable, knockabout style".

Looking back a quarter of a century later, Dougan told interviewers: "We were the first four people ever invited on television to actually speak about our sport. The chemistry was right and we used to spark off each other. Not once did we have a rehearsal. Malcolm was the only guy that I have ever worked with who could drink an excess of champagne and go on there and not slur his words. I used to admire him for doing that because I wouldn't try to do it."

McNab remembers: "We had some great fun and all my memories of Doog at that time are fond ones. People had never seen anything like it before although I am not sure we all realised it was ground-breaking at the time – Paddy and I didn't anyway. The BBC was very stuffed shirt and John Bromley was brilliant. Jimmy tried to control it, but Malcolm used to try to control Jimmy. He would take the p**s out of him unmercifully. Actually, we all ended up taking the p**s out each other.

"Without disrespect to Derek, he didn't have the intellectual football ideas of Malcolm, who was a brilliant coach. We noticed that he would start repeating some of the stuff Malcolm said off-camera so sometimes Mal would set him up and say the opposite of what he thought. It was all great fun and we all had a lot of respect and affection for each other."

McNab also remembers the group whiling away the afternoons at the Hendon Hall hotel before their evening broadcasts: "We used to play head tennis and nobody wanted to play on Derek's team because all you had to do was hit it to his right foot and you would win the point. Mind you, you never saw Bobby Charlton or Bobby Moore keeping the ball up and juggling either. I had a great regard for Derek as a player."

This group of articulate, stylishly dressed men enthralled viewers who followed football every day of their lives. They made the sport easily accessible even to those whose interest barely extended to the FA Cup Final, the one club game televised live each season. Fan letters and autograph hunters became an even bigger part of their lives. McNab recalls the group eating in a restaurant one night and being joined by Michael Caine who wanted to "have a drink with the lads".

Dougan had earned his place on the team by maintaining a public profile that he'd first cultivated with his 'Cheyenne' hair cut. He'd since written newspaper columns and articles in various football annuals, and had further enhanced his visibility by capitalising on the coincidence of his return to the First Division with the increased television profile of his sport.

He had even published his first book, *Attack!*, in 1969. It distinguished itself from many autobiographies of the period by giving an honest account of the frustrations he had encountered at almost every turn of his career, a contrast to the "jolly boys together" tone of many contemporary publications. The magazine, *Shoot!*, bless them, managed to miss the point by focusing on the book as being a humorous offering, even though it carried an overwhelmingly dark tone.

Dougan's summer on television increased the demands and opportunities away from the game. His raised public profile even saw him named as the best dressed man of 1972 by *Tailor and*

Cutter magazine. As well as the ability to use his name and presence to earn money by opening stores and endorsing products, there were numerous requests to contribute his time on behalf of charities and other causes in the town of Wolverhampton, where he enjoyed the status of favoured son.

Fundraising efforts for mental health research, motivational speeches to businessmen, appearances in local schools and ceremonial openings of fetes all became part of the weekly Dougan routine. He felt that players had a social responsibility to fulfil, to make a meaningful acknowledgement of the public whose support had helped to put them in such an enviable professional position.

It got to the point, however, where wife Jutta had to urge him to slow down and spend more time at home. He would end up admitting: "Throughout my career I have, at times, neglected my family because of the importance I have attached to my professional duties and responsibilities."

And, of course, when it came to seeking out players for comments, it was always Dougan who was top of journalists' lists, making sure that he was featured in every match report regardless of his on-field contribution. "The press realised that if they spoke to Derek then generally would get something good," says Northern Ireland colleague Sammy Nelson, "whereas from others it might be a bit naff."

It is understandable that the business opportunities Dougan attacked most vigorously were those that enabled him to develop his media portfolio. His World Cup appearances led to him being offered the chance to host a show on BBC Radio Birmingham, a half-hour slot at 5pm every Friday, during which he previewed the weekend action. Part of his role as presenter was to conduct one-on-one interviews with figures from a range of sports and chair round-table discussions in which local journalists were regular guests.

While teammates were resting for the next day's game by putting their feet up in front of the televised horse racing, Dougan would head to studio directly from training. "For those five hours while we are preparing the programme, the concentration is tremendous," he explained. "But it takes my mind off the match the following day."

Dougan was being paid to do what he loved almost as much

as playing football – talking. Inevitably, he showed a natural flair for the role, with the show's first producer, Roger Moody, saying: "Derek is at his best when he is chairing a discussion. He's a natural talker and his personality comes over well."

Nick Owen, who would go on to find fame as one of Britain's first breakfast television presenters, eventually became the show's producer, having been assistant producer in one of his earliest roles after moving from regional newspapers. Coincidentally, we talk two days after the consortium led by Owen has been confirmed as buyers of his beloved Luton Town, giving him a taste of the pressure that Dougan would have felt when leading the group that saved Wolves from extinction in 1982.

Dougan would doubtless have recognised the mixture of excitement and exasperation in Owen's voice when he says: "I have just finished writing my first programme notes. We only have 15 players for Saturday, which is a bit of a problem, but we can't sign any players until we come out of administration."

As conversation turns to the *Weekend of Sport* show, Owen recalls: "It was exciting to be working with Derek. I moved to BBC Radio Birmingham in 1973 and quickly got to meet him socially, and after a year or so I ended up producing him. We had some good banter and he would joke with me about Luton. Obviously the show majored on football but it would include anything else topical. Moseley and Coventry were among the leading rugby clubs at that time and supplied a lot of England internationals, while athletics was big with Birchfield Harriers and we had a horse racing spot.

"Cricket was very big and if there was a tour coming up we would have the likes of Dennis Amiss and Bob Willis in the studio. The producer, who before me was Jim Rosenthal, wrote the scripts and explained what was required and talked through everything with Doog, who would get in early afternoon.

"He would obviously have wonderful access to football stories and used his influence to get guests. In those days, access to players was difficult because clubs were not so aware of PR and the players could be quite remote. Doog was wonderful and had an easy way with people when he interviewed them. He was very charming and he was a bright enough chap that if he didn't know anything about athletics, for example, he could be fed by the producer. When he got going in an interview he could just roll along on his own."

When Dougan wasn't playing football or chatting, he was busy writing. In 1972 came his second autobiographical volume, *The Sash He Never Wore*, which ostensibly fleshed out the story of his upbringing in Belfast and which is discussed in a later chapter in the context of the reaction it caused, coming as the Troubles in Northern Ireland were approaching their most intense period.

Relating tales of his past was never going to be enough for someone with the literary ambition of Dougan and in 1974, Allison and Busby, who had published his previous book, took a chance on him as a novelist with the publication of *The Footballer*. Some sort of precedent had been set four years earlier when Terry Venables had paired with the noted screen writer Gordon Williams on *They Used to Play on Grass*, which offered a vision of British football's theoretical future.[11]

Dougan preferred to present the life of a professional footballer in the early 1970s. It is, however, little more than a hypothetical footballer's autobiography, from schoolboy starlet to England international, with tales of illegal approaches by rival clubs, clashes with authority and scrapes with newspaper men along the way.

Told mostly in flashback while the hero – Danny Stone of Branton United – has gone on a George Best-style walkabout from his club, it is, as a modern day read, painfully dated and lacks any discernable plot. There is no escaping the always clumsy nature of made-up football names and, as a supposed insight into the life of a professional footballer is little more revealing than any run-of-the-mill ghost-written autobiography. Certainly Dougan's own memoirs are a far more meritorious contribution to his sport's library.

The book did, it must be acknowledged, receive some praise from no less an authority than Melvyn Bragg, even though he pointed

---

11   Venables and Williams later co-wrote the popular ITV detective series, *Hazell*, while Venables helped bring his own vision of football's future to fruition when, as manager at Queen's Park Rangers, he oversaw the installation of English football's first artificial playing surface in 1981.

out that the construction was "predictable" and the characters "thinly drawn". Yet Bragg's review in *The Times* expressed a desire to see more of Dougan's work. "A first novel dealing with the stresses and delights of the author's own occupation must have the air of a one-off," he wrote. "Considering the narrative flair and the easy, unstrained dialogue, it will be a pity if that turns out to be the case." I suspect more people remain relieved that it was the author's only foray into the world of fiction.

The most interesting aspect of the book is that the central character's personality clash with his manager draws very clearly on Dougan's own fractured relationship with McGarry. The final few lines of the book – mentioning the manager Fred Jarman and his favoured son, club captain Charlie – were obviously written from the heart and it takes no stretch of the imagination to substitute the names of the author's real boss and captain.

"Jarman needs my talent. He would like to take it and give it to Charlie," the narrator states, going on to admit: "I shall have to put up with Jarman and he will have to put up with me. We are thrown together in mutual dislike." And he concludes: "There was a time I played the game for its own sake. Now I play for my sake."

In 1975, Dougan teamed up with historian Percy Young to produce *On The Spot: Football as a Profession*. The book is part social history of football, partly an attempt to offer an insider's view of top-level professional sport and part guidance for any younger readers who might have been considering the sport as a career.

The format of the book allows Young to demonstrate his skills as a researcher, while Dougan, as you would expect, offers opinion, insight, and illuminating anecdote. In a sense it is a more academic attempt at conveying the inside view of his sport that Dougan had somewhat clumsily presented in *The Footballer*.

Television work continued to come Dougan's way during the 1970s, although he was not expecting his half-hour in the spotlight when Eamonn Andrews surprised him with the famous red book for *This Is Your Life* early in 1974. Teammate Geoff Palmer recalls: "Bill McGarry had us in and said: 'Whether you like the bloke or not, we are all going down to London for the show.' Nobody complained."

Dougan was asked to reprise his performance on ITV's World

Cup panel for the finals in West Germany in 1974, by which time Clough's transfer had been secured from the BBC. After retiring as a player, he would secure a role in the late-1970s as analyst and presenter on Yorkshire Television's weekly highlights programmes.

Belfast broadcaster Jackie Fullerton has good reason to remember Dougan's calm professionalism when the two of them were assigned by Ulster TV to commentate on Northern Ireland's European Championship qualifier against the Republic in Dublin in the autumn of 1978. "It was my very first international as a commentator," Fullerton explains. "I had not yet learned to editorialise so I had about three suitcases of research. When Derek arrived from England he kept me calm. I was very taken by his assuredness and he clearly knew what he was doing."

Dougan had long been a proponent of allowing an increase in the amount of live football on television. Throughout the 1970s, the Football League maintained its stance on banning live broadcasts. Even radio coverage was restricted to one second-half commentary a week, with the choice of game unable to be publicised in advance. Similarly the television companies were strictly forbidden from giving any hints about what games would be coming up on *Match of the Day* or its ITV counterpart.

Dougan could never understand why the authorities were unable to see the benefits of promoting their product more widely and suggested the airing of one live midweek League game per week, along with important cup games. "Television coverage is woefully inadequate because of the Football League's negative, self-protective attitude, which in effect amounts to restrictive practice," he said.

As the end of the decade approached, ITV pulled off its historic coup of winning the rights to air its highlights package on Saturday nights, shunting the BBC to Sunday afternoons in what the press delighted calling the "snatch of the day".

Owen recalls the discussions that surrounded Dougan at that time: "Every ITV region did its own version and in the Midlands we had me and Gary Newbon in the studio and we wanted an in-game expert. We talked about it a lot and really wanted Derek but we came to the conclusion that he would not be available because of his work with Yorkshire. I happened to have Jimmy Greaves's number so we used him instead. So the Doog was indirectly responsible for getting Jimmy into television."

Dougan, though, was never short of platforms from which to air his views and in 1980, five years removed from the end of his on-field career, he released the third volume of his autobiography, *Doog*. Some of the book is a retread of the paths of his early life and career, but it is memorable for his frank account of life at Wolves under Bill McGarry, the kind of honesty that he'd not dared to offer when still a player. Dougan held enough opinions of all aspects of the game – not just his own career – that another book was inevitable and 1981 saw the publication of *How Not to Run Football*.

The tone for the book is set by the artwork on the dust cover, a depiction of the crucifixion of a bare-chested George Best by a hammer-wielding bovver-booted figure, while pound notes flutter across the page. The idea had grown out of a light-hearted comment by friend and business associate Bob Runham, whose company specialised in limited edition sporting prints.

"Derek would often ask why the press looked to crucify George Best the whole time," he recalls. "So I said jokingly: 'Let's stick him on the cross.' Derek loved the idea. It had been said in jest but he was like a dog with a bone and he wanted to court a bit of controversy."

Inside, the book's content is passionate yet erratic in its delivery, veering between constructive, prescient argument and a repetitive rant that drags up too much old ground from his previous works. He claims that the game's administrators are endangering football by their unchanging attitudes, describing them as "rooted in the past".

Supporters, he says, are fed up with the sport's "Victorian-Edwardian twilight world of artisan pleasures and backstreet folk customs" and he accuses football of failing to keep pace with social change. His warning that under the leadership of "men without vision" the collapse of professional football "as we have known it in England" is inevitable by the end of the 1980s does indeed foresee the implosion of football as landmarked most visibly by events at Bradford, Heysel and Hillsborough.

The world of all-seater stadiums and Sky's millions is not so far removed from the vision for the game's future that he outlines in his book, while his argument that going to decrepit grounds every Saturday was something that only a diminishing number of die-hard fans were prepared to endure hints at the evolution of the corporate fan who, for better or worse, characterises large swathes of the live audience for games in the modern era.

The example of Manchester United losing money in 1980/81 is used to urge the game to find new ways of bringing revenue into the sport, his main suggestion being redeveloping football grounds as all-purpose community centres. Rupert Murdoch, of course, eventually took care of that, providing the money that allowed for stadium regeneration and the kind of player wages that seemed other-worldly in Dougan's day.

But even in the early 1980s there were some who felt that falling attendance was in part due to the distance that inflated wages had placed between the players and the working man who stood on the terraces. As you would expect from someone who had not long completed eight years as chairman of the Professional Footballers' Association, Dougan takes the opportunity to counter that argument by pointing out the small number of players who enjoyed anything vaguely approaching a superstar lifestyle in 1981 and stressing that anyone other than a select few would be looking for employment at the end of their football career.

"A misleading impression is given that all, or most, footballers are getting inflated wages and this is a drain on the game's resources," he writes. "It is always worth remembering that without the players there would be no game."

The ability of Dougan to sit comfortably within circles outside of the game was evidenced in May 1981 when he was invited to appear on the BBC radio show *Robert Morley and Friends*, where the famous British actor discussed all manner of topics with a panel which, on this occasion, included authors Jackie Collins and Margaret Powell and dramatist John Mortimer.

Another book, written with BBC journalist Pat Murphy, was published in 1983. *Matches of the Day* looks at 25 historically significant games from the previous quarter century, with Dougan providing a historical, personal and anecdotal perspective and Murphy filling in the factual detail.

By the time Dougan had spent two and a half years trying to put his ideas on how to run football to the test as chief executive of Wolverhampton Wanderers (see Chapter 16), he discovered that televised football had more or less decided that there was no longer a place for him.

Former Leicester teammate Tom Sweenie comments: "Derek was so articulate and so smart dress-wise; I thought he was ideal for TV presenting. ITV ended up bringing in Ian St John, who I didn't think was a patch on Derek, who was superb."

As ITV remained married to *Saint and Greavsie*, there was a younger group of more recently retired players manoeuvring themselves into position to take advantage of the opportunities that the explosion of technology and media would offer in the multi-platformed 1990s.

But there were still a few of Dougan's contemporaries earning themselves a living by offering opinions on the game as the new century arrived – men such as Terry Venables, George Best, Frank McLintock, Alan Mullery, Rodney Marsh and Jimmy Armfield.

That Dougan was not among them perhaps owes much to two factors: that he had managed to antagonise too many influential people along the way and his refusal to allow an agent to construct a targeted career plan for him.

His niece Josephine Long, a radio journalist in Belfast, says: "Derek loved watching football. He wasn't one of these guys who, when they have stopped playing, want nothing to do with it. People have said to me they don't know why he stopped being a TV pundit because he had opinions and he could read the game really well. Well, I work on programmes where the presenters are real old hands, have been doing it for 30 years, but when the producer, who may be very young, tells them to do something they do it. Derek told me himself that if he didn't want to deal with the producer he totally ignored him. You can't do that and that's why he ended up going off the TV."

Maybe that comment refers to a piece of typical Dougan

bravado, or a trait that developed when he felt more established as a broadcaster. It certainly doesn't mesh with Nick Owen's recollection of working with him in the 1970s. "He knew that he was coming into journalism and broadcasting, which was not his main sphere of activity, so he bowed to the expertise around him," he says. "He was an absolute joy to work with."

Owen also believes that Dougan's television work dried up simply because of the passing of the years: "The powers that be probably saw him as a bit passé. Sky wanted to create their own personalities rather than rely on people like Doog and Malcolm Allison, who were associated with other broadcasters. To the next breed of producers, people like Greaves, St John and Dougan would just have been old players, like Stanley Matthews is to me."

But Josephine believes that Dougan's personality and name could still have found a home somewhere in the modern era of broadcasting. She says: "If I had been Derek's daughter I would have got some advice on how he could be reinvented. You see Rodney Marsh going on *I'm a Celebrity*. Why couldn't Derek have done something like that? But what would have been the point of having an agent if they are going to give Derek advice and he is going to ignore it? He would say: 'I am going to do it my way'."

Chapter 12

CAPTAINS AND CUP FINALS

I am discussing the nature of captaincy three days after an extraordinary display by William Gallas, the man nominated as the on-field leader of Arsenal. At the end of a game in which his team has seen one of their players, striker Eduardo da Silva, suffer a horrific broken leg and then been denied victory by a disputed Birmingham City penalty in the fourth minute of added time, Gallas has sat sobbing in the centre-circle, eventually having to be led from the field by his manager. Earlier, while awaiting the outcome of the penalty, he had been kicking advertising hoardings and being restrained from disappearing down the players' tunnel.

The reaction to such bizarre behaviour has, unsurprisingly, been one of widespread condemnation. Typical was Tony Cascarino in *The Times* urging Arsène Wenger to own up to his mistake in giving the armband to someone who appears emotionally immature and too eager to use histrionics to divert any criticism of his own performance.

Wenger has naturally defended his skipper, saying he expects to see commitment from his captain. It's impossible to believe, however, that clenched-fist Arsenal leaders like Frank McLintock or Tony Adams would have been reduced to such public disarray – and no one could ever accuse them of not being committed to the cause.

Sitting across the table in a City of London wine bar is a former Arsenal captain and manager, Terry Neill. He offers his take on events at St Andrew's: "I might not have reacted like that because I was a little bit calmer in those situations, but Tony would have wrecked the stadium and Frank would have wrecked the dressing room and everyone around him. We have all had our moments like that. Tony and Frank would have been kicking advertising hoardings and water bottles and anyone who got in their way, but sitting in the middle of the fucking pitch? No way."

The nature and role of a football captain has been given quite an airing in recent weeks. The new England head coach, Fabio Capello has appeared taken aback at the constant questioning on the subject of the identity of his skipper and the apparent importance attached to the position. Perhaps the job in relation to England is a special case, what with all the symbolism it carries, but it is easy to sympathise with his bemusement.

A football captain is hardly the equivalent of his counterpart in cricket, responsible for on-field strategy throughout the game. Today's managers are able to direct matters from the close proximity of the touchline rather than being confined to the dug-outs and ordered to keep their own counsel for fear of being banished to the stands. They can even pass along notes when shouts and hand signals won't suffice.

The captain, therefore, has little to think about but his own game. There is a bit of encouraging and urging to be done, but any experienced player worth his salt will willingly offer that regardless of whether his sleeve bears a piece of elastic with "captain" written upon it.

Adams was no less an inspirational figure in the England team when playing under the leadership of Alan Shearer. Conversely, Thierry Henry was no Terry Butcher when it came to bleeding for the cause but his lack of traditional captaincy traits passed without comment.

Derek Dougan acted very much in the manner of team captain wherever he played, freely offering opinion, criticism and encouragement, even though none of his clubs ever thought to offer him the job. However, Neill – as Billy Bingham had done previously – named Dougan captain of his country after himself being elevated to player-manager. "I don't think Doog was too happy with me taking over," he suggests. "But I was already coaching and managing. To try to soften it a little I made him captain and gave him some more responsibility."

Northern Ireland colleague Eric McMordie contends that Dougan's awareness of the needs of his teammates, particular those less experienced than him, earned considerable esteem in the dressing room and made him the ideal leader. "Derek was 'The Godfather' to us all," he explains. "He was so well-respected among the young players coming through. He looked after you with advice and in every other direction. He was an absolute role model. He tried to make sure the Irish boys would not get into too much trouble at times, but he could do that and still be one of the boys himself.

"The lovely thing about Derek was that he could be warm and kind but if that didn't work he had another side and he could be the tough man. He was very proud of where he came from and very, very proud to captain Northern Ireland. If you looked as if you were not doing the right job, Doog let you know – on and off the pitch."

At club level, Dougan played in an era when the role of captain entailed a lot more than holding hands with the schoolboy mascot and tossing the coin. And the complexity of his relationships with the men discharging the skipper's duties is a recurring feature of his story. When you consider the issues he had with his managers, it is little surprise that few of the captains under whom he played measured up to his idea of how the position should be executed.

This state of affairs arose partly through his perception that they failed to appreciate the responsibility they carried, but sometimes because of his own inability to recognise the complexities of the role.

At Portsmouth, Jimmy Dickinson might have played almost 50 games for England, but he disappointed Dougan with his reluctance to take the lead in team meetings, especially when the subject was the failures of the side. In an era when managers did not enjoy the dominance of their clubs in the manner of Wenger and Alex Ferguson, the captain had a heightened importance. He was expected to be the manager's representative on the pitch and in the dressing room, in the way that Billy Bremner became the on-field personification of Don Revie's will at Leeds. At the same time, of course, he had to retain his position as the man the lads looked toward to give them a voice.

Strong management could help the captain strike that delicate balance but Dougan rarely felt that his teams were the beneficiary of that, leaving Dickinson to breeze along with his non-committal, non-confrontational approach and Dougan looking for evidence of leadership.

At the same time, an immature and self-interested Dougan, in his frequent rages against injustices and inadequacies early in his career, often failed to consider the delicate position of a captain who had to fulfil multiple roles in the days before footballers were surrounded by agents and before managers could call upon expanded specialist coaching staffs. That was certainly true in the case of former England skipper Ronnie Clayton, towards whom Dougan admitted feelings of ambivalence during his time at Blackburn.

Clayton has told me: "When you were the captain, if any of the lads had something that needed to be taken up against the club then they came to me and I tried to see what I could do for them. If anyone had a bit of an argument, maybe about money, I could have a few words about it and try and do something."

It was not an easy situation for Clayton and his counterparts when their own jobs were no more secure than the next man's. In the days before players enjoyed much in the way of professional clout, any rocking of the boat could easily have seen them tipped overboard.

It was the status of club captain as the manager's chosen one that was at the root of the problem Dougan had with Mike Bailey at Wolves. Dougan confessed to the somewhat paranoid belief that club captains often acted as spies for the manager, reporting the mood and the gossip in the dressing room gossip. In particular, he stated in print, he suspected skipper Vic Crowe of colluding with manager Joe Mercer at Aston Villa.

Bailey was bound to suffer by association. When Dougan looked across the changing room he saw the representative of the man he detested, Bill McGarry. And this time, Dougan's determination to make a permanent home at Molineux meant that he could not just move on and forget about such annoyance, as he had done at his previous clubs. He had to live with it for eight years and, along with his ongoing battle with McGarry, it helped to characterise his Wolves career.

Bailey, either through a desire to set the record straight or because of generosity of spirit and a preference not to speak ill of the dead, says that he held no feelings of hostility towards Dougan: "I think people had the wrong end of the stick. Maybe he didn't like me, but I certainly liked him."

He also insists that his attachment to McGarry has been overstated by history: "People said I was very friendly with him, but that wasn't the case. Bill said what he wanted and I got on with my job – and part of my job as captain was to make sure his views were carried out on the pitch."

What is not in dispute is McGarry's opinion of Bailey. According to midfielder Steve Daley: "Bill McGarry loved Mick Bailey because he was a great captain, a great player and a great leader. If Mick was having a bad time himself it wouldn't prevent him from encouraging everyone else. He was brilliant."

To Dougan, however, McGarry's attraction to Bailey was representative of the insecurity he witnessed eating away at so many managers. "They need a player, some chosen favourite, to boost their self-esteem," he once wrote. "It is not usually the individualistic player they choose, but an ordinary, mediocre one, who is anxious to please."

Dougan would go so far as to suggest that Bailey's place in the team should have been given to Northern Ireland colleague Danny Hegan, who failed to cement a permanent place in the Wolves midfield during his three years at the club[12].

Hegan had played for McGarry at Ipswich and was signed from West Bromwich Albion in the summer of 1970. When he took

---

12   Hegan was 'sacked' by McGarry in November 1973 after missing two days of training. He was sold for a nominal fee of £5,000 to Sunderland, who released him after he went missing from the club the following January. He never played league football again.

over the number four shirt from the injured Bailey during the first part of 1972, Dougan felt his "exceptional talent" and sharp brain demonstrated that he should have been retained in that position in the centre of midfield instead of being moved back to the right when Bailey was fit.

He argued that he could see things more quickly than Bailey, who "was often caught in possession". The alternative view is offered by Frank Munro, who believes that Bailey rivalled the likes of Billy Bremner as the best in the country in that role.

It is a small manifestation of the division that Dougan believed existed at times in the dressing room and which was witnessed by others. That the Wolves team put such issues aside and worked together to win one major cup competition, one minor one, reach the final of the Uefa Cup and play in two other cup semi-finals in a four-season period says a lot for the collective professionalism of the team. Dougan, of course, would have had people believe that McGarry's poor management prevented them from doing even better.

"There were two factions in the club," says defender John Holsgrove. "The Dougan faction and the Bailey faction. Being totally honest, I was in Derek's faction, with people like Bobby Thomson and Les Wilson. When we went out on the pitch, if one scored a great goal we would hug each other. We worked together as a group and they called us the 'Tea Set' because we would go off and have a cup of tea together. The situation quietly simmered and sometimes in training there would be boots going in harder than usual, although neither Bill McGarry nor Ronnie Allen would stand for that."

Munro also remembers the classification of "the tea set and the drinkers", which had its origins in the numerous poolside cuppas ordered by the quartet while at the Los Angeles Sheraton in the summer of 1967. Yet as more young players came into the team as the 1960s gave way to the 1970s, there is a suggestion that the divisions became less obvious to the newcomers.

According to Derek Parkin, any differences were "a part of life" and were left behind in the dressing room. "It is human nature that you have some people you get on with and some you don't. You are professional footballers; you go in, do your job and go home. That era was the second most successful team in the club's history so I don't think you can say it was a factor."

Kenny Hibbitt says: "Being so young I was a bit naive and in awe of Derek, and I didn't know why the others didn't like him. I think he came in, did his job in training and didn't mix with all of them. I was one that he got on well with. He had a presence, a nice Irish accent and was very calm. I looked in his eyes and felt he meant what he was saying. A lot of people will say things and you know it's not coming from the heart. He was a character and did well for the other players. I always felt he was on his way to doing something with his life and he was a great guy to have at the club."

Dougan, however, stated his belief that "tensions caused by backstage pettiness" prevented his Wolves team from emulating the deeds of its illustrious predecessors of the 1950s. Such a comment also raises the question of how much the weight of the achievements of manager Stan Cullis's team – league champions three times – was a burden to the players that came after them.

Around the same time, for example, there were stories of Arsenal players pressing for pictures of the heroes of the 1930s being removed from the walls of Highbury's Marble Halls, but Bailey recalls: "I didn't look at it that way. They were fantastic achievements, something that was an inspiration rather than being daunting."

However, of more concern to Dougan than history – and the delicacy of his relationship with Bailey – was the ever-increasing contempt in which he held McGarry. Dougan reported for pre-season training in 1970 with his public profile heightened considerably by his World Cup television appearances and was determined to make the most of it.

Yet he felt McGarry was ignorant of the value of public relations and frowned upon the appearances Dougan made both on his own behalf and in order to support worthy causes. He was shortly to enjoy further elevation through his election as chairman of the Professional Footballers' Association, which he believed made life with McGarry more difficult than ever.

It irked Dougan that McGarry would allow only club captain Bailey to use the general office. He even recalled an occasion when he needed to make an urgent call to PFA secretary Cliff Lloyd at 9.45am, just as training was due to start. Warned that making the call from home and arriving late would earn him a fine and denied permission to use the club's office, he ended up getting changed into his kit and telephoning from a public call box in the social club.

Dougan felt McGarry had simply been flexing his muscles and reminding his centre-forward who was in charge. "I had the impression that Bill McGarry was suspicious of me because he never knew what I was doing away from the ground and could not tie me down," Dougan said.

So poor was their relationship, according to Dougan, that when a young Liverpudlian centre-forward called Peter Withe arrived at the club on his recommendation – having seen him playing for Arcadia Shepherds in South Africa – he was never given a fair shot and left the club for Birmingham after playing only 17 games in two seasons. Munro supports Dougan's view, saying: "Peter never really got a chance at Wolves, simply because McGarry wouldn't give Doog the satisfaction of being right."

The dynamic between manager and players proved interesting viewing for those who managed to adopt a neutral stance as they established their place in the team. Geoff Palmer explains: "Bill was really strict and wanted it done his way, with no half measures. I didn't think the way he treated young players was right but he made you get into good habits and I as I got older I had to thank Bill, whether or not I liked some of his decisions and the way he spoke. You could never have given Doog a b********g because of his age and he would never give Waggy a b********g because he knew you needed to gee him up. He would throw his arm round him and say: 'Come on, give me a bit more.' I thought his man management skills were quite good."

The 1970/71 season saw Wolves take a significant step forward, finishing fourth in the table and marking the start of a four-year period in which they could rightly be described as one of the leading clubs in the country. Admittedly they did not in that time challenge Arsenal, Derby, Liverpool or Leeds for one of the First Division titles that won, but this was an era where the gap between the top four and the chasing pack – the likes of Tottenham, Chelsea,

Ipswich, Manchester City and Wolves – was marginal and any of those teams could begin each season with genuine aspirations of a championship challenge.

Due to injuries and suspensions, the trio of Dougan, Hugh Curran and Bobby Gould, a summer signing from Arsenal, rotated in and out of the two central striking positions, scoring 45 league goals between them, of which Dougan's share was 12 in 25 appearances. Having lost their first three games while conceding ten goals, it was a considerable achievement to finish in fourth place, with a points total that in the competitive 1970s would on one occasion have seen them finish only one point away from the title.

There was also some silverware to celebrate when Wolves became the inaugural winners of the Texaco Cup, a European-style tournament for the leading teams in England, Scotland and Ireland who had not qualified for the real thing. As the years have passed, the tournament, which ran for five seasons, has become widely denigrated, but it was given a reasonably positive reception at the time. Dougan had even proposed exactly such a competition in his 1969 book, *Attack!* "Most clubs would welcome two games per week," he wrote.

It was something of a golden era for weird and wonderful competitions as clubs took the opportunity to throw open their stadium doors as often as possible and the burgeoning world of sports sponsorship sought inroads into football. The late summer of 1970 had seen the advent of the pre-season Watney Cup, a one-week tournament featuring the two top-scoring teams from each division who had not won promotion or qualified for Europe, while Wolves had a couple of months earlier participated in the Anglo-Italian Cup.

That particular event was the brainchild of the famous Italian football agent Gigi Peronace and had grown out of the original challenge game between England and Italy's League Cup winners, introduced as a way of compensating Swindon Town for their banishment from the Inter-Cities Fairs Cup. As a Third Division team, Swindon had been barred by competition regulations from taking their rightful place after beating Arsenal in the 1969 League Cup final.

Wolves had been one of the six English teams invited to play in the first expanded tournament in the spring of 1970. While three wins from four group games were not enough to see them advance to the final as the best of the English teams, home and away contests against Lazio and Fiorentina offered a taste of European football that would hold them in good stead. Similarly, the Texaco Cup would enable them to experience the nuances of two-legged knockout matches.

In particular, the away game in Lazio was a lesson in the harsh realities of playing foreign opposition at a time when venturing across the English Channel could still be akin to swinging open the doors of a Wild West saloon. With virtually no movement of players across international borders, the cultural differences between Italian and English football were vast. While the Italians were perceived to be skilful yet ruthlessly underhand, they saw England as a home of limited workhorses.

It all contributed to the Anglo-Italian Cup becoming notorious for a series of bloodbaths. In fact, the 1970 final had to be abandoned after 79 minutes with Swindon leading 3-0 in Napoli when the angry home fans decided to riot.

Dougan described the game in Rome as the most violent he ever played in, calling it a "fight to the death". The Lazio players appeared bent on taking physical revenge for a 1-0 defeat at Molineux and their brutality on the field ignited a furnace of spiteful intent among the fans. For the only time in his life, Dougan felt that it was not worth playing to win. "If they want it that badly they can have it," he was thinking. Getting off the field without having his leg broken by a tackle or being assaulted by a spectator was his chief concern.

The same Lazio team, incidentally, was responsible for the further worsening of Anglo-Italian relations later in the same year when their players attacked the Arsenal squad in the streets of Rome following a post-match banquet after a Fairs Cup tie.

By contrast, the Texaco Cup was a genteel affair, with Dundee United, Morton and Derry City all comfortably dispatched as Wolves earned a place in the two-legged final against Hearts. More than 54,000 fans took the competition seriously enough to show up for the pair of games, with Wolves – for whom Dougan made an appearance from the bench – virtually assuring themselves of the trophy when two goals from Curran helped them to a 3-1 win at Tynecastle. The win protected them sufficiently to survive a 1-0 reverse in the second leg, for which Dougan had returned.

And so to the real thing: the 1971/72 Uefa Cup, as the Fairs Cup had now been renamed after coming fully under the constitutional control of the governing body of European football. During preparation for Wolves' first season in Europe for 11 years, Dougan attempted to test McGarry, telling him during a summer tournament that he was thinking of retiring after one more season.

It was a pure fishing mission, used to gauge the true feeling of the manager, whose response was to tell Dougan that he could get a good price for him if he allowed himself to be transferred instead. He at least felt he knew where he stood – "some sort of merchandise with a price tag" – and sensed a temporary clearing of the air.

Besides, Dougan had another cause for satisfaction, a regular partner up front in John Richards, a young goalscorer from Warrington who had spent much of the previous season watching from the substitute's bench. Over the next three years the pair were to form one of the most effective combinations in the country.

Due to his own nomadic tendencies and the personnel at the clubs he played for, it was the only time Dougan was ever part of an established regular striking partnership in First Division football. His one regret was that such a state of affairs materialised in the latter years of his career. "If I had been ten years younger we would have set post-war records that no partnership would have equalled," he claimed.

The two men offered the classic combination, Dougan's guile and experience at the sharp end of the forward line complemented by the neat, well-balanced, poacher's instincts of the dark-haired Richards. Only the Liverpool pairing of John Toshack and Kevin Keegan, also established in that same season, provided comparable results in the top flight at that time.

"It was a fantastic partnership, as good as anything in England," says Munro. "Derek was very good in the air and at providing a target, while John was a great finisher."

§

Richards credits McGarry – in a way that Dougan never would – for getting the best out of the combination. The manager told Dougan, a lefty, to favour the right side of the penalty area with the right-footed Richards taking the left channel. It meant that each man could cut inside onto his stronger leg and, when the ball was delivered from the wing, the man at the far post would be poised to strike with his preferred foot.

Derek Parkin contends that it was the "best partnership in Europe", saying: "They used to frighten the life out of defences – Richards with his speed and aggression and the Doog floating around."

Geoff Palmer continues: "McGarry played to a system where the 'out' ball was to Doog so that was my main ball to look for. He was a fit lad, always in front at training, and would run for lost causes and make a bad ball into a good ball. He always said: 'Just put it into my area and I will go for it.' He and John knew where each other would be. We worked on it in training but they just hit it off. Richards had this uncanny knack of knowing where the Doog was going to knock it and would get on the end of things, even if they ended up going in off his knee or his backside."

Wolves' European campaign began with both Dougan and Richards, who combined for 40 goals in their first season together, scoring in a 3-1 home win against Portuguese side Academica Coimbra. Dougan's goal caused a two-minute stoppage as the home team protested that he had been offside. In the return game, Dougan scored a hat-trick in a 4-1 win, the fierce shot with which he scored his third being one of the most satisfying strikes of his career.

Four days earlier he had scored three times against Nottingham Forest. In one account, Dougan claims that the reticent McGarry had not offered a single congratulatory word; in another he said that the back-to-back performances prompted the only "well done" he had had received from his manager. Either way, the point is made. "If he felt that a few words of praise would have made me big-headed I could have informed him that this would have been better than the depression his silence caused," he said.

Dutch team Den Haag were taken care of 3-1 and 4-0, with

Dougan netting in both games. Three days after Dougan contributed a pair of goals to a 5-1 win over reigning league champions Arsenal, a Richards goal beat Carl Zeiss Jena on a slippery pitch in East Germany. Dougan's two goals in the home leg, after setting up the first in a 3-0 win, took his tally to eight in the tournament and saw him supplant Peter Broadbent as the club's leading goalscorer in European competition. Six games, six wins and 18 goals. This European football was a bit of a lark.

Reality kicked in when the quarter-final draw paired Wolves with Juventus, runners-up to Leeds in the previous year's competition and on their way to becoming champions of Italy.

Juventus were without their star forward Roberto Bettega, suffering from a lung complaint, for the first leg in Turin in early March but still put their visitors under intense first-half pressure. Dougan's ability in the air was Wolves' most likely source of success and he set up Jim McCalliog to volley the precious equaliser in a 1-1 draw. Dougan's style of aggressive play was a large factor in his success against European defences, in whose domestic football the big, British-style centre-forward was a rarity.

Kenny Hibbitt says: "They didn't like it up them. Doog took up fantastic positions and he liked to pull the centre-back around by coming out wide and making runs at full-backs. In those days centre-backs didn't like that. It helped make more room for me and Waggy."

According to Bailey: "Doog really came alive in those European games. The Uefa Cup was probably his best time as a player."

The team sheet Juventus turned in for the second leg surprisingly lacked the names of five first team players who were being rested before the following weekend's local derby against Torino. Wolves duly earned a famous 2-1 win that was considerably more comfortable than the scoreline suggests. Goals from Hegan, celebrating a run in the side in place of the injured Bailey by chipping in from long range, and Dougan had more or less wrapped up the tie before the Italians' late consolation.

A semi-final against Hungarian side Ferencvaros could not help but prompt memories of the famous 1954 floodlit challenge match against Honved, champions of Hungary. On that occasion, a 55,000 crowd at Molineux had cheered their team to a dramatic 3-2 second-half comeback against a team including the legendary Ferenc Puskas and several other players who had thrashed England 6-3 and 7-1 within the previous 12 months.

But by 1972, Hungarian football was in decline and Wolves returned from Budapest as firm favourites to reach the final after a 2-2 draw. They had taken the lead when Richards latched on to Dougan's back heel but looked in grave danger after the home side fought back to lead 2-1 and were then awarded their second penalty of the game for handball against Bernard Shaw. The tie turned again, however, when Phil Parkes saved the spot-kick and, five minutes later, Munro scored from a Wagstaffe corner.

Steve Daley, replacing the suspended Wagstaffe, opened the second-leg scoring in the first minute and Munro headed in McCalliog's cross two minutes before half-time. The Hungarians pulled one back after the break, but with Parkes saving another penalty a minute later after Alan Sunderland handled, Wolves held on to reach their first major final since beating Dougan's Blackburn at Wembley 12 years earlier. It was not, however, going to transport them to an exotic European location. Their destination would be north London, where Tottenham were lying in wait after overcoming AC Milan in the semi-finals.

Palmer admits: "I wasn't in the team in the final but a lot of the players who had travelled all over said it was a letdown to face Tottenham in the final. I know Waggy always said that to come back and play at White Hart Lane was a bit of an anti-climax."

The Spurs players, of course, felt no less disappointed at the thought of playing for European glory in the west Midlands. The biggest losers were the players' wives, who had been promised a trip with the respective teams if their men made the final.

Wolves fielded the same starting line up for both legs: Parkes, Shaw, Taylor, Hegan, Munro, McAlle, McCalliog, Hibbitt, Richards, Dougan, Wagstaffe. Perhaps because of the familiarity and feeling of letdown experienced by the two teams, the final was hardly a classic. Wolves had more of the play at Molineux and almost scored through an outrageous chip from Hegan, but went behind to a header by Martin Chivers after 58 minutes. They scored a contentious equaliser when McCalliog slipped a quick free-kick to Richards, who fired in off Pat Jennings while Spurs were still disputing the referee's decision. Chivers struck again to give his side a first-leg advantage when he smacked the ball past Parkes from 25 yards.

The return at White Hart Lane two weeks later was frenzied but lacking in quality. Both sides scored before half-time, with Alan Mullery's flying header being cancelled out by Wagstaffe's powerful effort into the top corner. Wolves' best attempt to save the game was denied by Jennings's wonderful save from Richards. Dougan lamented: "Wolves were capable of winning the championship, the FA Cup and other honours. But for Pat Jennings proving himself the best goalkeeper in the world at the time, we would have won the Uefa Cup."

Sandwiched between the two games against Tottenham had been one of the most infamous matches in the history of English football, when Leeds visited Molineux attempting to complete the FA Cup and league double. Two days earlier they had triumphed over Arsenal at Wembley, Dougan making the official post-game presentation of the Golden Boot to the scorer of the winning goal, Allan Clarke. Now Leeds needed a point on the Monday night to emulate the London club's achievement of the previous season.

§

Wolves' own First Division campaign had petered out to ninth place after they had been sixth in January. Having gone unbeaten in their first 16 home league games, they had lost four in a row by the time they kicked off in front of a crowd of more than 53,000 against Leeds. With some fans hanging off the floodlight pylons and others perched on neighbouring roofs they embarked on what Dougan described as the "most dramatic match I ever played in".

Munro scored following a corner just before half-time and after 67 minutes Dougan moved on to a pass from Richards to slip a low shot past keeper David Harvey for his 15th league goal of the season. The tireless Billy Bremner pulled one back within a minute and there followed a frantic final 20 minutes as Don Revie's fatigued, injury-depleted team sought the goal that would make history, although Dougan could have killed the game completely from a cross by Wagstaffe. The Leeds goal never arrived.

Nor, on the same night, did Liverpool get the winner at Highbury that could have seen them take the title instead, leaving Brian Clough's Derby County to receive the news that they were league champions while they holidayed in Majorca.

The real drama surrounding the Molineux game, however, emerged five years later when Danny Hegan claimed in the *Sunday People* that Bremner had tried to bribe Wolves players to throw the game. Bremner sued Hegan and the newspaper, winning £100,000 in damages for defamation. During the court case, Munro testified that Bremner offered him £5,000 to give away a penalty in those frenzied final few minutes and felt sure that he was acting on behalf of Revie. He maintains that claim even now.

Dougan, no great fan of Bremner, testified on the Leeds captain's behalf, saying that he had seen or heard no evidence or rumours of a fix. "If there had been any attempts to get the game fixed I would surely have known about it," he said later, noting: "Surely you nobble the guys who might score goals for a start?"

A footnote to the season was the rumour that Bill McGarry was about to move to Coventry City. Dougan claimed the manager had taken Bailey aside and told him after the Uefa Cup final, which had prompted singing and chanting on the team coach. They should have held their tunes. Joe Mercer went to Coventry to team up with Gordon Milne and McGarry was back on the cup trail in 1972/73.

Ironically, it was Tottenham and Leeds who were once again in at the denouement of Wolves' big storylines during that season. In the League Cup, a competition in which the club had yet to make a significant impact, Dougan scored in home wins over Orient and Sheffield Wednesday in the early rounds and, following a 4-0 cruise past Bristol Rovers, got the only goal in a fifth round replay success at Blackpool.

The two-legged semi-final against Spurs had a familiar feel to it. Seven months on from the European final, Wolves again faced a 2-1 deficit after the home game and, once more, could only manage a draw at White Hart Lane, 2-2 on this occasion after extra time.

Wolves had barely been given a scent of FA Cup final day in the

13 years that had passed since their last Wembley victory, but four home ties and four victories, all without conceding a goal, left them within 90 minutes of a return journey.

The third round offered them a timely meeting with a Manchester United in rapid freefall. Having started out the previous campaign like a runaway train and enjoyed a healthy lead at the top of the First Division, they had spent the whole of 1972 sliding down the table and wondering if George Best might ever show up and play some football.

An embarrassing 5-0 defeat at struggling Crystal Palace just before Christmas led to the dismissal of manager Frank O'Farrell. It was Tommy Docherty who was in charge by the time they visited Molineux; Mike Bailey whose goal ensured that there was to be no Cup run to ease the gloom at Old Trafford.

Richards, in the midst of a season that would see him finish with 33 senior goals – cementing his status as Molineux's "King John" and earning him his only England cap – scored the single goals that took care of Bristol City and Millwall in rounds four and five.

Before the quarter-final against Coventry, Dougan proved his own form by scoring a hat-trick in a 5-1 win against Manchester City, part of his 15-goal tally in all major competitions for the season, which also included his 200th league strike. More than 50,000 packed in to Molineux to see Wolves' showdown against their Midlands rivals, Richards taking only seven minutes to get on the scoresheet and Hibbitt completing a 2-0 win by converting a second-half penalty.

Semi-final opponents Leeds relished the opportunity of delivering some payback over the team that had denied them the double almost a year earlier. Bremner's goal, celebrated lustily in front of his team's supporters, settled a dour game at Maine Road and Wolves, for whom Richards hit the post late on, were stopped short of Wembley once again.

Two semi-finals and a fifth-place finish, coming on the back of a European final, was enough to confirm Wolves as a team worthy of mention along with the best in the country, but was little consolation for a series of near-misses. Nor was the meaningless 3-1 win over Arsenal before the start of the following season in the third place play-off for the FA Cup, a game in which Dougan scored twice.

Hibbitt remembers: "We had finished high up in the league a couple of times and been in a final and semi-finals. We were very close and yet so far, and nobody remembers the teams that come close. Doog knew he was running out of time to win something."

Parkin adds: "There was a very thin line between being number one and finishing fourth and sometimes it was just the difference between a couple of players here and there – and a bit of luck comes into it. We were a good side. I think that if you have a good keeper, centre-half and centre-forward you can build round that. We had that and then had someone like Mike Bailey who dominated the midfield, and brought younger players through at the right time."

Bailey believes that a taste of triumph earlier in the team's lifespan could have led to an ever greater record of success: "We were always competing and it's difficult to say why we didn't achieve more. We probably lacked a little bit of experience in the big time compared to the other top teams who had been competing in Europe for years and years. It was like a golfer just waiting for that first win. In the end, that win probably came too late because it was at the end of the great period we had together as a team."

Meanwhile, the temporary ceasefire Dougan had established towards his manager was severely tested when he faced a choice of obeying an instruction or setting in motion a chain of events that could have forced him out of the club. At least that was how the alternatives were laid out in the confrontational mind of the Doog.

Feeling fit and confident after his two goals in the play-off game at Highbury, he had a promotional engagement at a local store two days before the season opener against Norwich. Via coach Sammy Chung he heard that McGarry had ordered additional training, even though Thursday afternoons were usually kept free.

Dougan prided himself in never missing training for a personal appearance but was aware that his engagement had been advertised locally. He put the shop before some extra sprinting and phoned club secretary Jack Robinson to get his insurance cards ready for collection. He was expecting to be fined and had decided to refuse to pay on principle – at which point he believed he would be fired. "But I was determined to quit rather than be humiliated by a fine," he said. "I was part bluffing."

Dougan was banking on Robinson to warn McGarry that a fine could bring the situation to a head. He picked up his boots on Friday morning and went round saying goodbye to puzzled teammates. "I was leaving a trail and knew the alarm signals were reaching the manager's office." Sure enough, he was summoned to see McGarry and made clear his views on the extra training, accusing the manager of deliberately sabotaging his store appearance. McGarry said that had not been the case and Dougan was sent away without punishment.

The next day he scored twice in a 3-1 win against Norwich and continued his most prolific start to any season by netting in the next three matches. Conversely, Richards hit a barren patch, reaching the end of September without a goal to his name, which brought Dougan into conflict with McGarry once again.

Dougan felt that McGarry allowed press speculation about Richards's place in the team build to an intolerable level instead of giving him reassurances. He felt that the pressure was making Richards depressed and insecure, rather than motivated and stimulated in the manner that the manager was hoping. Richards at last found the net in a Uefa Cup tie at Portuguese side Belenenses, but the fact that he was later sent off for hitting an opponent was evidence to Dougan of an emotional state that could have been avoided.

The Uefa Cup campaign extended only to the second round – before Wolves lost out to Lokomotiv Leipzig on away goals after winning the second leg 4-1 – while the FA Cup brought another defeat to Leeds, this time in the third round. Yet the League Cup was to give Dougan and this particular Wolves team their finest hour.

The draw favoured them in the early rounds and after Halifax and Tranmere were dispatched, the feeling grew at Molineux that the fates might be with them this time.

Bailey says: "I always remember Jimmy McCalliog saying after

Halifax that when he reached the FA Cup final with Sheffield Wednesday they'd had a feeling they were going to go all the way. We started to feel the same."[13]

Richards was back in a rich vein of form, scoring twice as Exeter were beaten 5-1 in the third round. Dougan netted his second goal of the competition in the same game, part of his eventual tally of 17 for the season. The quarter-final against Liverpool at Molineux was won by another Richards goal, although only just over 16,000 saw the match because of the afternoon kick-off necessitated by the government's temporary ban on the use of floodlights. It was one of the measures introduced during the industrial action by coal miners, which had limited the availability of electricity and led to the imposition of the three-day week in offices and factories.

Norwich City, beaten by a Ralph Coates goal when they played Tottenham in the previous season's final, were Wolves' semi-final opponents. Richards couldn't stop scoring now, accounting for his team's 1-1 draw at Carrow Road and grabbing the only goal of the second leg.

The first Saturday in March saw Dougan back in a major final at Wembley. This time there were no injury problems and no daft transfer request. "Doog loved it," Palmer remembers. "All the euphoria and pictures and articles – everyone wanted to speak to him."

The Manchester City team that confronted Wolves might have descended from the peak it achieved under the Joe Mercer-Malcolm Allison partnership, but it still boasted the core of the team that had won every domestic trophy and a European competition within the space of three years and come close to a second title two seasons earlier. And it boasted an all-star forward line of Mike Summerbee, Colin Bell, Francis Lee, Denis Law and Rodney Marsh. Wolves, meanwhile, had shown league form that was only good enough for a mid-table finish.

Hibbitt remembers: "We were massive underdogs. We were

---

13   McCalliog would not be part of the later stages of the competition, having moved to Old Trafford to help in Manchester United's doomed battle against relegation.

standing in the tunnel in a straight line waiting for the referee to say 'let's go,' and there they were, all internationals who had played at Wembley many times, tossing the ball and flicking it around as though they were going out for just other game. Our bellies were churning."

Palmer has a similar recollection: "I remember going there on Friday and walking round the pitch so at least you knew what it was going to be like. But to go out in front of all those people was something you never forget. One thing that stood out in my mind was looking at their players in the tunnel and thinking: 'What the hell am I doing here?'"

The recording of the game makes for much happier viewing for Dougan-watchers than the embarrassment of 1960. There he is in the opening seconds, striding out in his black tracksuit top with comical-looking gold trousers, poking his tongue out at the camera, waving to familiar faces in the crowd and sharing a joke with the Duke of Kent during the player introductions. Commentator Brian Moore introduces the Wolves players, beginning with inexperienced goalkeeper Gary Pierce, celebrating his 23rd birthday by taking the place of the injured Parkes. The full line-up, showing four changes from the Uefa Cup final team, is: Pierce, Palmer, Parkin, Bailey, Munro, McAlle, Hibbitt, Sunderland, Richards, Dougan, Wagstaffe. Sub: Powell.

Wolves have the better of the early play. McAlle and Parkin make you wince with their committed tackling, while Munro shows composure and a pleasing desire to play football out of defence. City appear to have too many options for their own good, too many playmakers vying for their moment on the ball.

Dougan goes through the entire game without managing a single attempt on goal, but his contribution is a valuable one. Lay-offs, knock-downs, unselfish running and a series of bangs and boots in the back as he wins a string of free-kicks – all in a day's work for a leader of a 1970s forward line. He heads Wagstaffe's centre back across the box for Alan Sunderland to have his shot blocked before Munro has a header saved and Sunderland volleys against the post.

As the first half progresses City have more possession and Pierce tips away a Marsh free-kick, but a minute before the break Palmer's innocuous cross from the right falls behind his forwards, only to find Hibbitt running into the box. His first-time shot skews off the outside of his boot and drops beyond the left hand of goalkeeper Keith MacRae. "I drilled it in the top corner," Hibbitt laughs. "Oh, OK. I sliced it."

The second half maintains the unrelenting pace of the first and City begin making chances. Bell, quiet for the first hour, equalises with a simple low shot after Marsh's cross from the left reaches him on the edge of the six-yard box. The next 20 minutes are an exhibition of blocks, fingertip saves and safe handling by Pierce. Wagstaffe goes off injured ten minutes before the end, forcing Richards to remain on the field even though he is being slowed by a groin problem. With six minutes to play, Bailey, the best midfield player on view, slips the ball through to Sunderland, whose low cross from the right deflects off Marsh's foot into path of Richards and he scores with a low right-foot shot.

City's pressure comes to nothing and when the final whistle blows the director cuts immediately to Dougan, arms raised in triumph. His medal is clearly the human interest story of the day, at least on a par with that of Pierce, the unlikely hero who sits on the grass beaming in disbelief. Another scene has acquired new poignancy with the passing of the years: that of Richards jumping into Dougan's arms and planting a kiss on his head. Dougan is seen hugging his chairman as he receives his winner's tankard, but is a subdued and exhausted figure as the lap of honour begins. It is the tiredness of satisfaction and contentment.

Less than two years earlier, Dougan's international and club careers were in danger of being characterised by one appearance at the World Cup finals, after which he was dumped from the team, and the debacle of Wembley 1960. Now, two glorious Wembley occasions, one for club and one for country, have rectified that and given him happier memories to take into retirement, whenever that might arrive.

During my conversation with Derek Parkin he reveals that he has only recently watched the DVD of the full game for the first time. "I was really surprised at how good a side we were," he says. "We deserved to win on that day. At the time I was too young to take it all in but it was a bloody good game. The Doog was outstanding, Bailey had a great understanding with everyone and Gary Pierce was brilliant."

Hibbitt's memory presents a slightly different view to the recent observations of his teammate and may do his team a little disservice: "They gave us a right battering but we somehow beat them. Pierce gave the best performance I have seen from a keeper in my life. Even McGarry raced out to him at the end of the game and he never did anything like that. It was what you dreamt of as young boys. Doog was absolutely thrilled."

Victory at Wembley meant that Wolves had at last fulfilled the promise of the previous few years. Bailey says: "That was the defining moment" while Palmer adds: "McGarry always said that if we hadn't won the League Cup he would have upped and left."

But Wolves fans were never to have it so good again following that period in the early 1970s. And just as the happy days were ending at Molineux, so followers of the wider English game were being given plenty of cause for concern.

Dougan was particularly vocal in his fears for English football as 1974/75 approached after a World Cup tournament in West Germany for which England had been denied qualification by Poland. The gloom and pessimism surrounding the sport was reflective of the country in general, in the same way that the 1966 triumph at Wembley had captured, and enhanced, the optimism of the 'Swinging Sixties'.

Industrial unrest, which had brought about the downfall of the Conservative government, and the IRA's mainland bombing campaign provided most of the depressing headlines. Football hooliganism grabbed its fair share of column inches, while falling attendances and defensive football vied for space with the ongoing post-mortem of the end of the Sir Alf Ramsey era[14].

Dougan attempted to find some optimism in the performance of the Holland team that had finished as World Cup runners-up. "I

14   After the 1-1 draw against Poland at Wembley had seen England eliminated from the World Cup, Ramsey was retained for two friendlies before being fired, ending his 12-year reign as England manager.

would love the Dutch style of football to come to England," he said. "It was total soccer in the sense that there were ten outfield players with all the talent and skill to score goals. I think we might see some of that refreshing attitude coming into our game."

His hopes were based on observations that too many managers would opt to slavishly follow a successful system rather than attempt innovation. In the past he felt it had led to the effective functionality of teams like Leeds and Arsenal. Perhaps now it would cause an outbreak of Dutch impressionists. He had also been astonished at the comments of certain managers before the World Cup that they had nothing to learn by attending the event.

As it turned out, the First Division featured an enthralling title race in which eight teams were in contention until the final weeks, but it could hardly be said that the season was set alight by a host of Johan Cruyff clones. For his own part, Dougan spent the winter months coming to the realisation that 1974/75 would be his final campaign. The back trouble that recurred intermittently for the previous decade or so was restricting him in training and limiting his contribution in matches. What remained to be resolved was his exit strategy.

After eight years at the club in which his base salary, he claimed, had raised by only £20 to £100 a week, he was disappointed that McGarry offered him only four weeks as a pay-off. "That's mean of you," he told him. Having served less than ten years at Wolves, a testimonial was not an automatic right and he felt that he should have been credited for not hanging around for the final year of his contract and picking up his money when he was obviously not fit enough for the First Division.

Dougan reflected on the goals he had scored, the contribution he'd made on and off the field, and compared it with the praise he felt McGarry had wrongly been given for tactics and team talks. He felt that the manager had offered nothing more than a few half-time expletives and insisted that he never listened to McGarry because he could teach him nothing about centre-forward play.

Such thoughts helped convince him he was being short-changed, even when the offer was improved to £1,000. The pay-off McGarry would receive when fired by Wolves after relegation in 1976, reported to be £32,000, eventually left Dougan smarting even more.

His final season was one of frustration. Dropped by McGarry, he started only three league games and scored one goal as Wolves stuttered along in mid-table and suffered the earliest possible exit in all their cup competitions. Having played the final 20 minutes as a substitute against Tottenham over Easter he was retained for the next game, a home win against Manchester City. On the Monday after the game, McGarry asked to see him and said: "How do you want to finish your career, in the first team or reserves? I'm not going to play you any more in the first team."

Dougan's anger was centred less on the fact that he had obviously played his final first team game and more on McGarry's failure to tell him beforehand. He believed he had been denied the big send-off he deserved after becoming the first Irishman to score more than 200 league goals, chairing the PFA and helping establish Wolves at the forefront of English football. "It was up to me what I did, quit or play in the reserves. I had anticipated taking my last leave before the Molineux crowd in the last game of the season. It seemed I was to be denied this pleasure."

The path of Dougan's career rarely ran along its predicted course, however, and the day before the final game of the season at home to Leeds he was told he was in the squad. He put it down to the "undercurrent of feeling" that had been present in the local media. He was named as substitute and he got his final farewell in front of almost 35,000, being given a guard of honour by both sets of players as the teams took the field.

Dougan was brought on for a final cameo performance but even the way that was handled left him with a tinge of bitterness. He was given a 12-minute appearance – "a token farewell performance with a strict time limit", as he described it. The temptation when McGarry told him to remove his tracksuit was to refuse. "In the event I allowed him to humiliate me because I did not want to offend the biggest crowd of the season who had come to pay their last respects."

When the final whistle sounded, Dougan waved, blew kisses and fought back the tears. His career in English football, the most prolific of any Irishman, was over, with this final tally:

Club (goals)	Years	FL (goals)	FAC (goals)	LC (goals)	Other
Portsmouth	1957-59	33 (9)	3	-	-
Blackburn	1959-61	59 (26)	14 (4)	3 (4)	-
Aston Villa	1961-63	51 (19)	5 (2)	4 (5)	-
Peterborough	1963-65	77 (38)	10 (7)	3 (1)	-
Leicester	1965-67	68 (35)	5 (1)	3 (5)	-
Wolves	1967-75	278 (95)	12 (4)	22 (7)	31 (17)
Total	**1957-75**	**566 (222)**	**49 (18)**	**35 (22)**	**31 (17)**

In the boardroom after the game he shook hands with and was thanked by chairman Harry Marshall and his fellow directors, but McGarry was conspicuous by his absence. He said his last goodbyes and was gone. Molineux, though, had not seen the last of the Doog.

In the fullness of time he would be back as chief executive. Meanwhile, in the short term was a testimonial game in October between Wolves and Don Revie's International XI, when more than 25,000 fans took the opportunity to offer thanks to a man who had brightened up so many of their Saturday afternoons and Wednesday evenings for the past decade. Revie picked what was effectively a fringe England team and the match was treated seriously enough by the participants to end goalless.

His subsequent returns to the ground during 1975/76 were less happy occasions. Wolves were on their way to relegation, which caused Dougan to regret that he had not got himself fit and battled on. Secondly, he found himself barred from the main reception area at Molineux, which he felt was the work of McGarry. With typical bloody-mindedness he refused the offer of complimentary tickets as compensation.

Geoff Palmer, who remained at the club for almost a decade more, recalls: "We'd had a good run and Wolves had got a few more years out of Derek than they might have thought. But then he and people like Frank [Munro] and Waggy all came to an end at the same time. It was a wrench to lose experienced players and not bring in players to replace them. John [Richards] had to become more of the target man. I don't think they ever did replace the Doog."

Chapter 13

UNITED WE STAND

As you travel down Woodstock Road in the direction of Belfast city centre, the end terrace house, with its blue door, looks unremarkable. Stop a few yards beyond the cream walls, turn back and look at the side of the building and you are confronted by a two-storey image of George Best. The silvery blue paint and the unflatteringly paunchy and bearded figure it portrays create the somewhat ethereal impression of an ageing Best playing football among the clouds.

Nowadays he is flanked by two dates, the years of his birth and death in 1946 and 2005, picked out in black paint. Not so long ago, however, the wall was occupied in its four corners by other Northern Ireland footballers, including the great Danny Blanchflower; forward and one-time national manager Sammy McIlroy; and midfield player Tommy Cassidy. Occupying the berth bottom left was the head and shoulders of Derek Dougan, smiling back in his Wolves shirt.

Best's buddies were expunged from their mural existence after vandals once again took exception to Dougan's views on a combined Ireland football team, bringing together the best players from the north and south. He had been expressing such views since the early 1970s and when he spoke up again in 2004, protestors took black paint to his likeness during the night.

Only a couple of years earlier he had given a typically forthright interview after Northern Ireland captain Neil Lennon stood down because of death threats resulting from his transfer to Celtic, traditionally a Catholic stronghold. On that occasion Dougan described himself as "horrified at the intimidation that still goes on [in Belfast] to prominent people" and, when asked about the old chestnut of an all-Ireland team, added: "It would have done more than politics to bring the people together."

Dougan's stance was seen by some in the community from which he had grown to be disloyal to his roots. "I'm proud that I was born off the Newtownards Road," he said after the final act of vandalism against the Woodstock Road mural. He continued: "I genuinely believe that, like rugby, there should be a team from the 32 counties. There is nothing political about that – it's just a personal opinion… they want to segregate me into a category and I'm not allowed to have an opinion. Every now and then the minority seems to shame the majority."

East Belfast Ulster Unionist politician Jim Rodgers spoke up for Dougan by saying: "Derek is a guy who says what he thinks. Some people may not agree with his views but this is totally uncalled for and I would ask them to refrain."

It was not the first time the painting had been defaced in this way but on this occasion there was no attempt to clean and regenerate. When Best died in 2005, it became the easier option to turn it into a simple stand-alone tribute to the city's favourite son. The pragmatism of those controlling the mural reflected Dougan's own thinking: that speaking up for this particular cause was more trouble than it was worth. His stance had, after all, been misunderstood for more than three decades – dating back to the famous day in Irish football history when a combined side took on the might of the world champions from Brazil.

The insight of his niece Josephine Long is revealing, correcting the false impression that many held of Dougan's views. He was often considered to be attempting to be a political peace-maker when he advocated the all-Ireland team, a misinterpretation that was even used in tributes paid to him at his funeral and which he did sometimes contribute towards when offering a quick sound-bite without the opportunity to give the detail behind his thinking.

Josephine explains: "It's one of the common mistakes people make about Derek. He wasn't making a political point. When he was talking about an all-Ireland team he was talking players and competitions and trophies. He wanted to see Irish players play in European finals and get to the World Cup. He wasn't taking about a political union. He wasn't saying: 'Let's have a united Ireland.' Derek rarely spoke about fans from both sides of the community being united by supporting the team – he spoke about football and making a better team.

"I have never heard him talk about how someone from Dublin and someone from the Shankill Road can support the same team. That wouldn't have come into it. A couple of months before he died he told me he would never say publicly there should be an all-Ireland team again because it did him a lot of damage within his own community, the Protestant community. People had this misconception about him. Derek was very proud to be from east Belfast, very proud of his roots. I had many discussions with him about that."

Dougan became inextricably linked with the issue of a unified team in July 1973, by which time, after several false starts, his Northern Ireland career had finally achieved steady forward progress, culminating in the award of the captaincy of his country. Unbeknown to him at the time, it had also reached its conclusion.

Having been cast aside in the mid-1960s following his transfer to Third Division side Peterborough United, his return to the First Division with Leicester City had brought with it an almost instant recall. The fact that the Irish management had steadfastly refused to consider him while playing a lower level of football might have been extreme short-sightedness, but it should not be forgotten that the original banishment of Dougan after his drop down the divisions was understandable, coming at a time when he was struggling to make a meaningful impact for his country.

Almost three years after his last game for Northern Ireland in 1962, Dougan was back in the team at the first opportunity following his return to the First Division. The side was now managed by Bertie Peacock, a teammate in 1958, who had been in charge for four years.

Dougan admitted to nerves as he sat in the Windsor Park changing room, aware that his continued international career could rest on an effective comeback game. In the end, he need not have worried. He cracked a right-foot shot just under the bar in a 3-2 victory, saying later: "It still ranks as one of my most satisfying goals because of the circumstances and the timing."

Finally, he was an established part of the team, missing only three of the next 37 internationals. His goal-scoring return, however, was not prolific. After scoring in his comeback match it was almost three years and 12 games before he found the net again in a 3-2 win in Israel. In the meantime Northern Ireland had won only one game out of six in two seasons of British Championship games – which also served as qualifiers for the 1968 European Nations Cup[15] finals – and had seen Billy Bingham succeed Peacock as manager.

Belfast journalist Malcolm Brodie, who followed Dougan's international career from start to finish, says: "Internationally he never made the impact he should have. His international career had longevity, but he didn't have the goal-scoring capacity he showed as club player. I felt we didn't the see best of him as a Northern Ireland player. He just didn't seem to fit into the scheme.

"I had my battles with him and I know for a fact that he didn't like some of my material because I wrote it straight and he was not really turning it on for Northern Ireland at times. But he was prepared to accept that you were being honest and would accept criticism if there was no blarney or bluff about it. I knew his strength and weaknesses and I knew his egotism and yet I actually got on very well with him. When they made Derek they threw away the mould."

The most obvious difference between the Northern Ireland team that Dougan left in 1962 and the one to which he returned three years later was the presence of George Best, the Belfast boy whose genius had ensured his elevation to international football within

---

15   Later renamed as the European Championships.

months of his debut at Manchester United. Dougan had first met Best during one of Peterborough's visits to the Norbreck Hydro Hotel in Blackpool, where Best had made a point of telling Dougan that he could not understand why he was not in the Irish team.

Like most who played with Best, Dougan developed an instant appreciation and affection, likening it to playing with "a maestro". Few teams took the chance of leaving Best to be handled by one defender, which allowed Dougan to capitalise on the additional space he was afforded.

Dougan responded to those occasional critics who accused Best of being selfish on the field by pointing out that his vision and spontaneity allowed him to do things beyond the imagination of those whose first thought was to get rid of the ball to a teammate as soon as it arrived.

Dougan was also among those who saw the enjoyment Best took from playing for his country, a break from the highly-pressured and much-scrutinised world of Manchester United. "In the Irish squad he's treated as he likes to be treated, not as a celebrity but as an equal," Dougan explained. "He can muck in, horse around, feel for a while his Irish background and make contact with his roots."

Eric McMordie, who was one of Best's closest friends and accompanied him on their initial journey from Belfast as a pair of 15-year-olds, says: "George got on with Derek fantastically. Their families originally came from the same road and they knew the type of area each had been brought up in. Most of the Irish lads got on particularly well, like a large family, and Bestie loved Derek because he had wonderful sense of humour that matched his own dry sense of humour."

Turkey formed part of Northern Ireland's qualifying group for the 1970 World Cup finals in Mexico and following a convincing win 4-1 win in Belfast, with Dougan scoring the third goal, there was the daunting trip to Istanbul for the return game. Even though Turkish football had not reached the heights it would scale several decades later, the fervent support for the home team made the capital city an intimidating place for a young player like Bryan Hamilton, a midfielder with Linfield, to make his debut.

Predictably, it was a physical game in which Dougan gave his share of stick to his opponents. He admitted later that his tactics had come close to "hand to hand fighting". As long-time Ireland left-back Sammy Nelson says: "Derek never let anybody take liberties with him."

By half-time, the Irish players were growing concerned for their safety and two armed guards escorted Dougan from pitch, before watching over Bingham's team talk. As the Irish progressed towards a 3-0 win there were fears that the crowd, in a frenzy, would climb on to the pitch at the final whistle.

Hamilton recalls: "As much as we loved having George [Best] in the team, this was one of the games he didn't come to, so I got to make my debut. It was a hostile place and I was green as grass – only a boy. We played rather well and at the end I wanted to shake hands with everyone. Suddenly everything started to coming at us, so Derek, who was very experienced, put his arm round me and ran me off the park. He saw that I was not looking to get myself out of there quickly enough and he took care of getting me to safety."

The early months of 1969/70 saw two games against the USSR that would determine whether Northern Ireland returned to the World Cup finals after a 12-year absence. The trip to Russia was an ordeal from the moment that the Irish team was kept waiting in the airport for two hours upon arrival in Moscow without any explanation.

Attempts to gain information through an interpreter proved fruitless and Dougan put it down to "psychological warfare and part of their strategy". The night before the game Dougan and room mate Pat Jennings were attempting to sleep when someone entered through the unlocked door and began talking in German. Dougan, who could speak the language a little, ascertained that he was an East German delegate attending a conference, but could not get rid of him until another German voice called on the hotel telephone an hour later.

After the inevitable 2-0 defeat, the Irish team attended a reception at the British Embassy, where they were warned to speak in hushed tones for fear of the room being bugged. By comparison, the return game was uneventful, a 1-0 defeat sealing Ireland's fate.

The next international campaign, attempted qualification for the quarter-finals of the 1972 European Championships, opened with defeat in Spain followed early in 1971 by a pair of easy victories over

Cyprus. Dougan was on the mark in both games, won 3-0 and 5-0, with Best scoring a hat-trick in the Windsor Park match, for which Dougan was named captain of his country for the first time.

Single-goal victories against Scotland away and Wales at home were Northern Ireland's first wins in the British Championship for three seasons and earned them second place in the table. They had opened with a 1-0 loss to England at Windsor Park in a game remembered for Best having a goal disallowed after knocking the ball away from Gordon Banks as he prepared to punt it downfield.

Banks recalls the competitive nature of the Home Internationals of the time, explaining: "You could name some terrific players in every team. But they could all play when they were representing their country and for those games in Northern Ireland the crowd really got behind them. When we played on their ground we knew it was always going to be tough. They were not quite the same at Wembley, where they didn't gel the same as Scotland did."

Such a string of encouraging performances sent Ireland with confidence into another double-header against the USSR. This time they raced through Moscow airport, but found themselves placed in a hotel where the food consistently arrived late and hinted only marginally at what had been ordered. "We lost a match we should at least have drawn," said Dougan of a 1-0 defeat that was decided by a first-half penalty.

A couple of weeks later, the Irish could only draw the return game 1-1 at Windsor Park. However, to have held their own, all bar one penalty kick, over two games against a team that had been semi-finalists in major tournaments in 1966 and 1968 and reached the last eight of the 1970 World Cup demonstrates that the gap between the elite teams and the Northern Ireland side of the period, at least on their day, was not so great – especially when Best was available.

McMordie suggests: "We did not have a large squad and if we got a couple of injuries to key players it was a hell of a problem. We had a good side, with the Arsenal boys Pat Rice and Sammy Nelson at full-back, Allan Hunter of Ipswich in the centre, Jimmy Nicholson in midfield and Derek and George up front. But we struggled to get the same standard of player if we had injuries."

Neill remembers: "We should have qualified for the 1966 World

Cup but were beaten 2-1 by Switzerland, who were no great force in those days. It's easy to look at the players and say we should have done better. I think we all felt most sorry for George that he did not have that stage. A lot of us felt we had let him down a bit."

Hamilton adds: "We just loved playing for our country. It was about the fellowship and the coming together, even though some egos come into play there. At that time we had some wonderful players, a fantastic group, and not many countries get two world-class players at same time like we had in Jennings and Best. I suppose what we really needed was a David Healy to get the goals.

"Derek was not a prolific finisher. He was good in the air without being great and at about six foot twelve he should have been better. His game was more about leading the line and holding the ball up."

McMordie has a more sympathetic view of why Dougan did not score more goals at international level: "I was lucky to play with Best, who was world class, and Dougan, who as a centre-forward had everything. He was exceptional in the air, better than the average tall man, had wonderful ability on the ground and led the line with lots of aggression. As a midfield man I was very fortunate to have him in the team because he was very quick and you could rap it up to him.

"George could basically do the same; they could hold it up until other players came up. But some of the players were not as good as them. The Doog tended to cover a lot of ground and went into areas where he was not in a position to score goals. He and George had to cover a lot of ground up front and at times they had to go very wide to get the ball. If they had been able to get to the centre more and rely on other players making chances they could both have doubled their goals."

The first game against the USSR had been the final match of Billy Bingham's first period in charge of the Irish team.[16] It meant the departure of one of the few managers to have enjoyed a comfortable

16   Bingham, who became manager of Greece before taking charge at Everton, returned to manage the Irish team from 1980 to 1993, qualifying for the World Cup finals in 1982, when they came within one match of the semi-finals, and 1986.

relationship with Dougan. Bingham puts their rapport down to the bond they formed as players in the late 1950s.

"Derek was extrovert and talkative in a nice Irish way," he explains. "He could be an extremely volatile character, full of guts and the will to win. I knew him as a teammate and I think that gave me a head start as his manager. In a way he aligned himself with me. He had hung on to me when he was a teenager and we were good pals. I knew he was very opinionated and was quite vehement about things.

"He was always up on his hind legs giving his opinions, good or bad. He was quite funny and gregarious in the dressing room. You have a variety of people and different personalities and as a manager you have to adjust to them – and work them out. If you don't they will work you out, if you know what I mean. You have to get them on your side, use psychology and say the right thing at the right time."

The new man in charge was Terry Neill, asked to replicate the player-manager role he held with Hull City. After confirming Dougan as his captain, his next act was to name himself alongside the skipper in the forward line for the drawn game against the USSR. He never repeated the experiment, but it was his contribution in front of goal that created one of the most famous results in Northern Ireland football history a few months later, a 1-0 win over England at Wembley in the 1972 Home Internationals. Neill scored the only goal of the game from close range after 34 minutes following an inswinging corner by Danny Hegan.

"I happened to be leaning against the post," Neill laughs. "The Doog and I had done a switch we had worked on in training. He would make a run to the near post and then drop off and I would run in. It worked but if it hadn't been for Pat Jennings we would have been three down in the first 30 minutes. He was our saviour. Our centre-half Allan Hunter epitomised the spirit that night.

"Alf Ramsey threw on Martin Chivers with about 20 minutes to go. Big Chiv had pace and skill and we are on our knees because we have grafted like mad. Chiv trots on and says to me: 'Your boys are playing terrific tonight.' Allan Hunter is a couple of yards away and says: 'Kick the bastard.' Chiv spent the last 20 minutes out on the right wing somewhere. It certainly was a sweet moment but one of our first thoughts at the end was that it was a shame we didn't have George Best there that night to share in it. We all felt very protective towards him."

Also at the forefront of the Irish players' thoughts were the folks back home, their lives dominated by the atrocities happening outside their front doors on a daily basis. Neill continues: "The Troubles were at their worst and at Wembley that night we all felt as a group that it might have given the little province of Northern Ireland a bit of a lift from the day to day problems."

Team member McMordie adds: "The England game was our biggest result, one you always look back on. I don't think we were under extra pressure because of the Troubles but we obviously did think it would be a great help and we knew we were getting well supported by the people back home. It felt great to get that result because it helped the country."

Part of Dougan could not help but feel a wave of anti-colonialism, the satisfaction of the province having put one over on its rulers, its supposed superior. As much as he had embraced – and been embraced by – England, he still recognised the sometimes patronising and dismissive attitudes that prevailed towards his countrymen on the mainland. He accepted that football had won him an easy acceptance that many had been denied and saw it as ironic that to many he was "no longer regarded a real Irishman". On a broader theme, he likened the Anglo-Irish relationship to that of "stern teacher and an unruly pupil who never knows for what he is being punished".

§

His country's hopes of a successful qualifying campaign for the 1974 World Cup were ripped out before they had taken root, with a 3-0 defeat in Bulgaria followed in February 1973 by a 1-0 loss in Nicosia against Cyprus, the team that had been dispatched so easily two years earlier. Neill describes it as his most disappointing game as manager of his country, while for Dougan, it was to mark the end of a 15-year international career.

By July 1973, Dougan's homeland was in the middle of the bloodiest year since the outbreak of the Troubles four years earlier. A total of 163 people had already been killed since the turn of the year, with 100 more destined to meet their death by the end of it. Spring had seen the publication of the Widgery Report, which exonerated the British army for their actions on Bloody Sunday 16 months earlier, when 14 civil rights protestors were shot dead during a march in the Bogside area of Derry. On the sporting front, international football and rugby teams were regularly refusing to fulfil fixtures in Belfast and Dublin.

It was, therefore, the most sensitive time possible for someone to have suggested that the north and south should get together as one football team, and understandable that those who agreed with it were considered to be supporting a political cause. For most observers that is exactly what it was, although for the participants – from a profession notorious for its ability not to see the wider world – it was not necessarily the case.

Terry Conroy, a Republic of Ireland international who was part of the project, says: "It was at the height of the Troubles and we wanted to come together and make a statement that people at this level could get on." Yet others saw it simply as a chance to play in one hell of a football match.

The instigator of a game that has been elevated to almost mythical status in Ireland and did, for many, provide a beacon of hope in the darkest of days was Fifa agent Louis Kilcoyne, whose family owned Shamrock Rovers, one of the most revered clubs in the Republic.

He used his influence with Joao Havelange – the head of Brazilian football, who was then canvassing support for his ultimately successful campaign to become president of world football's governing body – to float the idea of his countrymen playing a game against a combined Ireland unit during an 11-week European tour, due to start in the spring. As the brother-in-law of Leeds and Republic of Ireland stalwart Johnny Giles, Kilcoyne also had direct access to the players themselves.

Kilcoyne's concept came to the attention of Dougan while he was in the process of discussing another project designed to bring the best footballers to Ireland. The victory of the Northern Ireland team against England in 1972 had emphasised to Dougan the potential healing power of sporting excellence.

To Derek, the issue of all-Ireland or north and south was less relevant in that regard than the simple fact that success on the sporting field or the opportunity to see the best players perform was a welcome distraction from the conflicts on people's doorstep.

Of that Wembley night, he wrote: "Sport, my sport, my soccer, was doing what sport should do and I knew that the possibilities were endless. Here with the victory much had been done… I knew instinctively that we had the power to change minds and hearts."

Dougan was fully aware that Ireland's sporting calendar was being decimated by the Troubles. In 1972, the rugby teams of England and Wales had refused to travel to Dublin to play in the Five Nations Championship after death threats were issued by Republicans against visiting British teams. Later that year, the Scottish FA insisted that their Home International Championship game scheduled for Belfast was switched to Hampden Park, while 12 months later Northern Ireland were forced to play their 'home' games against England and Wales across the water at Everton's Goodison Park.

Using his position as chairman of the Professional Footballers' Association, Dougan had discussed such a state of affairs with former Manchester United manager Sir Matt Busby, Liverpool and Leeds bosses Bill Shankly and Don Revie, and his own manager at Wolves, Bill McGarry.

They had talked about taking their teams to Belfast for a pre-season tournament in the summer of 1973. It would serve, Dougan believed, as an advertisement for the safe environment Northern Ireland offered to visiting sportsmen. Encouraged by the response from the clubs, Dougan met with initial resistance when he floated the idea with the Irish Football Association. "The reason given to me was that the timing was wrong and that the Northern Ireland of the 1970s was no place for the top teams of the English game."

Malcolm Brodie suggested to Dougan a possible way forward: positioning the tournament in support of a bid to get a new running track built at Queen's University in the name of Belfast's Mary Peters, who had won the pentathlon gold medal in the 1972 summer Olympics in Munich. The fund was still £10,000 short of its £60,000 target. Brodie also identified the £35,000 needed to finish renovations and the installation of a new floodlight system at Windsor Park.

According to Dougan, Irish FA secretary Billy Drennan was enthusiastic and suggested further discussions when the Northern Ireland team met up in London in February before travelling to Cyprus for the World Cup qualifier. In the meantime, Dougan was told to submit a written proposal.

Within days of dispatching that document to Irish FA president Harry Cavan, Dougan found Giles on the end of his telephone telling him all about Louie Kilcoyne. When the phone rang again minutes later, it was Kilcoyne himself. Dougan's excitement at the thought of the combined team taking on Brazil was tempered by the potential conflict with his own proposed tournament. He asked for, and was given permission, to mention it to the Irish FA at his forthcoming meeting.

When the time came to bring up Brazil, Dougan felt he was on a roll. Conversations about the club tournament were progressing positively and he felt that formal approval was within his grasp. Like a penalty taker stepping up in a semi-final, he took a deep breath and briefly outlined Kilcoyne's plan. It was as though he had dropped his pants and farted at the president. Silence filled the room. The committee men finally brought themselves to tell Dougan they would come back to him on all the issues. He died in 2007 without ever having heard back from them.

Dougan threw himself into playing his part in preparations for the all-Ireland game, with Conroy recalling the secrecy under which the historic scheme had been hatched: "The papers were not as proactive as they are now. You would get a call from one or two colleagues saying: 'They are trying to organise a game.' It was only then that it came to the attention of the newspapers. The first thing I knew was when Johnny Giles rang and said: 'Would you be interested?' He said that he was working on the southern side of things and Derek was working on behalf of the north. It all happened pretty quickly. It was summer time and most of us were at home – not many went to the beach in those days."

The fact that careers had removed the Irish players geographically from the volatile situation at home contributed to the easy mood among those invited. Conroy continues: "There were never any problems between the players. I am a Catholic from the south and Doog was a Protestant from the north but we never had any issues relating to the Troubles. It was never discussed. If you were living in the north at that time you would have found it harder to be friends [with a southern Catholic] – you were dissuaded from it. But it was your environment that dictated what you felt. Doog said he had never experienced any problems with teams of mixed religion in the north. He was no bigot."

Few observers were in danger of missing the significance of the event. North and south had been so irrevocably divided that the Prime Ministers of the two countries held not a single meeting from the 1920s to the mid-1960s. Any discussion between ministers of the two countries usually took place in Dublin under the cover of matches played by the still-unified national rugby team, so the notion of the two groups of footballers teaming up for a common cause was radical to say the least.

It appears the players themselves were the ones who failed to see history when it was staring them in the face. Ipswich midfielder Hamilton, one of those to receive a call from Dougan, says: "I think we were all non-political. When Derek asked me to take part in the game, I was looking at it purely from a footballing perspective and for the chance of playing against Brazil I would have played for the convicts. I saw it as football first, playing Brazil second, and third was the all-Ireland team." Hamilton attributes that to 'being blinkered' but it also supports the fact that Dougan was not selling the game as a political rallying point.

Conroy continues: "They would have been inundated by players wanting to play. Nobody said they couldn't make it. We had an impressive line-up. Quite a few of us would already have had a month off so fitness was an issue, but I am sure I speak for all the lads in that we felt we had to accommodate the Brazilians."

Harry Cavan was not in the mood to be so accommodating. Dougan recalled meeting FIFA president Sir Stanley Rous at the filming of a television programme in Wolverhampton and being asked: "What are you doing upsetting Cavan?"

Dougan was informed that Cavan was trying "every trick in the book" to get the game cancelled. He recalled: "The pieces on the board came together and I knew immediately that the man at the top of Northern Ireland soccer had tried to obstruct the possible progress of trust and togetherness."

According to Dougan: "Harry Cavan tried to get the match cancelled, purely and simply because he felt it was going to be a precedent; that the north and south was going to come together after that. It was very selfish."

Malcolm Brodie says: "The all-Ireland team created quite a stir and caused a bit of antagonism. Officials saw the dangers of unifying the players. It could have meant difficulties for both football associations at FIFA level. It could have led to pressure from them for a permanent all-Ireland team."

Tradition, vested interest, call it what you will. There were clearly many people without any desire to see such a situation arise. Dougan might have scoffed at committee men worried about losing their all-expenses paid trips to foreign parts, but even among players support would only have been expected from those who were candidates to be picked for a united team. Others, understandably, would have adopted the position of Charlton forward Ray Treacey, who Dougan claimed confessed to him that he would never win as many caps in a combined side.

Cavan proved unable to force the cancellation of the game, but he did manage to prevent the home team taking the field under any kind of Irish national banner. So it was that on Tuesday 3rd July the world champions took the field at Dublin's Lansdowne Road against a Shamrock Rovers XI, who were clad in the club's green and white hoops.

The invitation side was: Pat Jennings, David Craig, Paddy Mulligan, Tommy Carroll, Allan Hunter, Mick Martin, Terry Conroy, Martin O'Neill, Derek Dougan, Johnny Giles, Don Givens – six Northern Irishmen and five from the Republic. Brazil's squad lacked only three notable members of the 1970 World Cup team, strikers Pelé and Tostao and skipper Carlos Alberto, all retired from international football.

Conroy continues: "We only met up the day before the game, or maybe two days before. Preparation was very limited and we didn't even have time for a training session. There was no such thing for that game as tactics or systems. Players were just picked in the position they played for their club and country."

It might have been a friendly, but a mixture of professional pride, the nature of the opposition and the historic nature of the occasion ensured that everyone was playing hard. "It was Brazil and it was a packed house," says Conroy. "It wasn't a stroll for anyone. There was a lot of pride involved for us and a huge focus on it because of the reason for the game. Brazil wouldn't have realised what was going on in Ireland, but they would have known it was unusual and it that it was the best of the north and south. For them, the game had significance and they were not going to lose. They were certainly trying."

The Brazilians were given a helping hand when Jairzinho was brought down by Carroll's lunging challenge as he headed for the byeline, giving Paulo Cesar the opportunity to put a low penalty kick beyond the right arm of the diving Jennings. Rivelino brought out the best of the Irish keeper with a long range effort, but the world champions' march was temporarily halted when Carroll sent in a high cross from the left and Dougan's challenge on the notoriously lightweight Brazilian keeper Leao set off an untidy melee in the area that ended with Martin O'Neill netting an equaliser.

The exhibition that the crowd had been expecting manifested itself in three picture-book goals. The half-time lead was earned when the Irish defence was split apart by the strong running of Clodoaldo, who slipped the ball to his right to give Jairzinho an easy finish. That advantage was extended when Jairzinho raced away from Conroy and fed Paulo Cesar, whose shot flew into the net from outside the box. Then a raking pass from Rivelino found Valdomiro on the right wing and he cut inside Mulligan and beat Jennings with a cool finish.

Back came the Irish. Substitute Liam O'Kane fed another replacement, Hamilton, who stepped past a half-hearted tackle and knocked the ball into the path of Conroy on his right. He crossed to the edge of the six-yard box, where Dougan had timed his run perfectly to clip the ball past Leao. The final score of 4-3 came about when Dougan won the ball in the air from Craig's diagonal cross and Conroy scored with a diving header.

"Maybe Brazil took their foot off the gas," says Conroy. "And we didn't want to be humiliated. For the second goal, I crossed for Doog and then he set up one for me. A score of 4-3 was very respectable considering it was about 90 per cent of the Brazil team that people knew."

It had been a memorable day: an exhibition of typical Brazilian skill and a spirited Irish fightback. Only a late equaliser could have made it any better. And it had all gone off without a hint of any safety-related problems. Dougan's conclusion was: "What was proved that day at Lansdowne Road was not only could great sporting events be held without security problems, but that an all-Ireland side is a practical proposition."

The memories of the occasion remain vivid for all those involved, along with their gratitude to Dougan for his role in bringing the event to fruition. "Great credit must go to Derek," says Martin O'Neill, later manager of one of his international teammate's old clubs, Aston Villa. "For him to have that great foresight with the political backdrop of that time was really fantastic. People were telling him to be careful. It was an incredible event."

According to Paddy Mulligan: "The people lucky enough to play in that game will remember him forever. The game is most definitely his legacy. The previous day a few of us were sitting round chatting and he said: 'This is going to be a wonderful occasion and I've waited years for something like this.' He said privately to a few of us that he might have played his last game for Northern Ireland, but so what. He believed in this venture."

Dougan had been as proud as anyone to be part of such an uplifting event. Yet it was to be his final taste of international football. He was never again picked to represent his country, despite still being an effective First Division centre-forward at the age of 35 – although it should be noted he had not scored in his last ten games for his country. He firmly believed his banishment was because of his role in the organisation of the game and his freely stated opinion that the two Irish teams should be permanently conjoined.

He said later: "There was no hidden agenda that day as far as I was concerned. I just felt it would be a unique opportunity for us, bearing in mind the Brazil we were facing were the bulk of the

1970 World Cup-winning side. I never realised I would not play international football again and I only found out when the next squad was announced."

Dougan was convinced that Cavan had given instructions to Northern Ireland manager Terry Neill not to select him, a theory Conroy heard advanced by his friend on many occasions. He explains: "Derek and Giles and the organisers wanted an all-Ireland team but the powers that be at the Irish associations were very anti the game going ahead. He never represented his country again. At the time of the Brazil game he was still playing for his country and for Wolves and you don't just drop someone because of his age. I think it was because of his insistence on it being named an all-Ireland team.

"I spent a lot of time with him over the last eight or nine years. You just listened to Doog – you said 'how are you?' and he talked for an hour – and he mentioned the two people in blacklisting him. I am sure they tried to make things as difficult as possible because Doog was outspoken on everything. A friend of his one said: 'Doog was the greatest man in the world in opening doors and he was also the greatest at closing them.' He was opinionated, passionate and dogmatic and he could get things done. He would never take no for an answer and he was constantly back and forward, building bridges and getting people together, getting things done. He was always adamant that everything was possible."

Malcolm Brodie, however, refuses to believe that there was any kind of campaign to remove Dougan from the Northern Ireland team. He says: "Harry Cavan and him didn't agree, but Harry didn't leave him out. That was a myth. Dougan had an outspoken, cavalier attitude but there was no question of him being boycotted."

The man who ought to know the truth is Neill, who says: "That is crap. There was no way I was going to be influenced. I admired the entrepreneurial spirit of that game, even though there was no way I was going to be involved because Doog wouldn't have asked me. Harry Cavan was never involved in team selection; I would never have tolerated that. Doog either made a mistake or he didn't really know me."

The reason, Neill says, for leaving out Dougan was that their relationship had reached the point of no return: "I just wanted

Derek the player but in the end, he was a disruptive influence. There was always something inconsistent with Derek, some demon inside him. He had a need for conflict and could have started an argument in a graveyard. I had a letter from Peter Doherty saying: 'I know why you have left him out.' I had the same response from some others. I didn't need that but it was a bit of a comfort."

McMordie offers this observation: "Derek was his own man and not frightened to stand up. I don't believe I heard him have words [with Neill] during team meetings or training sessions but Derek was the most experienced player and always willing to say what he felt was right or wrong. He would not disagree with you and go behind your back; he would have it out with you. People did know at times there was going to be a bit of a set-to."

Nelson adds: "If Terry was saying something about tactics Derek wouldn't hold back. He would say what he wanted. He'd say: 'Hold on a minute. Can we go through that it again? It doesn't make sense.' He would put him on the spot."

Whatever role the all-Ireland project played, or didn't, in the termination of Dougan's international career at 43 caps and eight goals, there is no disputing the waves he had caused within his own community with his stance.

Conroy suggests: "On this occasion he might have upset a few people from his own side because they couldn't understand why he wanted to do what he did. Coming from an area that was 100 per cent Protestant, people might have said: 'You have got to look after your own side first.' That was not in his way of thinking. If there was a problem to be solved he would try to do it."

Interestingly, less controversial sporting figures have voiced similar opinions to those of Dougan without attracting the bile and abuse directed at a man who had such an ability to polarise opinion. Pat Jennings, for example, is critical of the lack of support given to the all-Ireland game by Northern Ireland's football rulers and speaks of the benefits of a combined team: "I wrote about it in my book that there is no doubt a united Ireland team would have a better chance of qualifying and going further in competitions." No one has been caught chucking paint at pictures of Ireland's greatest-ever goalkeeper.

But what contributed to Dougan's doubly precarious position among his own people was the controversial release the previous year of his book about his upbringing in Belfast, *The Sash He Never Wore*. The title, a contradiction of the Protestant ballad, *The Sash My Father Wore*, led many who did not read the book to believe that the tone of his work was criticism of his own religious community.

His sister Coreen states: "People condemned him for the title, but there was nothing in the book to upset anyone. People saw the title and thought it was offensive. You had to explain the book to them. Whoever picked that title, or let Derek pick it, advised him wrong. It was chosen to sell books and it was the worst thing he did."

Dougan, who compounded the controversy in 1997 when he released *The Sash He Never Wore – Twenty-Five Years On*, delivers in the main a simple family memoir of Belfast life. References to the Troubles are delivered without criticism of either side of the religious divide. More pertinent to Dougan is conveying his sadness at the conflict that had ravaged his hometown.

One typical passage read: "Not long a ago a couple of young players at Molineux went back to Belfast for a couple of days' break; one was a Catholic and the other was a Protestant. I don't have to say that here in England they are on the best of terms with one another. When they came back from their separated communities I asked them how it was. They had only been away from Belfast a matter of months and yet they saw a difference overnight. I was told that it was like a ghost town, where you could not go out at night, and there was no peace at all. It is tragic that this once happy-go-lucky town is now so full of tension, and that two young boys can notice the difference in a very short time."

Any criticism of politicians was aimed at both camps and expressed Dougan's desire for someone – anyone – to find a solution, whether from government or the church. "In the last three years it seems that an abscess has been brought to the surface; indeed it has come to a head and it has burst," he said. "Now we can clear the mess, clean the wounds and start afresh."

Dougan, who always maintained that he would "definitely do the same again" when he looked back on his involvement with the all-Ireland team, also maintained his stance on the Irish team throughout his life – even if he was finally dissuaded from voicing that view publicly.

In one of his last interviews, a previously unpublished conversation with his journalist niece Josephine, he maintained his dream of a united team, two decades after Northern Ireland's last appearance in the World Cup finals.

He said: "It's the oldest sport in this country and it is almost 85 years since the divide. Rugby plays together, hockey plays together and we swim together and it's really a nonsense that these two football teams divide. [The Northern Ireland manager] has got to make a silk purse out of a sow's ear. You are only as good as the resources you have. There is not one [Northern Ireland] player who is an outstanding footballer in the Premier League – they are second rate footballers.

"I was very lucky that I played in the last of the very good sides, the 1958 team and the team from 1965 to 1973, which was far superior to the team in 1958. The reason why we didn't qualify in 1970 was because we played possibly against the second or third best team in the world, which was Russia. Northern Ireland always had a nucleus of maybe nine players and we always carried two who were not quite up to standard, but tragically today there is not one who is up to that standard.

"I question the whole system and set up of the Irish FA. It really needs looking into why they don't produce any good players. They have good Under-16s and Under-18s and they don't go on. I don't know why they don't do it. They should have a clear-out and bring in somebody who has great experience and try to go forward. I never thought I would see in my lifetime when Northern Ireland would not score for 12 consecutive games[17].

"I do not see any future whatsoever and I regret there are not a half a dozen Sammy McIlroys playing for Northern Ireland. The people who run Irish football – the left hand doesn't know what the

---

17   A 1-0 defeat in Greece in 2003 meant Northern Ireland had played 12 games without scoring a goal, a run that finally came to an end when David Healy scored in the next match, a 4-1 loss at home to Norway.

right hand is doing. The most successful manager in Irish history is Billy Bingham, who delivered the goods. With all that experience he should be pulling the strings of everything. The people who run the game are beyond a joke."

The way the game was run had, of course, always been something in which Dougan had shown a passionate interest. For eight years in the 1970s he had filled an important role in the infrastructure of his sport. Inevitably, he had left his mark.

Chapter 14

REBEL FOR THE CAUSE

Derek Dougan, thinning hair plastered across his forehead by the sweat of 90 minutes' toil, took welcome support from the wall of the Wembley dressing room. Brian Moore, who had just described Wolves' League Cup final victory over Manchester City for the next day's ITV viewers, was deep into his post-match interview with the man with whom he had frequently shared a television studio when he asked: "Would you say this is the greatest moment of your career?"

Knowing that the watching nation would have been thinking "too damn right, Brian", the man who had played 17 years in English football without winning a thing, took great pleasure in replying: "Not really. Speaking personally, the greatest moment of my career – because football is a team game – the greatest for me was when I was made chairman of the Professional Footballers' Association four years ago."

Such an answer illustrates several aspects of Dougan's character: a hint of mischief, maybe, in his determination not to give his old pal the predictable answer to an obvious question; a selfish streak, perhaps, in that individual status is placed before team achievement. But to hear only the glibness of the reply does an injustice to the genuine pride Dougan was attempting to relate.

No one would ever dispute that he loved the cut and thrust of negotiation and enjoyed the eminence the title of PFA chairman bestowed upon him when he received it in 1970. But nor could it be denied that he felt real passion about the need for professional footballers to be given a voice, to be able to take charge of their own destinies.

As salaries increasingly distinguished them from the regular working man, Dougan, who had witnessed plenty of injustice in dressing rooms throughout his career, steadfastly refused to concede that money should come at the cost of the everyday employment rights most people took for granted. It was with such a battle in mind that Dougan had gratefully accepted the chairmanship of his union, completing a journey that had started when he saw the fear in the eyes of his Portsmouth colleagues, observed the drive of Harry Leyland, his PFA rep at Blackburn, and seen his profession standing on the brink of a strike in 1961.

He would write: "One of the reasons that I became involved deeply in my own profession and now help in the running of the PFA is that I had become conscious of the profession having been kept under, and inhibited, for the three quarters of a century professional football has been recognised."

Dougan's first step into the world of formalised football politics was the result of a phone call from PFA secretary Cliff Lloyd, inviting him to join the PFA management committee while a player at Leicester. To Dougan, well aware of the history of his profession, Lloyd, PFA secretary since 1953, was a legendary figure. His voice on the end of the line was hard to resist.

"Every professional footballer today owes a debt to a man called Cliff Lloyd," Dougan said when interviewed by the BBC's *Kicking and Screaming* programme in the 1990s. "[He] was the greatest genius I had the pleasure of working with, the finest administrator since the inception of the game in 1863, and yet he was maligned and abused by the FA and Football League, and a by a lot of directors and chairmen."

To Wolves teammate John Holsgrove, Dougan's deepening PFA

involvement was inevitable: "You could see where he was going and how he was going to develop outside the playing department. He had very strong views and felt that the players should have a strong union because we had gone through a period of doffing the cap. He felt that directors did not have a clue about football. He felt that there had to be a wind of change. He was fired up in his belly about it even before he came to our club and he hated players who were 'yes' men. That is where some of the factions came in."

The early part of the 1960s had been a momentous time for the PFA. Following the abolition of the maximum wage in 1961 there had still been a major battle to fight in an attempt to achieve that part of the new deal that was supposed to have gone hand in hand with the lifting of the salary ceiling – the players' freedom from the old retain and transfer system. That fight was to have a courtroom setting thanks to the willingness of England midfield player George Eastham to be used as a test case following his refusal to accept the right of Newcastle to deny him a transfer in the summer of 1960. He had been dissatisfied with his club house, angered by Newcastle's attempts to obstruct his participation in an England Under-23 tour and unhappy with the part-time job organised for him to supplement his football wages.

Newcastle's unwillingness to accede to his transfer request, however, meant he was stuck at St James' Park, even though his contract had expired. Unlike the thousands of players over the years who had found themselves similarly trapped by having to re-sign for their club or play nowhere, Eastham walked away from football, moving to Surrey to work as a cork salesman for Ernie Clay, later to become chairman of Fulham.

After several months of deadlock, Arsenal's £47,500 bid for one of English football's artists was accepted by Newcastle. Eastham's career was back on track but the principle at the heart of his temporary exile from the game remained. He went along with the PFA's proposal to challenge in court Newcastle's right to have made him an outcast within his own profession. The case was not heard until 1963, when Justice Wilberforce's historic ruling stated that Newcastle's failure to release him at the end of his contract was "restraint of trade". While it was not the precursor to complete freedom of contract, it was, as historian John Harding noted in his history of the PFA, *For the Good of the Game*, "a significant victory in a very long war".

The clubs still held the upper hand. Players could not simply walk out at the end of their contracts and could still be held to ransom by the wages being offered. All that had been won so far was the players' right to attempt to negotiate a transfer, not the end of the transfer system.

Football League secretary Alan Hardaker said in 1964: "If clubs pay the players, they are entitled to have some system – and it is accepted that this must be some system within the law – for their protection. If a player wishes to be a professional with all the benefits financial and otherwise of the present age then he must be prepared to accept conditions of service laid down by the people who provide his wages."

New rules governing players' contracts were established in April 1964, almost a year after the setting up of a Joint Negotiating Committee between the PFA and the League. Each contract gave the club the right to renew at a salary at least equal to that in the original contract and for the same period. If the club did not want to exercise the option, the player was free to leave without a fee being demanded.

At the end of a second contract period, the club had the right to renew again on equal terms. If the club decided to transfer the player instead, the original contract continued to run until the transfer was completed. If, however, the player was unhappy he could take his case to the League Management Committee and, if necessary, to an independent tribunal consisting of League and PFA representatives and an independent chairman. The tribunal would decide all aspects of the case, including the eventual transfer fee.

So even though the power of the options all remained with the club, the recourse to independent jurisdiction and the right to pick up full wages in the meantime was enough of an increase in the players' power to keep the union happy for now. Besides, having won one exhausting battle in the law courts, the PFA had neither the appetite or the funding – should it come to strike action – to push for further victories on the same battlefield. The prevailing attitude was not to further poke a monster that had already been riled by the Eastham verdict.

As everyone knows, English football wore a happy smile in the middle part of the decade, the victory of Alf Ramsey's England team in the 1966 World Cup prompting a boom in Football League attendance and a further strengthening of the sport as a media property. Some, however, looked hard enough to see below the shiny exterior that the game was displaying to the world. For Derek Dougan, the most significant event of 1966 was not Geoff Hurst's hat-trick against West Germany, but the setting up of the Chester Committee, which was charged by the Labour government to report into the state of football at all levels.

When the recommendations were published in 1968, Dougan grasped them to his very core and described the report as his "bible". The recommendation that resonated most was the suggestion that the contract system should be scrapped. Chester proposed the kind of freedom of contract that existed in other industries, saying: "On the one hand it will provide a better moral basis for the transfer system… and the new system would add to the dignity of the professional player."

While acknowledging the deep-rooted presence of the transfer system in football, the report said it was "not consistent with professional players' professional standing and must go", although transfers would still be allowed during the term of contract. In short, it proposed the kind of system that has existed since the European Court of Justice handed down its historic Bosman ruling in 1995.

Dougan's role as PFA committee member had whetted his appetite for greater office within his own organisation and when former West Ham and Manchester United full-back Noel Cantwell resigned as PFA chairman in 1967 in order to become manager of Coventry City, the vacancy was of great interest.

According to Dougan, another committee member, Coventry centre-half Maurice Setters, ruled himself out of contention for the post because he felt his disciplinary record made him an inappropriate candidate. Such niceties did not bother Dougan, whose own career had included no shortage of controversial incidents. Opposing him, however, was Arsenal and Northern Ireland captain Terry Neill.

Dougan felt it was because of Neill's safer image that he lost out on the position on this occasion.

He settled instead for being an active member of the PFA committee. Neill recalls: "He had a lot to say and a lot of it was very sensible and intelligent. But being the Doog, sometimes he wanted to bring the tanks in. But you don't mind that. You want people who will speak up."

Dougan would also find time to help support the efforts of Irish League footballers in forming their own union. Bryan Hamilton, who was a Distillery and Linfield player before joining Ipswich in 1971, recalls: "I had watched Derek playing for Distillery and followed his career in England, and when we were trying to start a PFA in Ireland we asked him for advice. Me and Jackie Fullerton and others were trying to start this association and I said I would get Derek to come and spend some time with us. He had some tea at my house and spent a long time talking about the PFA. He was instrumental in the association getting started."

Fullerton, who went from an Irish League career with Crusaders and Derry City to become one of his country's leading sports broadcasters, adds: "There was an international in Belfast on the Saturday and Derek stayed on to give us advice. It was a great gesture. I think his commitment to the PFA was part of his east Belfast working class roots. There was a trade unionist in him trying to get out. I always remember him trying to educate the players. He used to say that most of them never think the cheering will stop and all of a sudden, at the age of 35, they don't know what to do next."

Back in England, with Neill alongside Lloyd at the forefront of the organisation, the PFA – buoyed by the belief that the Chester Report demonstrated the bigger role the union had to play in the game – set about formulating a new strategy.

At the 1969 annual general meeting, Lloyd outlined the union's new demands, which included changes to options clauses in contracts to give players equal footing with their employers. Getting the 75 per cent of League clubs required to agree to such a change proved beyond the PFA and there had been no movement by the time Neill left office in 1970 to become player-manager of Hull City.

This time, Dougan's ambition was not to be denied, despite Neill's desire to determine Bobby Charlton's interest in becoming chairman. The two candidates could hardly have been more different: Charlton the English gentleman who had never been booked, Dougan the outspoken Irish rogue with a catalogue of controversy behind him.

Dougan also believed that his experience in the Third Division gave him an ability to empathise across his profession in a way that a superstar such as Charlton, used only to the pampered lifestyle of the First Division and the England team, could never have achieved. He used to tell Charlton as much during PFA committee meetings, saying: "Any player who has not played in the lower divisions does not know what the game is really like."

Neill recalls the events of the PFA committee meeting in Manchester in August 1970: "I had handed in my resignation and we were taking about who should be the successor. Dougan was very keen but Bobby couldn't make the meeting and I thought it would be a good idea, given his status, to have a chat with him, even though he might not have wanted it. Doog had the bit between the teeth and said: 'He is not at the f***** meeting.' So to cut it short instead of having a couple of hours arguing I said: 'Right, let's vote for you, Doog.'

"Your first thought in that situation is: 'Bobby Charlton: superb ambassador. Doog: bit of a loose cannon.' I felt we needed a little more clout and status at that time. The union had no money and a few of us had even chipped in to buy Cliff Lloyd a better second-hand car. But Doog subsequently grew into it. He loved to make a noise and thought he could get in there and rattle a few cages. And he did. He was a very hard working member of the committee and then chairman."

In his history of the PFA, John Harding notes that for once the union was to be led by one of the great individuals of the game, whereas characters such as Len Shackleton and Alex James had previously chosen to turn away from the PFA rather than join the fold.

With football and the media becoming ever more deeply entwined, Dougan was the perfect fit to head his profession. He had already seized for himself the opportunities that had been presented by the growing public fascination with the celebrity of football and was now in position to steer his peers through the same waters, deep with opportunity but with plenty of sharks lurking.

Future PFA assistant secretary Brendon Batson was a young player at Arsenal at the time, learning from Highbury's PFA representative Bob Wilson and preparing himself for when he could become a team representative himself, which he did following his transfer to Cambridge United. He recalls Dougan being a popular appointment among his profession. "He spoke very eloquently and, being Irish, he had a certain charm, even though he gave you a good kicking verbally. He did it well, attracted publicity and was very forceful in getting his argument across."

Terry Conroy adds: "He was ideal as chairman of the PFA because he was well versed in most things in life – more than most footballers, who are blinkered in most things. He would fight his corner and not feel inferior to anyone in any discussion."

Former Leicester teammate Peter Rodrigues says: "I think players do look and take note of who is in charge of the PFA. It was something Derek wanted to do throughout his life and he had the gift of the gab, that way with words. He was a good figurehead for the players and I am sure he would have fought your corner."

While Charlton would have been a more acceptable figure in the offices of football's ruling bodies, Dougan was happy to roll up his sleeves and come out swinging. This is not to say that he did not recognise the need for a touch of Charlton-like statesmanship.

He acknowledged as much in *The Sash He Never Wore* when he wrote about the "additional responsibility" he bore. "I cannot afford to be caught up in any sort of incident," he said, before adding: "Because of the coverage of the media any act of retaliation would be on the television screen and in the press for a week or more. I would then be in a position to be shot at, and it would not be much of an advertisement for the association if the chairman were to be sent off."

Player discipline was at the heart of one of the first major issues to confront the new chairman of the PFA, the infamous "Refs' Revolution" of the summer of 1971, which was launched when match officials were called to special meetings on the Sunday after the opening of the season. As a follow-up they received letters containing detailed instructions aimed at eliminating the foul play and gamesmanship for which the period has become infamous.

Highest on the list of evils to be eradicated was the tackle from behind, the standard weapon of too many defenders. The days of centre-forwards like Dougan and Geoff Hurst receiving the ball with backs to goal and having time to turn were in the past. Some, like Arsenal's John Radford, had taken to wearing pads on the backs of their legs as well as front. The "professional foul" and time-wasting tactics were among the other ills of which the game was to be cured.

On the face of it, these were all measures that Dougan should have welcomed. He was aware as anyone of the effects of the increased competitiveness and financial rewards within the game. Not only was there greater earning potential for individuals but the stakes had increased for clubs throughout the previous decade through European competition. The prospect of being able to qualify for a tournament such as the Uefa Cup by finishing in the top six had added to the level of competition right down the league table and made the battle to stay in, or move up to, the First Division an intense, often vicious, one.

The football authorities had shown their willingness to impose lengthy suspensions on those who found their way regularly into referees' notebooks. Since Dougan's eight-week ban in 1969, high profile figures such as Alan Ball, George Best and Peter Osgood had spent long periods on the sidelines but such punishment seemed to be ineffective as a general deterrent.

Dougan would have been fully supportive of the new measures had his members been given warning of what was about to occur. Instead they were left to read hints in the Sunday newspapers by Football League secretary Alan Hardaker, who spoke of a "campaign" to come. The realities of the new regime confronted the players on the Tuesday night, the first big midweek programme of matches. On that night 32 players were cautioned in 15 games – an insignificant number by the standards of the card-happy modern era, but enough to create headlines in the brutal world of 1971/72.

At Portman Road, six men, a phenomenal amount for one game,

were cautioned by Tonbridge official Ron Challis in Ipswich Town's victory over Coventry. "The game won't continue if they keep booking people like this," said Ipswich manager Bobby Robson.

The following night, seven players were booked as Tottenham and Newcastle fought out a 0-0 draw, after which Newcastle captain Bobby Moncur commented: "We will be going out there with handbags soon. The referees are turning it into a game for cissies." Spurs manager Bill Nicholson insisted: "It is time we were told what was going on. It seems the Football League are giving the referees books and pencils and trying to get them to frighten the players. It was impossible for players to concentrate in circumstances like those tonight. We have been told nothing about the new policy."

Elsewhere that night, three players were sent off and 38 more booked. Under a back page headline that read "Soccer on the brink of revolt," the *Daily Mirror* asked: "What is football trying to do to itself?" and commented on the "lunatic decision to operate football to the letter of the law".

In the first 11 weeks of the season, 715 players would be cautioned. By 15th December, the number would rise to 1,000. When top referee Brian Daniels failed to book anyone in a game between Fulham and QPR a fan sent him a get well card.

The reaction of the players was a promise to fight against suspensions caused by the referees' new-found willingness to reach for their notebooks. Vernon Stokes, chairman of the FA's disciplinary commission, countered: "We will work through the night if necessary to get through all the appeals."

It was all getting rather silly. PFA secretary Cliff Lloyd entered the argument with comments that illustrated the growing absurdity of the uproar over something that all parties agreed was, in principle, good for the sport. "We know that the game can only be better for the removal of the tackle from behind and dissension," he said.

"We have never argued against that. I have been accused of painting players whiter than white. That is nonsense. If there had been prior discussion of those points, there could have been no complaints. I don't know where we go from here."

The players might have wanted prior consultation but their extended sulk about the new guidelines does suggest that had the

Football League waited for agreement between the referees, players, managers, coaches, directors and tea ladies on the best method of cleaning up football, strikers would still be feeling defenders' studs in their calves almost three decades later.

Meanwhile, it was the referees' turn to get hot under the collar, threatening a revolt if their name-taking activities were not backed at forthcoming disciplinary hearings. Lloyd in turn voiced his fears of a hard-line by the authorities sitting in judgement on his members: "I shall shortly have to appear on behalf of players at hearings. It has been hard enough to get players off in the past – I would think that would now be impossible. I fear for the game if the present policy persists."

On the final day of August, Dougan had his name taken against Crystal Palace, one of 75 players booked in the space of three days. He appeared merely to have put his arm round Palace defender John McCormick as they tumbled to the ground.

"If I was to say what I really felt about that booking I would be suspended *sine die*," he said. "It is the first time I have been booked in two years. There were no hard tackles tonight yet three players were booked. The players are simply bewildered by it. If this continues we will have 85 minutes of stoppages and five minutes of football. It seems that there is no longer any room in the game for physical contact."

Dougan was asked about calls by some of his more militant members for strike action, but argued: "Striking is not the answer. We appreciate that something needed to be done to improve the game, but we are getting away from common sense and instead finding chaos and confusion, It is imperative that we get around the table and talk with the League and FA as soon as possible. The livelihood of our players is being put in jeopardy."

Several weeks into the season it was becoming clear that English football was a safer environment for the more skilful, less robust, players. Watford manager George Kirby went as far as trying to lure Jimmy Greaves out of premature retirement, while former England inside-forward George Eastham was enticed back to Stoke from South Africa and would help them win the League Cup.

England goalkeeper Gordon Banks commented: "The new

refereeing code has helped players like him. Now they can do their job without being hit from behind. Players like George Best are coming into their own again."

On the first Sunday of September, Dougan chaired a seven-hour meeting of the PFA committee, after which Bobby Charlton warned of the problems of making players change long-established habits: "We've been playing this way since we were kids kicking tin cans in the streets. It is very difficult for players to re-educate themselves in a matter of weeks."

Early in September, some light became visible at the end of the tunnel of threats and rhetoric when FA secretary Denis Follows announced that a summit meeting would take place with all parties represented. As the day of the talks neared, Charlton said with resignation: "The message has already got across to the players. Whether they like it or not, this is the way the game has to be played from now on."

On 7th October, Dougan and his PFA committee colleagues gathered in London with officials of the FA and Football League, the Association of Football League Referees and Linesmen and the Secretaries and Managers' Association. It was only the second time in 108 years of organised football in England that members of all those bodies had been brought together.

A statement issued at the end of two and a half hours of talks said there had been unanimous agreement that the bodies "should consider a suggestion for a committee of study – without executive power – to examine such matters put forward for discussions by the parties concerned".

It was hardly the Treaty of Versailles, and the players were denied the amnesty they had sought over the early-season bookings, but the meeting was harmonious enough to provoke a vast change in the attitude of Dougan, who described the day's events as "a marvellous step forward".

He continued: "I am disappointed we did not get an amnesty but otherwise we are all very happy with the outcome. The steps the League took were needed but we felt the way they took them was wrong. Everything now has been cleared up. I am sure there will be a great deal more understanding between players and referees from now on. We only wanted to work in harmony with everyone. Now we are."

Dougan was so happy he was even moved to comment: "It is only when I go abroad that I realise the high standard of refereeing we have in this country."

Spokesmen for the other organisations voiced similar satisfaction, with Hardaker, typically, providing the best sound-bite when he remarked that the game had been given a "much-needed cold shower". Follows even gave the players some hope of leniency when he explained: "The FA Disciplinary Commission agreed that no amnesty would be granted but every individual case would be considered in the light of the new conditions at the time."

Matters of player punishment continued to call upon Dougan's time. In 1972 he and the PFA found themselves in the Royal Courts of Justice on behalf of Ernie Machin, who had been sent off for allegedly kicking an opponent while playing for Coventry two years earlier.

Television replays proved that the referee's report was wrong in the case of that particular offence, but the FA commission noticed another misdemeanour so upheld the dismissal and subsequent suspension, even though Machin was not given the opportunity to defend himself against the new charge.

Dougan felt the case was typical of the FA's haphazard judicial process. "Disciplinary procedures in the game caused a great deal of heartburn," he said. "The courts run by the FA were often no more than the kangaroo variety. Justice was not always done or seen to be done. Players were resentful, feeling that they would not get a fair hearing."

Dougan also looked disapprovingly at the way clubs arbitrarily imposed their own internal disciplinary measures, taking advantage of the fact that most players were too fearful for their own livelihood to take on their employers. He felt that such a situation also diminished his professionals in the eyes of the public, who were used to hearing players referred to as "the boys" or "the lads" and thought nothing of it when they were treated in the same patronising manner. He wondered aloud what other profession could so casually fine its workers two weeks' wages for "flimsy reasons".

Progress was made, however, when the Conservative government's Industrial Relations Act said that all employees must have the right to legal representation in cases of disciplinary action, while the football authorities introduced a new system in 1972 that made the accumulation of disciplinary points the basis of uniformly-applied suspensions, rather than relying on the whims and moods of the members of a commission.

From the moment he showed up at Distillery in his Teddy Boy jacket, Dougan had shown himself to be image conscious. He now felt the need to prove that footballers could be smart, articulate professionals. Steps might have been taken by the authorities to stamp out thuggery on the field, but the general public's view of many footballers was still characterised in the *Monty Python's Flying Circus* portrayal of fictional footballer Jimmy Buzzard, played by John Cleese, who tells his interviewer: "I'm opening a boutique, Brian," and: "I've fallen off my chair, Brian."

Appearances of the brainier of each team's players on shows like *Quizball* could only go so far in altering public perception and were frequently countered by inarticulate post-match interviews that had by now become a staple of *Match of the Day* and *The Big Match*.

An air of sophistication, Dougan believed, could be achieved by the introduction in 1974 of an awards night, where players would swap their Afghan coats and bell-bottom jeans for dinner jackets, and vote for their own Player of the Year, rather than rely on the football writers to be the sole arbiters of such an award.

"The image of the footballer as a thick-headed yokel who needs constant discipline and can not be trusted to manage his own affairs is a distant throwback," Dougan stated. "The real image belongs to the PFA Awards night. Anyone who doubts the social progress of the modern footballer has only to switch on the Player of the Year Awards on ITV, without doubt the best night on the sporting calendar."[18]

Dougan demonstrated to Andy Gray his desire to put on a good

---

18   There was a predictably ironic reception, particularly from satirical football magazine *Foul!*, to the award of the first PFA Player of the Year Award to Norman 'Bites Yer Legs' Hunter, who to many was the antithesis of the sporting sophisticate that the PFA was trying to project.

show after the Aston Villa centre-forward was voted winner of both the Player of the Year and Young Player of the Year awards in 1977. Having injured his ankle in Saturday's League Cup final, Gray was forbidden from travelling to London for the dinner by manager Ron Saunders, who was anxious about his fitness for the replay. Even the persuasive Dougan could not change the mind of the notoriously dour Saunders, so his next option was to call Gray and ask if he would give up one of his awards so that the PFA at least had one winner present at the event.

Gray, angry with Saunders and indignant at Dougan's suggestion, refused. With time ticking away, Dougan finally got all parties to agree to a film crew visiting Gray's home to record the presentation of the awards.

Trophies aside, Batson believes that the real benefit of the dinner was the opportunity to bring players of all levels together and forge a unity that would prove important in the battles to come over the ensuing years: "It was the first time in my experience that all players in all divisions were together on a social basis. As a lower division player, you only encountered the top players if you were lucky enough to play against them in the cup, but that was a competitive setting, not social.

"The first dinner in 1974 was the first time I really encountered Derek and I saw him in his pomp. He was a great speaker and to see someone slagging off the football authorities on behalf of all the players was enlightening. It was like he was just talking among friends and you knew that those in power would have to take notice of him."

By the time of that event, those in football's positions of authority were aware of battle lines being drawn as Dougan and Lloyd prepared to push for greater contractual freedom for their members. The notion had floundered at various Football League annual general meetings and the PFA believed that an approach to government was its best hope of success.

In May 1973, the PFA had made representation to the Departments of Employment and Environment, whose ministers had referred matters to the Commission on Industrial Relations. Any judgements the CIR passed would not be binding but would add weight in any case brought to an industrial court. For some critics of the PFA, this approach was not radical enough. Reports of the union's 1973 annual meeting had noted "ripples of discontent with the lack of progress" among some members, while Eamon Dunphy, the Millwall midfielder forging what would be a highly successful career as a writer, accused the PFA leadership of lack of aggression.

Publicly, Dougan, never one to passively accept any kind of slight, pointed out the achievements of the PFA since 1960 and could not resist a dig at Dunphy, noting that his subscription was overdue. Privately, he accepted that there was a certain truth to the comments and was increasingly feeling the need to see the battle through, resolving to remain as chairman of the PFA until the fight was over – regardless of when he ceased to be an active player.

Foul!, the forerunner of modern-day publications like *When Saturday Comes* and unafraid to take the kind of stand unthinkable to reverential magazines like *Shoot!* and *Goal*, heaped further disapproval on the PFA, citing 'feeble leadership' and 'faintheartedness'. Even the CIR had been critical of the union's delegate system and had found in interviews that many players were ignorant of the PFA's activities.

Writer Alan Stewart described Dougan as "smug" and expressed the belief that he really wanted to be a manager. Betraying a startling lack of insight into the current head of the union, he wrote: "Chairmen of the PFA never seem to be men with radical views."

Lloyd spoke up for Dougan, describing him as hard working and pointing out that his PFA duties were carried out for no pay in his free time. Lloyd and the PFA wanted to progress their case through building a platform for negotiating with and educating the Football League, rather than confronting them. Batson – who sat through two decades of similar discussions with football's ruling bodies after becoming right-hand man to Lloyd's successor, chief executive Gordon Taylor, and a series of PFA chairmen – is well placed to discuss the dynamic between the union's two leading men in the 1970s.

"Derek liked a good argument," he says. "Particularly if he felt he was in the driving seat. He took a lot of experience from

Cliff, but he was the voice. The players would have been putting forward their views and setting the agenda it and then it was up to the chief executive or the secretary, who were dealing with the Football League all the time, to guide the management committee, who are representatives of players from all the divisions. In those negotiation meetings it would have been Derek who was leading."

Bruce Bannister, the former Bristol Rovers striker who was a member of the PFA management committee under Dougan, recalls: "I think Cliff was a very clever fellow. I won't say he manipulated, but let's say he directed his chairman excellently. There were very few times when the secretary and chairman disagreed. I honestly can't remember one. Everyone's opinion was passed around in executive meetings. We had people who were not afraid to voice their opinions and it was not a matter of everybody doing what Derek said.

"Derek had his opinions too, but he would bounce them off Cliff before he bounced them off the media. Cliff knew how good Derek was as a spokesman. Derek would say things more strongly than Cliff would, but if he ever needed pulling back a little Cliff could do it. That is why they worked so well together."

Dougan was determined to lead the union as far as necessary in order to change a system he believed still "enslaved" the players. He explained his desire to achieve greater independence for his members when he wrote: "The system we have accepted for far too long treats players as serfs, reducing them to the cattle market."

Bannister says: "Freedom of contract was the only place it could go. We suffered restraint of trade any which way you want to look at it and it needed to be put right. Footballers were still slaves, even though some were well-paid slaves. A good step had been taken through George Eastham and eventually the Bosman case put it right completely but there were a myriad of steps between them. There needed to be a change in the thinking. Someone needed to say: 'That is not fair or reasonable'."

According to Bannister, the profession needed someone to take that step for them, because the country's changing rooms were not exactly abuzz with talk of rebellion: "Players knew it was not fair but quite simply they couldn't see things being changed, so what was the point in it being discussed?"

The PFA appeared undecided how far they wished to push their cause. At the annual meeting in November 1974, the union's chief lawyer, George Davies, said that "anything short of total freedom would be an imposition on players". Yet a year later Lloyd, sensing the tide turning in his members' favour, told the same meeting that compromise was desirable.

The League had accepted the CIR's recommendation to set up the Professional Football Negotiating Committee, which would have an independent chairman. The committee, upon which the PFA was represented by Lloyd, Dougan and Terry Venables, began a series of quarterly meetings, at the second of which an agreement was formulated, based on four points: the transfer system to remain for players under contract; players to have the right to seek employment at another club at the end of their contract; a system to be devised to compensate a team losing a player at end of his contract; and agreement that the compensation system should not be a hindrance to players finding new employment.

Agreeing the principle of compensation was one thing; reaching accord on a formula was another thing entirely. Alan Hardaker recommended the multiplier system used in Holland. It was based on a player's wages, which was considered the best indication of his worth, and also took into account his age, division in which he played and whether he was moving up or down in status.

In October 1975, though, the League suggested that the wage used in the multiplier should be the wage being offered by the new club rather than the pay packet he was leaving behind. The players held firm and at their 1975 AGM gave their negotiators a mandate to pursue the original formula.

Early in 1976 the League began pressing for the multiplier to be dropped completely, suggesting instead that clubs should have a month to agree a fee before going to a tribunal to fix the transfer fee. The game of bluff and counter bluff continued when the PFA maintained its insistence on a multiplier, but conceded it would be based on wages being offered by the buying club.

By now, the issue was becoming so all-pervading that even *Shoot!*, whose most contentious question was usually asking a player which famous person he'd most like to meet, was devoting two pages to the debate in the week before the Football League's AGM in June 1977. Inevitably, Dougan took the opportunity to have his say: "When we met the League Management Committee in 1975 we were looking for complete freedom of contract with no compensation paid to clubs whose players moved on. In the 26 months of negotiations since then, we've compromised and conceded and yet still the League chairmen won't agree the deal we have thrashed out with the Management Committee.

"What I think it really boils down to is there are a few mavericks abut who consider it to be against their interests to implement it and they've convinced other clubs to do the same. I can't understand the objections of the chairmen. In fact, it's they who should be pressing for this move more than us, because it will save clubs a lot of money.

"What we are trying to do as a professional body is to take the heat out of the transfer system and save clubs from irresponsible buying. At the moment you get clubs chasing a title or fighting against relegation who spend out X number of thousands of pounds on a player who might not be in the side a year later. We feel no industry can afford that kind of irresponsibility and if that's not protecting the interests of the club, I'd like to know what is.

"I'm still hopeful the chairmen will see sense before the annual meeting next week and accept the proposals before them. But the one question I would ask them to think over in the meantime is: 'Do they think the game is healthy at the moment?' To me, the answer is clearly no, and if they'll only look at it more closely they'd see the changes we are proposing are in the industry's interests."

Differing views came from various sources, including Coventry City chairman Sir Jack Scamp, who accepted that freedom of contract was inevitable but added: "It has to be a sensible and satisfactory agreement and the one that has been put before us so far isn't. The deal that has been proposed is far too complicated, a legal nightmare."

And he somewhat missed the crucial point of the players' desire to take control of their own careers when he asked: "Why can't clubs be left to negotiate things between themselves as they have always done. It's not as if the new arrangements would change the status quo that much. The only real change would be player's right to move at the end of his contract." Which, for the PFA, was a pretty big "only".

Millwall and former QPR manager Gordon Jago argued that the Dutch system had led to a small number of teams dominating and warned that small clubs like his own must not end up as mere training grounds for the richer clubs. West Ham midfielder Trevor Brooking spoke up for the players but his view that personal geographical ties would protect against the big clubs acquiring all the best players seems very naïve when viewed in the modern era of football without frontiers.

The League failed to pass the proposed new deal at its meeting, despite apparently agreeing to the principle of it. In September of that year, a meeting of the Midlands clubs suggested that the compensation formula could be manipulated to prevent teams having to pay the full amount of the player's value. Cliff Lloyd rightly pointed out that such manipulation was only possible because the clubs had insisted on not using existing salary as part of the equation, but the clubs agreed to push ahead for an agreement free of any mathematical formula.

Dougan was individually dragged into the controversy when it was subsequently revealed that the League failed to vote in favour of a new agreement in the summer because they believed he and Coventry managing director Jimmy Hill had agreed that if a player decided to leave his club at the end of his contract the clubs concerned should be free to negotiate the fee – an arrangement that obviously ran counter to the compensation formula.

Dougan stated that at no time did he make such an agreement with Hill and found it deeply ironic that a man who had played such an important role for his profession during his term as PFA chairman should now be standing in the way of its further progress. Dougan said he was "prepared to settle the matter on the holding or buying club's offer being the basis of how the compensation was negotiated". He said it had not been suggested to him that the two teams should be left to negotiate the fee.

The PFA management committee backed its chairman by recording: "In view of Mr Dougan's remarks it appeared that Mr Hill had completely misled the meeting of the Football League clubs."

Hill contended that the multiplier system was a false constraint on a free market, writing later: "The proposition to impose artificial levels of compensation, which the clubs were supporting, would have meant that if the Sky Blues had sold Larry Lloyd at the end of his contract they would have received only £100,000, having paid a hefty £240,000 for him."

Meanwhile, players such as Charlton stalwart Keith Peacock and future PFA chairman Alan Gowling agreed that the existing transfer system should be retained to prevent all the money going into the pockets of a few top players.

Dougan remained adamant that the transfer system was the game's biggest problem and saw his personal commitment to the multiplier formula as the best answer to those who said he did not have his heart in the struggle once he had become chief executive of Kettering Town (see Chapter 15).

"It would have been impractical to get the negotiations under way and then resign as chairman to pass the complicated issues to another chairman," he responded. "I was interested only in continuity which meant remaining until negotiations had been completed and the new deal implemented."

In April 1978, the League clubs issued their final rejection of the multiplier system, with Hardaker warning that if it was insisted upon by the PFA the whole deal would fall through. In the meantime, the PFA management committee had received a mandate from its members to go all the way to a strike.

Batson recalls that the players would willingly have followed Dougan and Lloyd down such a path: "Derek was fantastic as we moved towards freedom of contract in 1978. I went to a regional meeting at the Sobell Centre in Finsbury Park and the players suddenly realised that we could control our own destiny. There were a lot of doom and gloom merchants in the game saying it would be the death of the lower divisions and that players would be out of work, but I was one of those players at the lower levels and at Cambridge we said we would take our chances."

Dougan would subsequently maintain that there was never a real threat of such extreme action, acknowledging that a strike "would have disrupted the game and driven away supporters on whom the game depends". He continued: "At every stage of negotiations we had the good of the game at heart and showed that the PFA is not a militant movement but a progressive organisation which values the interests of all that the profession represents."

Something had to give and the PFA management committee voted to accept the proposal that tribunals should be used to settle disputed transfer fees. According to Dougan, he and Bannister were the only members of the management committee who wanted to push on for full freedom of contract. But he conceded: "I decided it would not have been circumspect to take on the rest of the committee, so a watered down version of freedom of contract was agreed upon."

The PFA's annual meeting of 1978 formally accepted the deal that was on the table. Dougan's disappointment at not gaining the complete victory he desired should not diminish the significance of the giant step forward his union had achieved. As Lloyd pointed out, the right of a player to leave at end of his contract had been established – which was the overriding principle of the PFA's battle – although lawyer George Davies warned that "time will tell whether the arrangements spelt out in the new regulations offer a reasonable freedom for your members".

Dougan's final word on the subject before stepping down from his position as chairman was his own warning to the clubs: "I predict they'll live to regret not implementing the multiplying formula devised by the PFA in the long-term interests of the game."

The death of Derek Dougan occurred, ironically, only a few months before the PFA began a series of retrospective events to mark the centenary of the organisation, spearheaded by chief executive Taylor. Among the last acts of the Lloyd-Dougan partnership had been the start of the formal grooming of the former Bolton and Birmingham midfielder, a long-time member of the PFA management committee, to succeed Lloyd as secretary at the date of his planned retirement in 1980, serving for two years as Dougan's successor as chairman in the meantime.

Three decades later, Taylor remains in his post. "Derek was one of the game's most colourful characters and I was very proud to have served with him and under him," he said at the time of Dougan's passing. "I had eight years under him as chairman and he led the PFA, along with my predecessor Cliff Lloyd, all through negotiations in establishing a constitution and a collective bargaining agreement which have stood the test of time.

"At time he was a very controversial character, never frightened of taking on authority, which got him into trouble in his playing career and, needless to say, off the field as well. He led as chairman and brought in the players' right to move, which was the forerunner of Bosman."

Batson adds a reminder that there are other important parts of the current PFA structure that have their roots in the Dougan era: "In addition to freedom of contract, there were things within that, like the players' cash benefit scheme, which meant that as a player [in need] you would get something from the game irrespective of your earnings. While the modern-day player might not be fully aware of Derek's contribution it is there for people to read about. He has left a legacy and the PFA centenary has brought a lot of that to the fore again. We should recognise the huge contribution he made to the well-being of players of the modern era and former players."

Dougan's unsuccessful attempt to win the position as the head of PFA Enterprises meant that his formal involvement with the union ended in 1978. The final word on that relationship goes to Alan Merrick, who had the chance to witness at close quarters his contribution to his profession when serving as the PFA representative for West Brom.

"The guy was a breath of fresh air," he says. "He was always very articulate and thoughtful and he was real – there were no fabrications. He was very opinionated but his opinions were invariably solid and well thought-out and you had to analyse them before you questioned him. He was a principled person who stuck to his guns and was on a crusade at times. He upset the authorities and the stalwarts of their boardrooms because nobody had ever confronted them like that before.

"He came from the era when players lived from pay cheque to pay cheque and had no rights or security. Whether they got paid enough often depended on whether the team won and they got their bonus. The Doog broke down barriers. He spoke up for players across the whole spectrum of the game and a lot of people were very influenced by him. He gave a lot to the game."

Chapter 15

GETTING SHIRTY

Logging on to the official internet site of Kettering Town Football Club during the final weeks of the 2007/08 season reveals that the spirit of Derek Dougan is still alive. As I surf the club's site, reading about their march towards the Blue Square Conference North title, I go into the match report of the latest game. And what are the first facts detailed at the top of each report, even before scorers and team line-ups? Match sponsor, ball sponsor, programme sponsor and even sponsor of the game report itself. The Doog, I reflect, must be looking down with satisfaction.

Through Dougan's foresight and willingness to take on the established order, Kettering Town is forever associated with the introduction of the concept of club sponsorship to English football, in particular the notion of branding on shirts. It is the legacy of the 18 months he spent at Rockingham Road as chief executive, team manager and occasional centre-forward, his first job after the conclusion of his professional playing career.

Dougan's arrival at Kettering in the autumn of 1975 was the result of a phone call from club chairman and local businessman John Nash, who was quickly left in no doubt that Dougan's ambition was not merely to manage a team but to run it from top to bottom, including financial, commercial and development activities. At a subsequent four-hour meeting, Nash clarified that he was not proposing a sale of the club to Dougan but assured him he would have the power to operate without consulting the board.

Managerial duties would be included but Dougan wasted little time in appointing former Wolves colleague Brian Thompson to assist in that area, while he concentrated on other matters. At Kettering, the role of manager was accepted as part of a bigger package that allowed him to be "in control of my own destiny", but he had already established in his own head that the position, answerable to boards of directors, was not one he craved for its own sake.

According to Dougan, he'd already turned down one opportunity that had been put to him by Aston Villa chairman Doug Ellis during the celebration banquet for Wolves' League Cup final win more than a year earlier. He recorded that Ellis's initial offer had been to go as player-manager, but his own doubts about his long-term fitness forced him to tell Ellis he was not up to the dual role – at which point Ellis asked him to go purely as manager.

Dougan was aware that incumbent manager Vic Crowe would have his contract terminated if he accepted Ellis's offer and wondered how long it would be before he found himself in the same position. Before long, he was also dismissing newspaper talk of possible managerial jobs at Bournemouth and West Bromwich Albion, whose players were reported to have named Dougan as their choice of successor to the sacked Don Howe.

Dougan, though, was more interested in the wider workings of club football, having seen enough mismanagement by directors to believe he could do better. His first target had been Third Division side Walsall, the West Midlands club that had been saved from extinction in 1972 by Ken Wheldon. After requesting a meeting with Wheldon, he explained his vision for redeveloping Walsall as a community centre with the football club at its hub – the blueprint he had carried close to heart ever since the publication of the Chester Report.

"I felt the time was right for football clubs to change their approach and I wanted to try to give them an insight into how a football club could and should be run," he said. He had approached Walsall not only because they were down on their luck and drawing crowds of around 4,000, but because he wished to remain in the Midlands. Dougan's account gives no mention of any kind of financial offer to Wheldon, who called Dougan two weeks later to say: "You have no chance of taking over."

It was not until two years later that Wheldon spoke of Dougan's bid for Walsall, when he claimed: "I told Dougan he would need a quarter of a million pounds to get this club and he was offering nothing. He wanted to take over Walsall to prove that players could run a football club without directors. We treated it as a huge joke."

However, Kettering Town, whose status as a top Southern League team made them one of the forces in non-league football, were giving him his opportunity to activate his ideas. Announcing that "I am going to put this club on the map", he went to meet an excited group of employees.

Defender Sean Suddards remembers: "We were one of the best non-league teams at that time and it was magnificent to think that a national figure like the Doog was coming. He was one of the most mild-mannered friendly characters I have ever come across in football. He was soft spoken and as he was playing as well he just acted like one of the lads, even though he was a world figure in the footballing sense, instantly recognisable. He certainly attracted media attention and raised the profile of the club and that was positive for everyone.

"As a manager he led by his own example and you couldn't help but warm to his style because he had been one of the top players in the UK for many years and yet was putting his reputation on the line at lowly Kettering. You listened and were respectful and he tried to bring a sense of fun into the game, which wasn't there with a lot of other managers. We were glowing. He had a charismatic approach, he treated everybody equally and you just felt like you were in his company rather than being an employee. He made you feel important."

Goalkeeper Gordon Livsey remembers Dougan making sure there was a tangible sign of how importantly he regarded his players: "He was not a good manager in terms of his knowledge of football and tactics. That was poor. He never knew how to sort out a problem on the field. But he was a great motivator. He was interested in the players and had them at heart. He would do anything for us. For a start, he came in and doubled the wages. At that time I worked for the club chairman, John Nash, and I went to see him about a rise at work.

"He asked me what I was getting at the football club and I told him I had gone up from £16 a week to £32. 'What? Since when?' he said. I told him Dougan had just doubled our wages and he sent me straight to the club secretary to get the wages book. He didn't put them down again, though. I don't think he would ever have knocked Doog down. People wanted to play for Derek Dougan and you knew that he meant business by doubling our wages because he didn't feel we were in the right bracket."

In this regard, Dougan was making sure he didn't fall into the trap that had ensnared other managers in forgetting their past. "As former players, managers ought to know better but at times they represent the biggest hurdle," he said.

It didn't take long for Dougan's personality to make its mark in other ways, as Livsey recalls: "He didn't really have time for an initial training session. It was straight into the game on Tuesday night at home to Bedford, our big rivals. We were both doing well in the league but it was misty night and it was dubious whether the game would be played. The referee made the decision to go ahead and we went 1-0 down, which was a shock.

"Doog had been chuntering on to the referee for most of the first half and when we went in at half-time there was no sign of him or any team talk. Just before we were due out again, he came in and said that the game was abandoned. He must have spent most of the half-time convincing the ref to call the game off because he didn't want to start with a defeat."

The moment for which Dougan's Kettering career is remembered most vividly occurred on 24th January, 1976, when his team ran out for a game against Bath City with the words Kettering Tyres spelled out across the chest of their maroon, white-sleeved shirts.

Despite displaying generosity towards the players, Dougan had become increasingly worried about the tenuous financial state of the club he had taken on. The glee with which the club directors had accepted the abandonment of that opening game, offering them the chance to rake in the gate money all over again, had alerted him to the extent of the problems. Every passing week bought further supporting evidence, including the horror of the local bank manager when it was reported that Dougan was earning £15,000 a year – even though the reality of his deal was £600 per month plus 50 per cent of any commercial revenue he generated. He discovered that the club operated five bank accounts and would fund one by borrowing from another. On six occasions, he would claim, his monthly pay cheque bounced.

One solution was sponsorship. English football had been awash with corporate endorsement of minor cup competitions since the turn of the decade, but the branding of a club by one company, although commonplace in Europe, had yet to be introduced. Dougan told Kettering Tyres that for £2,500 its name could appear on his players' shirts. "The euphoria over Kettering Tyres' sponsorship was increased by the knowledge that we would be pioneering something which other clubs had only talked about," he said.

The furore that the episode caused would ensure that the company received publicity worth many times their investment. It is hard to believe Dougan did not foresee, even relish, the battle he had instigated, even though he would insist, 'It was not a confrontation of my seeking.'

Dougan claimed that his first inkling of the row to come arrived in the form of a letter from the Football Association, informing him that the new shirts breached FA rules. As he could find nothing in the association's regulations relating to the issue, he ignored the letter.

Livsey remembers arriving in the dressing room for a Southern League Cup quarter-final at Weymouth early in February: "Doog had negotiated a deal and I don't know how much the chairman knew about it. I remember the FA being against it but we went down to Weymouth on a Tuesday and these shirts were laid out for us. We were all a bit surprised but our trainer said: 'This is the right kit.' We thought we'd been told we couldn't wear it, but Doog said: 'Nobody tells us what we wear. I am the one who tells you'."

Publicly, Dougan's stance was not dissimilar. "I could end up in Sing Sing or Strangeways, wherever the food is better," he said. "I find it inconceivable that petty minded bureaucrats have only this to bother about."

Suddards says: "You don't realise at the time what a big thing it is: to actually be the first to wear a sponsor's name. It is only later that you realise that he was miles ahead of everybody else. You take it in your stride, although it got us a lot more coverage."

Letters flew back and forth between FA headquarters and Kettering, while the shirts had several more airings, although Dougan had affected a compromise by changing the wording to "Kettering T". He insisted that the scheme had been planned "tastefully and discreetly" but the day before the 1976 FA Cup Final found Dougan and Nash up before the heavy hitters of the FA.

Feeling like naughty schoolboys, they explained the rationale behind the shirts, which, it transpired, none of their interrogators had even seen. Dougan exhibited a new shirt bearing only the legend "KT" and maintained his stance that the rule book, produced in 1972, did not specifically forbid such attire.

"Do you know we could close down your ground?" asked Vernon Stokes, head of the disciplinary committee. Dougan was as taken aback by such a comment as he was disappointed that no FA officials had visited Rockingham Road to witness the efforts the club was making to solve its own financial problems in a professional and discreet manner.

After a break for deliberation, Dougan and Nash were given a stern warning and told that the shirts must not be worn again. What particularly riled Dougan was the fact that the FA had been raking in money from kit manufacturers Admiral over the previous two years for having its corporate logo placed prominently on the breast of every England player.

The postscript to the episode was that in June 1977, the FA would announce its decision to allow clubs to carry a 2.5 inch square logo on their shirts, which was not allowed to be "detrimental to the image of the game". FA secretary Ted Croker added that if Kettering had approached their case in the proper way "it could have been granted 12 months ago". Ironically, Kettering would be unable to find a sponsor to take advantage of the new regulations.

After seeing his team finish the 1975/76 season in third place in the Southern League, Dougan took the opportunity to combine his position of authority at an English club with his passion for seeing visiting teams crossing the water to his homeland. He had relished travelling to Northern Ireland with Wolves to face Derry City in the Texaco Cup five years earlier – despite being frighteningly close to a bomb explosion during the trip – but, undeterred, he enhanced Kettering's preparation for the new season by having them board a plane to Belfast for four games against Irish League teams.

Suddard recalls: "It was at the height of the Troubles so we did think: 'Whoa, where are we going?' The place was being bombed. Only Derek would think about taking an English team there. We had a team meeting and a wives meeting about it, and we went out there even though it was not the thing to do at that time.

§

"When we got there, soldiers were waiting at the bottom of the steps of the plane and we were transported in an unmarked Belfast bus. The whole thing was surreal, although you think nothing if it when you are in the middle of it. We stayed on the north coast of Ireland one night and the next seaside town along, about five miles down the road, was bombed that night.

"But we had a fantastic reception everywhere. We went to a golf club and the locals were meeting us off the bus and offering us their clubs so we could play. Wherever we went in Ireland, Derek was presidential in his status among the people."

Good form in those games led into a storming start to the season. Kettering reached New Year as the only unbeaten team in professional or semi-professional football in England before crashing at home to Margate. By that time, the club was making national headlines once again, by virtue of having secured a place in the third round of the FA Cup. "This little place has come alive," Dougan purred. "We have scaled the mountain for them."

Dougan himself scored six goals in a run of ten games, including a close-range winning goal at Oxford United in the first round of the FA Cup after a 1-1 draw at home. "I'm deadly from one yard," he joked.

Livsey says: "Derek still had his deft touches and he was a poacher for goals and was in the right place at right time. But he didn't play as many games as he would have wanted to."

The reward for a 1-0 home win against Tooting and Mitcham was not exactly the dream third-round draw against one of the major teams. Instead, it was the visit of Fourth Division Colchester United. Perhaps remembering Wembley in 1960, Dougan made the decision not to play on the morning of the match after missing a month's worth of games through injury. A 3-2 defeat in front of 5,020 meant there was no further opportunity for heroics on the national stage.

"It was a disappointment to get Colchester," Livsey admits. "We believed we could beat them, but I think the actual game got the better of us. We could have won if we had played to our true potential. It was the biggest crowd Kettering had had for a long time and we probably froze a bit and maybe already thought we were going to the fourth round."

Helping to bolster the Kettering defence during the FA Cup run was Alan Merrick, whom Dougan signed on a match-by-match deal after he completed his first season in the North American Soccer League with the Minnesota Kicks. The former West Bromwich left-back, who stayed in Minnesota to become a successful coach, attaches great significance to the lessons he learned playing under Dougan.

"He gave a sense of confidence, belief and hope," Merrick recalls – a gift not to be underrated when dealing with non-league players who have probably taken their share of knock-backs from the football world. "He stuck up for the underlings and the down-trodden. He put backbone into people. He got a few players to re-emerge in football and resurrect their careers because he got them mentally and physically correct."

A prime example of that was Billy Kellock, a forward who had been with three league clubs before slipping down to Chelmsford City, from where Dougan signed him. After three years with the Poppies he went on to play more than 250 league games with a variety of teams, including Wolves in the 1980s.

Merrick continues: "I was back in the Midlands tying up the sale of my house before going back to the States and Doog would pick me up from my parents' home in his Jaguar and drive us both to Kettering. We had some great conversations, although sometimes it was odd going to and from games with him with all the emotions that involved. But he showed me several different sides of management that bore fruits for me later on. He was determined to give this little club a presence within the community and take them to another level. You have to give him credit for the way he went into that type of challenge."

Kettering's season lost momentum and the title challenge dissipated, but it was finances that concerned Dougan, particularly after the resignation of Nash as chairman in May 1977. Players' wages were often not be paid on time and Dougan told new chairman Tom Bradley that the club could not move on to a more secure fiscal footing without taking a long-term view and transforming itself into a sports and community complex.

While initial discussions took place with the Sports Council, the initial funding would have to come from the Kettering public. Yet Dougan's appeal met with ambivalence. As he put it: "The scheme fell through at the very moment the club had an unprecedented opportunity to rid itself of the mistakes of the past and prepare itself for new concepts in the future."

Faced with such disappointment, Dougan had no choice but to move on. He did so with the satisfaction of having improved the club's finances to a significant degree and achieved his goal of putting the club on the map. Life was going to be a lot less interesting for a while for the Kettering fans, one of whom would write at the time of Dougan's death: "I loved the time he spent at my club. He was great for us and a really nice guy. Every away match he would come and thank us for coming. He would come out to the coach before we left. He was a nice guy and had time for everyone."

Chapter 16

WOLVES AT THE DOOR

Flicking through newspaper files from late-1970s and early-1980s, it would be easy to believe that Derek Dougan had been camping outside Molineux waiting for an excuse to walk in and hang his jacket on the back of one of the chairs. Media were constantly intrigued by the possibility of a return to his former club, with the strongest opportunity appearing to arise in 1978 after the departure of manager Sammy Chung.

Dougan responded to the urging of the fans by applying for the vacant position, yet he believed chairman Harry Marshall, who had succeeded John Ireland in 1975, merely went through the motions of an interview before appointing the man he had earmarked all along, John Barnwell.

By 1982, Marshall's own position was under threat. The League Cup triumph of 1980 seemed a long way in the past as First Division status was lost and the club faced an increasing struggle under the weight of debt caused by the building of the new Molineux Stand. This was hardly an uncommon state of affairs in the days before TV's millions poured into the game.

Chelsea's construction of its cantilever main stand had precipitated their cash-strapped descent from the First Division and begun a period of yo-yoing between the top two levels. The Stoke team Tony Waddington had built to challenge for the league title in the mid-1970s had been dismantled because of the need to pay for repairs to a storm-damaged stand.

Now the £1.5 million cost of development at Wolves found Marshall facing a challenge from local insurance broker Roger Hipkiss, who tried to galvanise his fellow shareholders into unseating the chairman through a vote of no-confidence. Dougan's name was mentioned as possible new director, but such was his ability to split opinion that Hipkiss and his supporters felt having Dougan on their team might actually damage their chances of affecting the change they desired. Even those who wanted Marshall out might have felt that the introduction of Dougan, who had proved to be a spiky executive since the end of his playing career, was too heavy a price.

Among other potential saviours were former Aston Villa chairman Doug Ellis and ex-Wolves keeper Malcolm Finlayson, whose presentation at the club's EGM in June 1982 prompted Marshall to respond that the goodwill attached to his name was all that was keeping creditors at bay. His proposed solution was to sell space within the new stand for offices, find a buyer for Scotland centre-forward Andy Gray, the club's most saleable asset, and develop a supermarket next to the ground.

After the rebel group won the support of the meeting, they were narrowly beaten when the shareholders voted on the meeting's recommendation. They issued a writ claiming that 500 votes were invalid, prompting the resignation of Marshall, allowing Ellis and Finlayson to become chairman and vice-chairman.

Describing the accounts as "hopelessly and irretrievably bankrupt", Ellis took only a matter of days to ask Lloyds Bank to appoint a receiver. It was announced that unless a buyer could be found by the Football League's deadline of 5pm on 30th July and guarantees could be given that the club could fulfil its fixture obligations, then Wolverhampton Wanderers would fold after 105 years.

The scramble for a saviour was on. While names like future club owner Sir Jack Hayward and Walsall chairman Ken Wheldon were mentioned as potential investors, a lower-profile group was being constructed by Wolves season-ticket holder Doug Hope, a businessman who had moved down from Scotland in the 1960s and done well in the world of cars and property.

"Everyone was bemoaning the fact that Wolves were being allowed to go to the wall," he recalls as we sit surrounded by newspaper cuttings, a picture of Hope bearing Dougan's coffin looking down on us. "There was a lot of huffing and puffing and hand-wringing from the local establishment who were shareholders in the club – like the *Express and Star* and Butler's Brewery – but not much action. I had got to know Derek socially over the years. He was a good PR man and knew how to treat people. I said to him one day: 'I have got somebody who reckons he can fund a takeover if you are interested in becoming involved'."

The spider web of Hope's contacts had begun with a previous business acquaintance, Mike Cornwell, who connected him to someone in Manchester who was friends with John Starkey, an architect involved with Allied Properties, whose principals were Mahmud Bhatti and his younger brother Akbar. By the time Hope and Dougan met with the Bhattis, the deadline for saving the club was less than a month away.

"We saw them in Manchester," Hope explains. "We'd had two meetings with their people, a chap called Mike Rowland who ran Allied Properties, and John Starkey, and then we went to Manchester to meet the Bhattis. It was the one and only time I saw them dressed in Arab garb."

Dougan later told author Peter Lansley in *Running With Wolves* that they had happily offered the impression of a connection with the Saudi Arabian royal family and added: "When you see Mahmud Al-Hussan Bhatti drive up in a Rolls Royce at his own aviation company, and know of luxurious offices in London, you can't help but feel impressed."

Hope continues: "They said virtually nothing. They were sitting in this Portakabin at the airport and they just listened. Derek outlined what his ideas were for the club and how he felt it was viable and what could be done. We had already had discussions with the council by that time about a proposal for a superstore.

"Derek was the football man and the spokesman. He was the

man to open the door. We went for a meal in the Four Seasons restaurant with Starkey and Rowland, who was up and down on the phone the whole time. It was clear what Derek had said had impressed them.

"We felt from that meeting it was a goer. We then had to sit in Derek's house in Wolverhampton waiting for the call to say that this was a viable situation and after that we met with the receiver, who told us he wanted £2m."

Hope adds ruefully: "We didn't do sufficient due diligence in relation to the Bhattis and a lot was taken on trust. But we didn't have much choice as far as we were concerned. There was not much time before the deadline and we were up against a lot of other people and no one really knew the strengths of the other bids. We knew that Doug Ellis probably thought he would be able to buy the club pretty cheaply."

The day of the Football League's deadline was full of drama, tension, frantic phone calls and finally, breathlessly, triumph for Dougan and Hope, who recounts: "We arrived at 9am at the offices of the receiver in Birmingham. It was most of our people, while the Bhattis were in London. We had previously agreed the offer the day before and the purchase price was £2m, plus we added another £50,000 because we had no idea what else was being bid. We had been told that if we had produced the money we could buy it.

"The Football League also wanted various assurances and at the last minute, once everything was done and dusted, they said they wanted the directors to guarantee the fixtures. Derek and I were to be the only directors at that stage because the Bhattis naively thought they could remain in the background. Derek and I signed a guarantee for £50,000 each that the fixtures would be completed.

"Also, the Bhattis wanted a Liberian lawyer at the last minute and we found one in New York. But it came half past four and they came from the Grand Hotel and signed the bankers draft and three minutes before the deadline the job was done."

Hope can't resist adding: "At two minutes past five the phone rang in the office and it was Doug Ellis calling to see if it was his!"

Dougan was introduced to the media as the club's chairman and chief executive, claiming that "in the space of a few weeks a miracle has happened". He said he would not be paid for his role and continued: "I will have total control of the club but I have no desire to influence whoever is in charge of the playing side."

Addressing the speculation over the future of Gray, linked with a move to Manchester United, he said he would discuss a £1m fee and added that he would also consider a swap for United forwards Lou Macari, Norman Whiteside and Garry Birtles. The mischief of such a comment demonstrates how Dougan loved being back on centre stage, especially at a club that meant so much to him.

Despite obvious questioning about the consortium's backers, Dougan protected their anonymity, saying only that they were Wolves fans based in Manchester. He then told *World of Sport* viewers that they were "most creditable and responsible people", adding: "I would like to think they have made this cold calculated decision on the ground that we are going to make it work at Wolverhampton." It would be several months before the identity of the Bhatti brothers as the mystery investors was revealed by dogged reporters.

Dougan's next performance was at a public meeting at Wolverhampton Civic Hall, where he was in his element, his audience eating out of his hands. "Give us your support for a year and judge us after that," he said, announcing that John Ireland was returning to the club as president and would have the Molineux Stand named after him.

With the new season fast approaching, Dougan wasted no time in making his personnel changes, appointing former Aston Villa executive Eric Woodward as general manager. Commercial manager Jack Taylor, the former World Cup final referee, was asked to resign and club secretary Phil Shaw also left after 33 years at the club. "There were various people Derek wasn't comfortable with," says Hope. "Derek's view was he wanted it to be a club with Wolves people."

The day after reportedly having been asked to re-apply for his job, manager Ian Greaves met with Dougan and departed Molineux. Under the former Huddersfield and Bolton boss, who had succeeded Barnwell, Wolves had won only five of 20 games.

The surprise selection to replace him was Graham Hawkins, a Wolves teammate of Dougan's in the 1960s who had previously been manager of Port Vale and was assistant at Shrewsbury under Graham Turner.

"People thought my friendship with Doog was a factor in me getting the job," Hawkins relates. "But after leaving Wolves I hardly bumped into him, apart from the PFA dinners. We were not close at that time and I don't know how he even got my number. I had not followed what was happening at Wolves. We had just performed the miracle of keeping Shrewsbury up and you live in your own little world. I was just leaving for work and Derek called and said he wanted me to go and work for him.

"I said: 'Where?' When he told me it was Wolves and he wanted me to be manager I was absolutely taken aback. I drove to Shrewsbury in a dream. The club I had supported and played for wanted me to be manager. I had to pinch myself."

Hawkins, who had left Wolves to play at Preston and Blackburn, laid down his one condition to his new boss: "I would not accept anything unless Derek agreed that it was me and nobody else in charge of the team. I was not going there as a 'yes' man. He kept his promise all the way through even though some people thought he was pulling the strings. I remember nearly bashing a reporter one night because of that. We were at a dinner and he made that statement. The red mist came down and I had him pinned against the wall with my fist clenched when Doug Hope grabbed me."

Hawkins recalls being unconcerned about the financial plight of the club in accepting his new role: "I didn't even ask what the money was or who the players were – it was all adrenalin and enthusiasm. I knew some of the players and I knew Jim Barron, the assistant manager. It was obvious we did not have much money to spend and the staff had been pruned dramatically."

What was left was a small squad of veteran players concerned for their careers and young players who had barely discovered whether they had a future in the game. "We had a lot of seniors, no middle and then the youngsters," says Hawkins, who gave four teenagers their first-team debuts in the opening game of the season, a 2-1 home win against Blackburn.

"I didn't have to pick the teams at that time. They picked themselves. My only thought was: 'How do I play these 11 players?' In the end, some of those boys ended up getting ruined because of the pressure they were under. But they had great attitude and showed the older lads what could be achieved through skill and determination and then the older ones took over."

Hawkins encouraged his team to play attractive, open football, building from the back rather than lumping the ball downfield at the first opportunity. He recalls: "Derek took me a bit under his wing when I was a player at Wolves and I shared a room with him in America. I learned a lot from him and one thing that stuck with me was what he said when I left: 'Do everything with style.' That always stuck with me and I liked my teams to play that way."

Having watched the second half of that first game among the fans on the terraces, Dougan saw Wolves compile a nine-match unbeaten start to a season that, against the opinions of most so-called experts, ended with them gaining promotion as Second Division runners-up.

Full-back Geoff Palmer, into his second decade at the club, recalls: "We had young kids thrown in at the deep end and a tinge of experience. We got off to a great start and were better than people had thought."

Most of those players had welcomed the arrival of Dougan, who'd immediately made a point of assuring Andy Gray that he would not accept a knock-down price for him. "To me, he was the right man at the right time," Gray recalled. "His presence lifted the club, inspired the fans and briefly put us back on the right track."

To midfielder Ian Cartwright, one of the opening-game debutants, the chairman was an inspirational figure. "You would always see him around," he remembers. "He was full of life and he encouraged all the young lads. He knew everybody's name. When you are young you are not that concerned about money issues. I was 18 and I lived with my parents. I suppose the situation was a worry for the bigger players who were on thousands a week and had mortgages, but to me it seemed like a great club and we'd see Derek most days.

"He would often pop his head in and encourage us. He was a very passionate man and I don't think he wanted to be one of these chairmen you don't get to know. He wanted to show he was there for us and that, as a player himself, he knew everything we would be going through."

Palmer adds: "You never had to call him 'Mr Chairman'. You'd see him and say: 'All right, Doog?' That is how he wanted it; he didn't change. He said: 'Call me Doog and if you have a problem come and see me'" There was no closed door."

Hawkins continues: "Derek was in every day. I always saw him on Fridays but not until after I had put up the team sheet. He might ask why I had done certain things and we would sit and have a Scotch together. And if I ever had a problem I would go and see him."

Another long servant, Kenny Hibbitt, says: "Derek got on well with Graham Hawkins and we saw quite a lot of him. He was a big influence in that first season. But we could sense something wasn't quite right and it turned out he didn't have the finances to take the club further. He ended up having to write his own cheques. I got one that bounced, which I kept. I had never experienced that before. Doog was let down big time."

The truth was that the promotion campaign had been played against the growing realisation among Dougan and his colleagues about the plight of the club. Within weeks of the takeover, they discovered that the Bhatti brothers had, in fact, only put up £500,000 of their own money. The rest had been borrowed from Lloyd's Bank against club assets and the future health of the club now rested upon planning permission being granted for the superstore development behind the north end of the ground.

Hope explains: "We assumed we had got a substantial company behind us so whatever we required would be provided. But by the first Christmas we began to have doubts that everything was as it had been presented to us. We thought we had a deal that the council, subject to planning permission, would support us in developing a supermarket on the site and that would generate a great deal of money.

"But due to local opposition, mostly from the owners of the local shopping centre, that plan became frustrated. And once it was turned down we knew we had problems because the funding wasn't there from the Bhattis. They were reluctant to fund it even if they were in a position to do so.

"We always felt there was a bit of animosity towards the Bhattis because they weren't part of the local establishment. It would have helped if they had spoken to people and the media but they weren't prepared to do it. It was not negotiable. They wanted to remain in the background and they were almost naïve. They didn't think the press would dig into who was behind the club."

Dougan said he spoke to the Bhattis 20 times a day, while Mondays were taken up with management meetings involving the two brothers. There had been little money available for new players, despite the figure of £1m being bandied around in some quarters. Instead, Hawkins had been forced to make do with investing a total of £141,000 in Stoke defender Alan Dodd, QPR goalkeeper John Burridge and Luton midfielder Billy Kellock, one of Dougan's Kettering old boys.

Hawkins acknowledges the positive influence his boss had in such transactions: "That is where Derek's skill came in. He was in front of his time in terms of how football clubs are run as he was basically a technical director. He used his links with other clubs to find out who was available."

For the start of the 1983/84 campaign, the Wolves cupboard was barer than ever. Hawkins warned Dougan and the board that he needed between £750,000 and £1m if the team were to compete in the First Division, listing the likes of goalkeeper David Seaman, defender Mick McCarthy, midfielders Paul Bracewell and Micky Gynn and young Leicester forward Gary Lineker among his targets.

Hope recalls a £110,000 fee having been agreed with the Filbert Street club for the future England captain, while Hawkins adds: "We had done our homework and spoken to one or two of the players. We spoke to Bracewell at length and knew the terms he wanted. The board said we could not afford it so then we knew we weren't going to get guys like Lineker and McCarthy."

Instead, Dougan signed Rotherham winger Tony Towner for £100,000. "It was the only thing Derek did that I didn't totally agree with," says Hawkins. "I was on holiday at the time. We had seen Tony play and he was on our list but I didn't agree with the way it was done. Another winger was a low priority for me. Derek thought he would be another Dave Wagstaffe."

Without the desired influx of new blood, Wolves made a flying start to the season when they took the lead after 60 seconds in their opening game at home to champions Liverpool through a Palmer penalty. But after being pegged back for a draw, it was not until the 15th league game of the season that they recorded their first win with a 3-1 success at West Brom.

By that time Gray had been sold to Everton for a cut-price £180,000, Preston had dumped Wolves out of the League Cup and the die for the season had been cast. A steady stream of players found themselves up for sale as the team remained stuck to the bottom of the table, winning only six league games in total. A remarkable victory at Liverpool in January had been a rare bright spot, the lowest point being when only 7,481 saw them lose at home to Notts County.[19]

Hawkins did not quite make it to the end of the season, replaced for the last few weeks by Jim Barron. Hawkins believes that a knowledgeable football man like Dougan understood and sympathised with the hopelessness of the manager's situation: "I knew that from about September or October the powers that be wanted me out. I wanted them to pay up my contract. I was only on £21,000 a year, which was bugger all. Some players were on more than me and I remember a big argument after I left a player out and he said he was losing money because of it.

"That got me blazing. I told him: 'If we are talking about money I will swap my pay packet with you now. If you want to talk about football you can come in, but if you want to talk about money don't bother.'

"I knew what was coming but I was very upset it had finally happened. The offer made to me [£10,000] was not acceptable

---

19   To put the crowds of the era in context, the steady decline in attendance experienced by football during the 1970s had continued into the next decade, with Wolves' game at Liverpool in this season watched by only 23,325 and the match at Arsenal attracting 18,612 – less than a third of what it would draw in the modern day.

and it took me seven years to get what I'd wanted. But that was the Bhatti brothers mainly – there was no money for Doog to pay anyone off.

"He was supportive all the way through. Once I was called into a meeting with Derek, Dougie Hope and Roger Hipkiss. I knew Roger wanted a new face, Doug was in between and Derek didn't want me out. He knew that, whoever he brought in, it would not be any better than with me. It was proved that nobody could have got any more out of the players than me.

"That meeting had come from the Bhattis and Derek said they wanted him to take a more active part in training. I said: 'You know what the agreement is. If you take one step on the training ground I will sue.' Derek didn't contest it; he just gave Doug a kind of knowing look. He knew what I was going to say and he never did get involved in training."

Eventually Hawkins got the call from Hope to say that he had been dismissed. "Maybe Derek found it too difficult to do it himself as he was an old friend," says Hawkins, who was frustrated that the full extent of Wolves' financial plight was never made public while he was in charge. "Not long before he died, Derek referred to me at a dinner when he said: 'There is somebody here we should have supported more, but I didn't have the money. If we had money it would have been a different story.' That needed to be said at the time."

Early in June 1984, the club announced Tommy Docherty as a surprise choice as manager. Docherty's managerial career had been on something of downward spiral since leaving Manchester United following the FA Cup victory of 1977, spells at Derby, QPR and Preston having failed to produce much in the way of success. It was a decision upon which Dougan had been outvoted by Woodward, Hope and Hipkiss following an interview process that had included several other candidates, including former Wolves players Mike Bailey and John McAlle and established managers like Alan Mullery and Alan Durban. Docherty did nothing to endear himself to his new boss by taking up his position with the quip that "Derek Dougan is to football what King Herod is to babysitting".

Hope recalls: "Doog felt that in Graham he had somebody he

believed in and could talk to. He wasn't keen on having Docherty, but we felt he was an experienced manager, a character, and felt he could lift the club after we had been relegated. Derek and Tommy had crossed swords in the past but I don't think there was any problem while they were both there."

Docherty's hopes of re-establishing his own fading credentials were undermined by the worsening finances at Molineux. Not only was there no money for new signings, but the PFA had to step in to pay the players' wages when the club ran into cash-flow problems. Future England goalkeeper Tim Flowers even remembers paint peeling off the walls of the cockroach-infested dressing-rooms.

According to Dougan, the club had needed to twist arms to acquire a ground safety certificate, while he'd been required to give a personal guarantee of £30,000 for a new public address system. He said he ended up putting in more than £150,000 of his own money.

Relegation was inevitable, secured by a run of 21 games without a win and followed, just as inevitably, by the dismissal of Docherty. By that time, however, Dougan was no longer at the club, having resigned in January 1985. "It was an acrimonious departure," says Hope.

Dougan had become frustrated at the increasing remoteness of the Bhattis. Those numerous daily calls had petered out to the point where he was struggling to get them to answer his calls. Rumours were circulating that they no longer wanted Dougan to be running the club. He didn't want them at Molineux either and late in 1984 he tried to get funding for a takeover, although the Bhattis' asking price meant it was never a realistic option.

Hope explains: "We were under a lot of pressure and Derek felt he couldn't do any more so he resigned. He and John Starkey tried to offer the Bhattis money to buy the club and once he had shown his hand in that way the relationship had deteriorated to such a point that it was inevitable he would go. He felt he had been let down."

Newspaper reports suggested that Dougan had lost the support of his fellow directors, while stories would emerge later that year that Allied Properties and Wolves were to sue Dougan over his undertaking to guarantee losses and claims that he had not returned his company car and borrowed money.

Hope insists: "There was all sorts of silliness. Derek and I had each put in a bank guarantee of £150,000 and I think there was comment, no more than that, that he could be taken to task. It was all posturing. I don't think the guarantee was ever claimed."

The episode of Dougan's tenure as chief executive of his beloved Wolverhampton Wanderers remained the saddest professional chapter of his life. He'd had regrets before – the FA Cup final transfer request for example – but nothing like the deep-seated, unshakeable frustration and sorrow he felt at being unable to bring his vision of how a club should operate into full, vibrant life at Molineux.

In his book, *How Not to Run Football*, he had expressed unhappiness that his old club had "failed to recharge the batteries of supporters who in the 1950s were among the most committed and passionate in the country".

He genuinely believed he was the man who could make that happen. He had made the fans believe it too. However much events might have spiralled out of his control, he wore the guilt and disappointment like a shroud for the rest of his life.

Chapter 17

FRIENDS AND ENEMIES

It is the final day of the 2007/08 season in the Coca-Cola Football League Championship, or the Second Division as it was in the days of Derek Dougan. Inside Molineux, the vast majority of a crowd of more than 26,000 are cheering and screaming in the increasingly forlorn hope that their vocal exertions will produce the miracle of two more goals in stoppage time against Plymouth Argyle.

A Wolverhampton Wanderers campaign that began with an emotional tribute to the Doog at the opening game against Watford is ending with older fans regretting the absence of a Dougan-Richards style partnership that could turn a 1-0 victory into the three-goal margin needed to secure a place in the play-offs for a place in the Premier League. Thirty-odd miles away at the Britannia Stadium, Stoke City's fans are beginning to surround the touchline as they wait for the final whistle to blow on their own successful promotion campaign.

It is the kind of drama that Dougan used to thrive upon as a player, the type of occasion when he would have done everything in his power to make his mark. As someone who never lost his passion for his sport, it was also the kind of finger-biting excitement he loved as a spectator. Had he lived to see this season, he would probably have been there at its denouement, passing opinion to anyone who would have listened. The chances are, however, that Wolves would have had to do without his support. It is Stoke's goalless draw against Leicester that he would have attended.

"It didn't matter who we were playing," Terry Conroy tells me. "He would like to come and have a drink and relax." Conroy, who still works for Stoke organising activities of former players and serving a match-day host, continues: "There were always autograph hunters coming up to him and he said: 'I can't believe after all these years how I am welcomed here.' I told him it was because of who he was and what he'd done."

It wasn't that Dougan ever fell out of love with Wolves. While watching and enjoying the success of his friends at Stoke, his heart would have ached for the near miss of his former team. He simply fell out of love with going to Molineux, his links with the club being maintained chiefly through his relationship with the London Wolves supporters' club, of which he was proud to be president. At the heart of his absence was the fear that fans had never forgiven him for events at the club in the mid-1980s.

Doug Hope, his vice-chairman at that time, says: "He was very upset and he felt that people would think he had failed because the full story wasn't available. His view was that people don't look beyond the fact that the club was relegated. It always niggled him that things had not gone the way he had hoped."

London Wolves chairman Stuart Earl says: "Derek loved the club. I am convinced of it. He always phoned me to talk about the games. I remember I had been round to his house the night before a play-off game against [West Bromwich] Albion and he gave us a rollicking for still being there at midnight. He said: 'What time will you lads be up for the game?' We told him we would be in the pub at 9.30am. He phoned me to check!

"I know a few Wolves fans turned against him because of what happened during the Bhatti brothers era. We never really spoke about that because I know he was planning to write a book explaining what went wrong. I was totally convinced he took over and ran the club in good faith. I called him at the club on the day he took over and he said: 'Stuart, this is the proudest day of my life.' But he ended up convinced that many of the fans were against him. He had also fallen out with Sir Jack Hayward over a testimonial for Frank Munro and just felt he would not be welcome."

Former teammate John Holsgrove recalls: "A few years ago Ernie Hunt did a signing session for his book on a Saturday at Molineux. Derek actually turned up for that, but would not come into the ground to watch the game."

Chris Westcott, the author who worked on Hunt's book, adds: "To get Derek to the launch was a very big deal as he did not go to Molineux. It was terrific of him to support Ernie – he always had a lot of time for him."

Earl continues: "Derek eventually went along to a couple of games with Dave Dungar [from club sponsor Chaucer] and Dave finally persuaded him that the majority of supporters were for him and not against him. He got a standing ovation when he took his seat."

Dougan's partner Merlyn Humphreys explains: "The fans meant everything to him and he still got a huge postbag. But he had been the one who had said he could save Wolves and didn't know it would be him with egg all over his face. The fans didn't know the Bhattis, they knew the Doog and he felt it was he who was supposed to have saved them.

"Dave Dungar asked him one day to come to Molineux and said: 'You will see the fans still love you.' Doog thought they hated him and, of course, they never hated him at all. He drew his own conclusions and took to the grave his belief that the fans thought he had let them down."

Speaking to Wolves supporters and witnessing the show of affection after his death, it has become evident that Dougan clearly underestimated the place he continued to occupy in hearts and minds of the Molineux faithful. His play on the field, together with the personal touches experienced by many fans, ensured that his legacy as a player survived the influence of the Bhatti brothers to a far greater extent than he believed.

Robert Goddard explains that he is sitting on his staircase with a commemorative 'Doog' scarf hanging next to him as he recounts tales of his hero's thoughtfulness: "One day I was reading *Soccer*

Star magazine and decided to write a letter. I asked if through their columns I could thank the greatest footballer I had ever seen for the way he had spoken to the fans and helped other players around him. They used it as their star letter under the heading 'Dougan makes the day perfect'.

"It was just before Christmas 1968 and I got this card through the post with a photo signed to me from the Doog. A while later I bumped into Derek before a game and thanked him. He said he'd read the letter and got my address from that. I couldn't believe somebody would do that.

"At the end of one season I saw him outside the ground and said: 'Have you got a shirt I could have as souvenir?' I forgot all about it until the following season when I saw him at Manchester City and wished him well. He had reporters all around him and he put his arms round me and told everyone: 'He comes all way from London.' It made me feel big. Then he said: 'I have got a shirt for you.'

"The following Saturday he gave me a parcel and said: 'Don't tell too many people.' It was his shirt from the Northern Ireland v Wales game in 1967. On another occasion he took the time to meet my mum and dad before a game. When I saw him at a dinner a few months before he died I finally got him to sign the shirt and thanked him for being one of the biggest parts of my life."

Of particular pride to the London Wolves supporters club, of which Dougan was life president, was the fact that their floral tribute, in gold and black, was chosen to be placed on his coffin.

"Doog always said that the first time we met was at his Wolves debut at Plymouth," Stuart Earl explains. "But I can assure you that you never forget the first time you met the Doog and it was, in fact, at his home debut against Hull a week later. At that time, John Ireland let the London Wolves supporters go in the main entrance and the Doog came in, his usual bubbly self, and said hello to everyone.

"His hat-trick endeared him to the supporters instantly and he was one of the few players I have seen in all my years going there who could make a mistake and the crowd would laugh it off. He had this ability to turn everything into a joke. If he missed a chance he would pick up the ball and return it to goalkeeper or have a laugh with the crowd. He was my hero and will never be surpassed by anyone."

Yet, despite such endearment, most of Dougan's live football in later years was enjoyed at Stoke, where in 1998 he had been reported to be part of a consortium considering a takeover. Doug Hope was once again involved and he explains: "We tried to buy Stoke just before the owners from Iceland came in. We had got potential funding from a group in Ireland but it never really got beyond discussion."

Conroy, Dougan's match-day companion, recalls: "The Stoke fans had fond memories of Derek. He knew they had no need to welcome him so he was warmed by the affection here. It was their way of saying 'We will never forget you'. He came to a dinner here when I organised a reunion of the 1972 League Cup winning team. Unfortunately John Ritchie had died and we had buried him three days earlier but the dinner went ahead. It was a sell-out and we invited Doog and Merlyn. I asked him if he would say a few words.

"Well, if you said 'a few words' to Doog you could leave the room for an hour because he would go on and on. I look back and think that if I had known that only three months later he would have been dead, I would have made sure I made the most of that evening. The tribute he paid to Stoke was fantastic. It was all unscripted and he spoke for about 20 minutes – a tribute from a rival club.

"People there would not have known his affection for Stoke and it came out that night. His speech could not have been better, it was from the heart and he was inundated by people visiting his table for signatures and photographs. When we spoke the next day he kept saying what a fantastic night he'd had."

There is an old American proverb that says: "The more arguments you win, the less friends you have." Dougan proved that you didn't always have to win the argument for the same effect to take place. He was never short of friends, but he also managed to lose plenty along the way. He was never prepared to compromise his beliefs or his passions for social niceties. If he upset people along the way, so be it.

At the root of it all sits the nature of the competitor. Dougan spoke many times of players not knowing what to do when the cheering stopped. He fed his own sportsman's craving for competition through his union work, his leadership of football clubs, his adoption of causes for former players. When no such avenues presented themselves, even a dinner conversation with friends could become a suitable battle ground. He was prepared to play the role of devil's advocate just to get his fix.

His sister, Coreen Long, admits: "Knowing Derek the way I do, I don't think he would have been the easiest person to live with. If he knew your Achilles heel he was in there. He would wind people up and they fell for it. He used to do it with me, until eventually I got the measure of him and said: 'Derek, I am not biting.' He just laughed.

"But that is when he fell out with people and if he didn't like you he would just not bother with you. I will give you an example. Some guy he got friendly with had a car place and always would lend Derek a car if something had happened with his. One time he couldn't lend Derek a car. Oh well, that was the end of the relationship; this guy was every name under the sun. If you didn't do what Derek wanted you were out. If he took a huff he took a huff."

His niece, Josephine Long, tells a similar tale: "I know people fell out with him, but I would just not let him get away with it. If he was in bad form I would tell him to eff off, or I would send wee text messages telling him: 'You are such a w****r,' and he would love that.

"Derek didn't give you an answer, he lectured you. He just hammered on and he loved holding court. He was not a gossip and would not say anything malicious about anyone but when he fell out with you there was no middle ground. Sometimes you would have to say to him: 'For God's sake, he is not that bad,' and then he lightened up a bit.

"He certainly wasn't a horrible man and if you got annoyed with him he could take offence and be the wounded one and say: 'Put your bright face on.' You almost needed someone to come behind Derek and say to people: 'He doesn't mean it. He is just joking'."

Such a trait meant that people would often be deterred from

getting close enough to Dougan to get past the bluff. And, besides, he wasn't always joking. The contempt in which he held some of his managers, notably Bill McGarry, has already been discussed and, significantly, some teammates I have approached about this book have made clear their preference not to be part of the project. It is easy to guess why. In the case of John Richards, there is no need to surmise about the nature of their relationship. Two men who formed such a lethal on-field partnership ended up being unable to be in the same room.

Richards has placed on record the root of his fall-out with Dougan, who was in charge at Wolves when his former teammate's career at Molineux came to an end. Having been loaned to Derby after failing to gain a place in Graham Hawkins's team, Richards was recalled in March 1983, expecting a run in the side as it chased promotion.

Yet he returned with a brief appearance as a substitute at Grimsby followed by only two starts and one more run-out off the bench, prompting him to write in the *Wolverhampton Express and Star* that a picture of him in a Wolves shirt during the current season was "rarer than a penny black". He added that "the Christians in the Coliseum had a better chance than I've had".

Dougan, who called Richards to his office to explain his comments, had written enough of his own outspoken columns in his time and had even been a paid-up member of the National Union of Journalists. Dougan's argument was that he'd never said anything detrimental about any of the clubs employing him or any of their policies. Richards, who felt that his column had been fair comment given the way he had been treated, told Dougan he could see no point in seeing out the final two years of his contact.

Richards was angry, though, that he had no chance for a farewell game because his departure was not sorted out until the summer. He felt Dougan should have been able to sympathise, having almost been denied the same honour by McGarry. Richards claims that Dougan then withheld the agreed pay-off on his contract when he left for Portuguese Division Two team Maritimo. Again, he saw irony in the situation given Dougan's background as a champion of players' rights and his fight for his own settlement when he retired.

Richards had looked up to Dougan during their playing careers, learning much about the art of forward play from his older partner and taking up the mantle of the club's PFA representative when Dougan was called to higher office. Yet Richards says he has never forgiven Dougan for an unpleasant telephone exchange with his wife, with the result that "our relationship has never mended".

Such memories are in strict contrast to those of Geoff Palmer, whose long career at Wolves ended during Dougan's reign with a transfer to Burnley. He recalls: "I had a problem with some money that was owed to me and it was getting on a bit. The club wouldn't pay it but one day I had a call from the Doog telling me to go round to his house. I asked if there was any reason and he said: 'I have got something for you.' I called in for a cup of tea and he threw an envelope at me. It was a cheque for the money the club owed me. That was the sort of thing he would do."

During the course of a couple of phone calls, Richards has politely informed me that he does not wish to elaborate on his falling-out with Dougan, a telling commentary on the state of affairs between two men who once happily posed in cowboy gear as football's equivalent of Butch Cassidy and the Sundance Kid. Dougan died without the situation ever getting anywhere close to being fixed. It hardly prompted reconciliation when Richards became non-executive director of Wolves in 1994 under owner Sir Jack Hayward, becoming managing director three years later and holding the position until 2000. Dougan even declined to attend a reunion dinner organised by Richards for the 1974 League Cup winning team.

Conroy believes that Dougan was uncomfortable with Richards having become the first Wolves player to be awarded two testimonial games, in 1982 and 1985. "It was a terrible situation, but I wouldn't point the finger at anyone here," he says. "Derek felt he wasn't welcome at Wolves, although it could have been resolved quite easily with one phone call between the two of them. Derek felt a strong feeling of injustice over the testimonials. It was OK if Richards had more than one, but Derek felt some other older players had been forgotten about and the resentment built up over the years."

Frank Munro, for example, had signed for Celtic only a few days short of completing a decade with the club, but said he had been promised a testimonial, which he attempted to claim via the PFA after returning from a 12-year stay in Australia. He was told that the agreement had been with a previous company, a new one having been formed when the club went into receivership.

Conroy continues: "Derek was philosophical about his own feeling of being shunted aside by the club over so many years, but he knew that one or two of the lads one would go to their graves feeling hard done by. He was close enough to go and fight on their behalf and was perceived as a troublemaker by some at the club."

Coreen comments: "He really did p**s off Wolves. I don't know what happened but they are still bitter to this day – you know what Derek could be like. He was happy but he wanted something in his life to replace football. He paid in his chips as far as football and the media was concerned. That was Derek's expression. He did get a lot of jobs at one time, but if you upset people in life, well…"

Niece Josephine believes Dougan could have filled a role at Wolves or some other club had he been more able to kiss, make up and compromise. But she explains: "If someone like Portsmouth had said to him: 'Derek, you can coach the under-16s,' I don't think it would have been good enough for him. He would have wanted to be manager or chairman. He had to be at the top or nothing.

"I believe there was a place in football for Derek but that place might not have been where he wanted to be. He was never going to be the manager of Arsenal or Chelsea but he could have been successful at something. He could have been at Wolves being a matchday host and would have been fantastic at that, but because he pissed them off that never happened."

Whether as an occasional employee or a fan, Dougan should have been a regular visitor at Molineux in his later years, enjoying the reverence that most fans still afforded him. But the rift was too deep for him to attempt to cross it. It had even extended to him turning down an invitation to join the Wolves Former Players' Association in 1991 when the organisation expanded its membership.

Originally restricted to players who were at the club before 1960, personal invitations were sent by WFPA chairman Billy Wright to all those more recent players who had appeared in 200 Wolves games. Dougan never responded, his antipathy towards Wright contributing towards his reluctance to sign up. "I never thought Billy Wright was that outstanding a player," was his view of the Molineux legend.

Holsgrove was saddened by Dougan's stance: "Life is too short and we should stick together. It was an affront to the players he played with. He could have said: 'I am going to join because they are my mates and I have been through the mill with most of them.' It is difficult because we were friends, but Derek had this ability to clam up and keep to himself.

"It all goes back to the time when he was chairman and then he fell out with John Richards. Derek was very stubborn. But if you were his friend and you were in trouble you could pick the phone up and he would be there. He would never let you down. He had his dark side and you either accepted it or you had nothing to do with him, which is what a lot of people did."

Conroy conveys the same sentiment: "You can't say 'if only he had been a little bit different'. He was an all or nothing guy. If you minimised him you were not getting the true character. He thrived on confrontation and loved nothing better than debates. He was always adamant that he was right. That was the warrior in him. But he could have a barnstormer and then it would be forgotten. That is why so many people liked him and had respect for him. He had principles."

Bryan Hamilton adds: "Derek had flaws like the rest of us and maybe he didn't do things as well as he should have done, but none of us are perfect."

Meanwhile, Geoff Palmer remembers, 'You could never have a conversation where he agreed with anybody. It was the just the way he was. He gave you his views and a lot of people listened. But he never changed. He was not like some people who change like the weather and you wonder which face you will see each day."

Sammy Nelson considered Dougan "a really lovely guy" and says: "I always enjoyed his company and could have a bit of a *craic* with him. I could understand some people finding him argumentative and no doubt he did start things up, but he was not being nasty and it wasn't personal. Some people didn't get that."

Terry Neill often wondered what caused that need for confrontation. It might have sustained Dougan in his retirement from the playing field, but it was hardly a new development. "People like Pat Jennings, Billy Bingham, Jimmy McIlroy and Dave Clements were more consistent players on every level," he ventures. "They seemed more comfortable in themselves. There was always something in Derek that made him say 'I am going to change Ulster' or, 'I am going to right this wrong'. It was almost as if on a daily basis he was howling at the moon and something was eating away inside of him."

Perhaps it was inevitable that Dougan should eventually take his love of a good argument to the highest possible debating platform: the political stage.

Before that, however, Dougan's desire to correct perceived injustices and instigate change saw him become involved with medical matters. Invited to speak to members of the health profession, he discovered that his wish to see the establishment of a centre for the treatment of sporting injuries was shared by two prominent physicians, surgeon Irshad Ahmed and Dr Terry Pinfold. Russell Hall Hospital in Dudley was the site of the two men's occasional sports clinic but Dougan discussed with them the possibility of raising funds to launch a full-time medical centre.

Named after the town's most famous sporting son, a victim of Manchester United's air crash at Munich at the age of only 21, the plan for the Duncan Edwards Sports Medicine Centre Appeal took close to a year to come to fruition before being launched in November 1986. Dougan announced plans to raise £665,000 and expressed his vision that the clinic would offer free treatment to everyone with a sports-related injury, not just professional athletes.

Dougan delighted in claiming that the Charity Commission had told him it was "the finest charity of its kind in history", a comment he made in a book entitled *Duncan Edwards*, which was published as a money-raising venture for the fund and featured content from Edwards's own book, *Tackle Soccer This Way*.

A variety of events were staged, including an auction for one of Billy Wright's England caps, a sponsored walk and a celebrity football match. But as momentum was lost it was clear that insufficient funds had been raised. It would emerge that about £70,000 of the £90,000 realised had been used to finance the administration of the charity, a fact that is widely agreed to be down to poor, over-ambitious management on the part of Dougan rather than any dishonesty.

Such an outcome echoes the views of all those who have told me that Dougan's big-hearted desire to be in the vanguard of such initiatives – and smaller, less public, schemes – was too rarely matched by an ability to organise and delegate.

Dougan stepped down as co-ordinator, another blow to his esteem after the events at Molineux earlier in the decade. He was even questioned in court about the collapse of a local company connected with a businessman, John Ferriday, whom Dougan had claimed would underwrite the fund to the tune of £1 million.

Add such events to the failure of his own promotions company in Wolverhampton; the break-up of his marriage some years before, when Jutta had returned to Germany; a one-year driving ban; and a temporary involvement with the cash-strapped Uttoxeter racecourse, and it is hardly surprising that Dougan sought escape. He began spending more time in Belfast, from where he would launch a claim against Wolverhampton Council that they owed him £25,000 that he had put into his former football club and which he had never been repaid following the club's placement in the hands of the receiver in 1986.

The happy aspect of his return to his homeland was the re-establishment of family ties. Coreen recalls: "I really got to know Derek in the late-1980s and early-1990s when he came to stay with us when he was running some soccer schools over here. He stayed with us and went home at the weekend. But then that went pear-shaped. It was his way or no way. That was the first time I had a real insight into Derek as my brother and that is how we became close.

"He stayed for a while with our brother Morris and there was a fall-out there. Out of all the brothers and sisters it was me he took to and in the end it was just me he was in touch with, although when Dale's daughter got married [in 2007] Derek was invited but couldn't go because he was getting his foot [operation] done. I think he was closest to me because I was always there for him if he ever had troubles."

Niece Josephine recalls fondly the closeness Dougan felt and displayed towards her family: "My Daddy passed away in 1999 and Derek always had us over on Christmas Eve and that was us until 2nd January. We had a fantastic time. Most of the people at the funeral I knew because I went everywhere with him and I could go to parts of Wolverhampton where people would know me because of Derek.

"One of the nicest things said to us at the funeral was that in Derek's eyes Coreen was the queen and I was the princess. We were there for Derek if ever he went through setbacks. And he never missed anything I did – exams, driving test – and he came over for my graduation. When I was younger I had a wee job at the Co-op and he wanted me to give up the job. He didn't think you should be working and doing your A-levels."

Josephine ignored his advice, even after the arrival of a card bearing the printed words: "If you think you are beaten, you are" and in which her uncle had written: "I told you 'give up your job and revise, revise, revise'. I don't want you or your mother telling me in September 'Derek, you were right'. Lots of love, Uncle Derek. PS I am only thinking of your future."

The time Dougan spent in Belfast in the 1990s had done more than reconnect him with parts of his family. It had fired him with political ambition. Not that he was a stranger to such an arena. In 1975 he had lent his name to a campaign to keep the United Kingdom in the EEC – the 'Common Market' as it had been known when Britain had joined a couple of years earlier – and stood alongside politicians and other stars of sport and show business. In 1976 he said: "think the EEC is terrific. I believe that if it is handled right the EEC is probably the greatest community we could wish to be a member of. I just wish we could throw away some of our vested interest and parochialism."

In 1978, he had used his position as chairman of the PFA to comment on the political regime in Argentina, hosts of that year's World Cup, after certain journalists had suggested that the event should be boycotted in protest at the country's poor human rights record. Dougan wrote to *The Times* to oppose such action but said that the media should "insist that all facets of a country are fully reported and exposed". He continued: "Footballers, sportsmen and journalists need to join together to ensure that whatever the sporting occasion in whatever nation none of us forget essential human rights and the constant need for their defence."

To the amazement of those closest to him, Dougan announced in March 1997 that he would be contesting the East Belfast seat in the upcoming Westminster general election, taking on incumbent MP Peter Robinson, who held an imposing majority for the Democratic Unionist Party. "I'll work for a community based on trust and togetherness," he trumpeted. "We all deserve a better future after years of political stagnation. Drumcree[20] sent me over the top. No one wants to talk to each other. This is the greatest country and could be the land of opportunity."

Even those who recognised Dougan's love of debate were concerned at his willingness to become involved in such a volatile arena. Eric McMordie remembers: "He used to stop at mine some weekends and we had fantastic times, but he was not an easy-going gentleman and could upset people. He was a very bright guy who had educated himself and we would often speak about Belfast. He talked about people back home who were well known as people you didn't want to upset – people in top organisations."

As well as surprise, there was concern among Derek's family, as only two months before announcing his candidacy Dougan had, according to doctors, come close to dying after suffering a heart attack. Newspaper reports of the incident, which took place on a Sunday evening in Belfast, stated that doctors at Belfast's Royal Victoria Hospital had been forced to resuscitate him after his heart stopped beating. A local friend, Frank Bannan, was quoted as saying: "I think he is doing too much lately. He does a lot of after-dinner speaking and still has business interests."

Dougan, always with a flair for rhetoric, used his brush with death in his electoral manifesto, saying: "When I drove myself to hospital in January I knew somehow that I would come through and I would

---

20   Rioting and violence, resulting in one death and hundreds of injuries, broke out in 1996 after the Royal Ulster Constabulary blocked the annual Orange Order parade at Drumcree.

offer myself to serve the people of East Belfast. I am one of them…
when you have come back from the door of death you see life and the
future in a very different light."

Election day saw Tony Blair's new Labour sweep the Conservatives
out of office after 18 years, yet Belfast proved immune to such a mood
of change. Robinson was returned to Westminster with 16,640 votes
– 42 per cent of those cast – followed by the Ulster Unionists' Reg
Empey, whose 9,886 represented 25 per cent of the turnout. Dougan
trailed in seventh of the nine candidates, totalling only 541 votes.
It was the kind of heavy defeat he'd rarely been on the end of in his
football career.

Belfast native Terry Neill comments: "What was he thinking? He
was a great footballer, a bit of a national icon at the time. But he knew
nothing about those guys [in politics] and they would have eaten him
– not for breakfast, he would have been just a snack. But Doog was
a strange individual, a bit of a pseudo intellectual. There is nothing
wrong with people looking to improve their knowledge or education
or taking an interest in the wider world, especially footballers, but
Doog got a bit carried away at times. When he embarked on his
political career I remember thinking: 'Is this the same fellow who as
a young player just into the Northern Ireland team I had get into a
cab or get to bed legless?'"

§

Belfast broadcaster Jackie Fullerton, meanwhile, recalls Dougan's
campaign receiving more amiable approval than might have been
evidenced in the polls: "I think the reaction of most people was
probably to smile and say 'that is the Doog being the Doog'. He
was always in the public eye and the people looked upon him with
great affection. He was one of us and had made a name for himself.
Despite his growing fame he was always a people person and was
great at mixing. I always admired Derek because if he thought
something he said it. He would have garnered a few enemies because
people don't like to hear the truth."

If nothing else, the campaign offered a timely publicity platform
for the revised version of *The Sash He Never Wore – Twenty Five
Years On*. Maybe that had been the motivation all along, although

one of his Belfast friends, Alex Lattimer, recalls the book being used against him during the campaign: "There is an awful lot of bigotry in Belfast and people didn't read the book. They judged it on its cover and some of the top people started throwing it against Derek. Anybody who read the book would know that Derek was a genuine person."

There was a postscript to Dougan's ill-fated election efforts two years later when Belfast printing firm TH Jordan claimed that he still owed them £3,000 relating to printing costs during his campaign. Another loose end. Typical Doog.

Chapter 18

LOVE FINALLY

It has been almost a year since I sat here in the home of Merlyn Humphreys, 12 months she has spent largely in a frenzy of activity aimed at keeping alive the memory of Derek Dougan.

Once the funeral had been arranged, there was a project to compile a three-hour DVD of the highlights of his life. And as we chat, Merlyn sits beside a thick looking file containing the paperwork and planning for a statue being commissioned from Andy Edwards, designer of the Gordon Banks memorial unveiled by Pelé at Stoke City. "I needed to keep the Doog on the stage because that is what we wanted," Merlyn explains, although adding: "I was foolish to think he would ever go off the stage."

The DVD – an idea conceived and funded by Peter Bartlett, webmaster of the London Wolves supporters' group, who then contacted Merlyn looking for material – has been a cathartic experience. "I got to know all the lads and they said that on Saturdays I should go and have a drink or a meal with them. It was fantastic. Everywhere I looked there was someone I knew. It was like being with Doog again because he had projected these people into my life. It was like communicating with him and I heard so many stories about before I met him."

Merlyn supplied hours of video and radio footage that she and Doog had collected. She then secured the appropriate copyrights, offered photographs and helped in the editing process, eventually being listed as executive producer when the DVD went into the shops – on the back of sales and distribution deals she had set up with the likes of HMV and WH Smith.

"It has been therapeutic and it has brought in a lot of friendships," she says. "I had lost Doog, but here I was getting him back in a funny way. It forced me to look at him and listen to him almost prematurely. I can listen to Doog now and it is like me listening to someone who loves me. It doesn't hurt."

Sales of the DVD have been raising money to carry on the work of XPro, the organisation to help and support injured former footballers that Dougan was battling to fully establish at the time of his death. And no sooner was the finished product in the stores than thoughts turned to a lasting memorial in the form of a statue.

Merlyn shares with me the documents and ongoing discussions about possible sites – either in Wolverhampton or at Molineux – plans for funding, and thoughts about how and when it might be launched: "We want the launch to be a focal point for the Doog's work in getting XPro established as a charitable foundation and to be a celebration of his life."

Turning back the clock, we discuss how Dougan became a part of Merlyn's own life: "I knew of him, of course, and in the 1970s we would go to Wolves matches, although if Doog wasn't playing we would come away."

In 2003, having been let down on an appointment in St Albans, Dougan was lunching in a pub called The Mitre, where Merlyn and a friend had also decided to visit. Standing at the bar talking to an acquaintance, Merlyn recalls: "I could see this other person moving around in the background. Then I said: 'Oh, my goodness, you're Derek Dougan.' It turned out he had never been in that pub before and neither had I and we had both lived in the area for 30 years without our paths crossing.

"He was all chuffed because he loved being recognised. I said: 'My husband absolutely worshipped you,' and his smile got bigger and bigger. My friend ran down and took a picture and that was it as far as I was concerned. But about an hour later they came and joined us, sat themselves down and we had the jolliest afternoon imaginable."

Having refused Derek's persistent request for her number, Merlyn accepted his business card. "I pondered on it and then a week or so later decided to call as a surprise; a bit of a laugh really. I thought: 'He has a place in my life in the sense that my husband and I adored him, so what is wrong with going out with him?'"

Laughter accompanies the memory of what happened next: "He asked if he could pop down and see me. It was about midday and when I opened my door he had on a white suit and sunglasses. He was standing there posing, trying to create an impression like John Wayne!"

A lunch date the next day at the Greyhound pub in Lower Penn was followed by numerous phone calls from Derek while he was away in Spain. When he returned, he told Merlyn: "I think I am growing quite fond of you. I would like to start seriously going out with you."

And, for her part, Merlyn confesses: "Unashamedly, I fell for him. He was a bit of a rebel, powerful and emotional, and he would take up all the air in the room when he entered. He was a great raconteur, always outspoken, never dull and he had got it all going on. He had all the one-liners and he had probably used them all before, but we knew it would be the last time he used them."

Linda Westcott, a friend, endorses the qualities that Merlyn fell for: "I first met Derek seven or eight years ago when my husband Chris and I sat for ages in his kitchen. I was bowled over by him. He was a very warm human being with so much charisma and so nice to talk to. On another occasion when he was leaving our house he looked right in my eyes and at the front door and said: 'You remember this. If ever you want to stay with us just give me a call.' You could tell he was being very sincere."

According to Derek's sister, Coreen, it was not just love that Merlyn brought into his life, but organisation and stability, becoming his business colleague as well as his partner, attending all his meetings and helping to organise his daily routine. "We all breathed a sigh of relief when Merlyn came along," says Coreen. "We didn't have to worry about him so much."

It was the kind of anchoring influence he could have done with during previous years as he had lurched from one mishap to another. No sooner had he recovered from his heart attack and the ill-advised foray into Belfast politics than he'd been forced to spend several months anxiously waiting to clear his name after being charged with assault on a former Vietnam veteran who went by the nickname 'Rambo'. Dougan had been accused of using a pool cue to attack Eylande Mason at the home of a friend, Patricia Thompson, but the jury at Wolverhampton Crown Court took only 30 minutes to unanimously endorse his explanation that he had used only his hand and had been acting in self-defence. "It's been a very difficult nine or ten months that I've been through," he told reporters.

Merlyn's eventual influence also provided a foundation from which he utilised talents and beliefs that, while so valuable to him in earlier life, were being wasted. "He should have got an agent years ago," says Coreen. "He had a talent, but his family didn't nourish him in that way. His two boys didn't have a clue. He had everything but it wasn't channelled in the right direction. He needed someone to come along and make him listen. Derek was not even in a pension scheme. He had no money from football once he came out of it. He never made a will because he had nothing to leave."

Merlyn continues: "For three years, ours was a full-time relationship. We weren't leaving each other at nine and coming home at six. I was there on every level – partner, secretary, housekeeper, entertaining for important people."

And, amid all the meetings and paperwork, Dougan was "very, very romantic", which will come as no surprise to those who witnessed his passionate approach to the game and the mutual love affairs he had with fans up and down the country. He'd always cut a somewhat romantic figure on the field, much like an early-day Eric Cantona.

"He would never speak to me without saying he loved me," says Merlyn and to emphasise the point we browse through the birthday, Christmas and Valentine's Day cards he sent her and listen to the numerous answerphone messages she salvaged after he died, on many of which he bursts into song. "He was very emotional. Sometimes I would catch sight of him and the whole of his face would be contorted. It could be a film or something that someone was telling him."

On Christmas Eve of 2004, Derek had gone down on both knees – "he was never one to do things by half," Merlyn laughs – and proposed marriage. A friend in Belfast, Alex Lattimer, remembers the excitement caused by Merlyn's acceptance: "Derek asked me over for dinner and I couldn't believe what was on the table, liqueurs and everything you could think of. It was like a five-star hotel. After he gave me a few depth charges – large vodkas – he asked me into the lounge for a talk. He said: 'Would you do us a favour. Would you be best man for me?' I said I would and he ran to the door to give the thumbs-up to Merlyn. He lavished everything on us that night."

Marriage plans, however, ran into considerable obstacles. Apart from the legal complications and expense of attempting to complete divorce proceedings between England and Germany, Dougan spent much of his final three years fighting debilitating health problems. Most serious was the blood clot that came close to killing him early in 2005, caused by the fibrillating heart that had been the legacy of his attack in 1997.

It was only Merlyn's insistence to Derek's doctor that the pain in his leg was too serious to be treated by antacid tablets that led to a check for a clot. When the results were revealed, he was ordered immediately to hospital. "The doctors said it was a massive clot," says Merlyn. "They caught it just before it left his leg and entered the main blood stream. If that had happened he would have been dead."

Doug Hope recalls: "Merlyn saved his life. She knew perfectly well what it was and told them. She could make Florence Nightingale look inadequate and I think she prolonged Derek's life with the way she looked after him."

Other ailments that struck down Dougan included cardiac asthma and gout. He had to undergo manipulation in hospital for a bad shoulder and spend six weeks in plaster because of the old ankle injury he'd suffered at Portsmouth. He was on medication to regulate the thickness of his blood, prevent build-up of water in the heart chamber and counter high blood pressure.

"He had a million hospital appointments and had to take ten tablets a day," says Merlyn. After spending the summer of 2006 on elbow sticks because of gout-related arthritis in his feet, Derek had an operation early in 2007 to remove the middle joints of his toes and have them pinned in place. As the tenth anniversary of his heart attack had approached he was given an angiogram to assess its state.

Merlyn explains: "By now they were describing it as worn out. It was becoming 'floppy' because it compensates for trauma by growing and losing its shape."

It was during the course of such procedures that doctors made the startling revelation that Dougan had completed a successful sporting career with only one functioning kidney. Either it had simply never grown or, the medics surmised, had been damaged in some kind of childhood accident.

Dougan had always been a proud man. To have people know of his sometimes frail state would have been unthinkable to him. As he continued his campaigning work for former footballers and his frequent fund-raising efforts he was able, as Merlyn puts it, to "leave that tired person in the house".

She continues: "He filled himself up, he energised himself and he said 'let's go for it'. That is what the world would see and a lot of people were surprised to learn later how ill he had been. He put on a face and adrenalin got him through. But as soon as he stepped out of the spotlight again he would be exhausted."

Terry Conroy wishes that Dougan had been willing to slow down a little, but accepts that it was not in his friend's nature to do so: "He was always fighting battles, mainly for other people. He would always have another cause and was shooting for the stars. He could be all over the place, but for the right reasons. From what the medical people said, in the end his heart was absolutely rotted away. Yet if you had said to him ten years earlier that this would happen, I think he would have carried on the same way."

As well as pride and a competitive spirit – which so often took him headlong into confrontation – Dougan had compassion. Professionally, he had combined all those traits to battle for the rights of his fellow footballers; now, in his final years, family, friends and former colleagues were the ones who benefited. Only two days after his blood clot, Derek and Merlyn took in his 11-year-old grandson Alex for several months after Dougan's son Alexander, a widower, was taken ill.

Dougan made sure he was regularly on hand to speak and appear at the London Wolves' fund-raising events, although chairman Stuart Earl recalls: "He also phoned me asking me to take a table in one of his events – and then phoned back asking if I would take two. He was always interested in other people's misfortunes, even though he had his own troubles. Merlyn will tell you how happy fellow former professionals were to turn out in bulk for Doog and one of his events."

Derek Parkin, whose wife died of cancer late in 2007, says: "If any of the old players ever had any problems he was always the first there to help out. We were good friends right to the end. I might not see him for six months and then he would ring out of the blue. Derek was always the first one on the phone to ask how my wife was and he always rung whenever there had ever been any upset. Whatever people say about him, he was always a good friend to me."

Teammate Geoff Palmer recalls: "If you wanted anything arranging the Doog would do it for you. It was typical of the bloke – he never forgot anybody. After Frank Munro had his stroke, Doog rang me one Saturday and said: 'Pick me up, we are going to see Frank'."

Dougan's desire to see his peers given greater support from within the football community was such that he eventually gave it a formal outlet through the establishment of XPro.

His long-time friend and co-founder of the organisation, Bob Runham, explains that its genesis dates back to the late 1980s: "I had got to know Derek when he was a player through the company I had designing football and sporting prints. I spent some great times in his company and with people like Pat Jennings and Gordon Banks. I remember we spent the whole of one afternoon drinking tea with George Best.

"One day Derek and I met Paul Fletcher, the former Burnley centre-forward, at a motorway service station. He had cleverly kept a record of his entire career and at first I thought it was just a scrapbook. But then it became clear it was a medical record book, including notes of when he had been made to play when unfit, all signed by the club physio.

"He had obviously thought about this and he went to the DHSS when he finished playing and put in a claim. He got a disablement benefit. Derek said himself that he had lost about £100,000 in entitlement for injuries during his career and said that the PFA didn't know about entitlements for football injuries until he and Paul Fletcher told them about it."[21]

Dougan spent a good deal of his time following that meeting taking up various causes for retired players, many of whom he felt either didn't know their rights or were lacking the finances to fight for them.

"We put a lot of players on the right road," says Runham. "Players who were having to go to the PFA with their begging bowl." Typical was Dougan's representation of a former Everton player whose family needed an additional £40 per week to have him placed in a home where he could receive the care he required. He also helped Larraine Astle, the widow of former England centre-forward Jeff, with her claims that his death in 2002 at the age of 59 was related to the thousands of times he had been required to head the ball.

Runham continues: "Derek also spoke in front of a committee for industrial injuries and argued that osteo-arthritis should be recognised as an industrial disease. And memorabilia was another area he was into. He was tired of players being ripped off and having their medals sold for a few bob."

While offering his personal support wherever possible, Dougan knew it was not enough and developed his plan to create a fully-funded organisation that could expand such work. He also acknowledged that money-raising events such as golf days could never produce enough to offer the kind of service he wished to provide.

"It was a dream of Derek's that one day there would be an organisation to help former footballers that was recognised and supported by the football authorities," says Runham. "He was unable to get Gordon Taylor to agree to let us be XPFA, and I think a great opportunity was missed. The chance was there for Gordon but for some reason he wouldn't take it."

---

21   PFA chief executive Gordon Taylor disputed that latter point in subsequent correspondence with Dougan.

So it was XPro that was officially launched at Villa Park in June 2005, with Dougan named as chairman and former Aston Villa player Neil Rioch as chief executive. In the brochure published to mark the event, Dougan wrote: "I feel very strongly about the fact that the vast majority of my former colleagues are unaware of the rights, benefits and entitlements due to them as ex-professional football players. Many ex-professional footballers will have very strong grounds for industrial injuries claims and will not how to pursue these entitlements. Many do not know they are entitled to access the huge amount of funds available to them for treatment of injuries, operations and benevolent support."

Following the launch, Dougan set about making the rounds of football organisations, presenting his ideas and looking for backing. But, as Runham explains: "It's difficult to start something when you have no money and no one grasped the nettle. So many people said they would help us if someone else did, and then we found ourselves back in the street. We were going round in circles. We did get great support from Steve Cavalier at Thompson's, the industrial injury lawyers.

"Derek's head was almost bursting with ideas. He could be frustrated beyond all belief with the thought that he could run football and look after the players better than those in charge. He never tried to get back into the administration of football, though, never went cap in hand for a job or sought any position.

"Some people said XPro was just a way of putting himself back in the public eye and maybe it is a fair accusation, but I think it was wrong. It was something he truly believed in."

Dougan presented the aims of XPro to an all-party Parliamentary group at the House of Commons and continued to correspond regularly with Gordon Taylor, who, in the letters I have seen during the writing of this book, emphasises his position that the objectives of XPro "are very much part of the ambit of the PFA".

Yet even Taylor had been forced to admit in a letter to one former player that "our funds are under tremendous pressure and so we have had to reduce the help we can give from the Benevolent Fund". Dougan accepted that the PFA's first priority had to be to current players, but that merely increased his dissatisfaction at the

PFA's reluctance to embrace his organisation as a possible additional resource to aid the old boys.

Taylor's former deputy at the PFA, Brendon Batson, says: "I dealt with Derek a lot and he was very passionate about former players. What we were trying to say was that he was part of building up of the PFA and it is there for former and current players. Our view was that we should encourage clubs to have former players' associations that dovetail with the PFA and the first port of call when players are in need should be the PFA.

"And the reason the PFA can do that is the work that was done by people like Derek. I think it is a little harsh to say he wanted to take on the PFA. He wanted an involvement and he wanted to do what he felt was right."

Shortly before his death, Dougan saw signs of a breakthrough after being invited to speak in front of various UEFA executives in Barcelona at the European Former Players' Associations Congress. Runham finds it ironic that Dougan's vision should find such easy acceptance on foreign soil. "As a result of that, the Spanish equivalent of XPro is now getting €30,000 a year from UEFA and €50,000 from the Spanish PFA," he says. "The Europeans are steaming ahead of us and that is a route we are going down now."

As XPro seeks recognition as a charitable trust[22], with the idea of having various prominent ex-players as vice-presidents, even Runham has to concede that it lost its biggest asset when its founder died: "We often felt we were rolling a big ball up the hill and it kept pushing us back. But that is why Derek was so important. He had a passion for it and I think it kept him going in his later years. He was impetuous and maybe he could have done more if he had directed himself better – we often shouted at each other over a table about that.

"But without that you wouldn't have got the little bits of magic. With limited resources we desperately need a footballer of the same leaning and ability to challenge the establishment. If there was a

---

22   This was achieved in 2011 (see Postscript)

fight to be fought, you could bank on Derek. He walked with a swagger and even when we were down at the FA he treated them with a little contempt. He never had a discussion, he spoke at them.

"But there was no one better at opening doors and getting meetings with important people. One day he and Merlyn were in with his friend Mervyn King, the governor of the Bank of England, and were so busy talking about Aston Villa that eventually Mervyn said to him, just before 8pm: 'You'll have to excuse me, but I have got to go and sort out the Budget for tomorrow.' Derek thought he could phone the Queen and she would listen. If anybody came up in conversation during a meeting he would pick up the phone and try to call them. The meeting would stop and we would have to try to call, say, Sepp Blatter."

Another interesting insight into Dougan's drive comes from Chris Westcott, with whom Derek and Merlyn stayed when participating in hearings on behalf of former Portsmouth teammate Norman Uprichard.

"One evening we spoke for about three hours about Derek's life and career," he recalls. "I don't think I had to ask more than about two questions. He was in fantastic form. He had gone through a phase in his life where he had been to quite a few players' funerals. The most recent had been John Ritchie and he had been shocked at how quickly John had fallen away after getting Alzheimer's.

"He was questioning mortality and life after death and the actual impact you can make on this planet. He was a very modest chap and it was quite clear that even though he had shaped and touched an enormous number of people's lives, he didn't see it that way. He just saw it as part of his mission to support to his fellow ex-pros and give back as much as he could."

One former professional footballer whose plight Dougan became deeply involved in during the latter months of his own life was Ian Cartwright, a young Wolves player during Dougan's chairmanship in the 1980s who was in need of funding for the cancer drug Sutent, unavailable via his own local health authority in Dudley.

It was through Cartwright's friend, Simon Dunkley, that Dougan discovered that Cartwright was being forced to pay £3,000 per month to treat his renal and spinal cancer. Dunkley explains:

"We'd had no joy with the local health trust in Dudley so we wanted to get pressure on them to get the drug we needed to help Ian. We went to the *Express and Star* and explained that here was an ex-Wolves player with cancer who was getting no support and was asking for something back.

"Next thing I had a message on my phone saying: 'This is Derek Dougan. Please give me a call.' I rang him back and it was like a young schoolboy being told off by a teacher. 'How the f*** do you know he only has two years to live?' he said. It put me on the back foot. He wanted to know what my experience was in regard to medicine and he wanted to talk to Ian's surgeon. We got permission from Ian and once Derek understood the background he became passionately involved. He explained through tears about his mum passing away through this disease and how much it had affected him."

Dougan was quickly into action, assisting in the organisation of a fundraising match between the former players of Wolves and West Brom. Dunkley continues: "I just wanted him to do a rally call in the paper to get more people there and I also I wanted him there on the day to make presentation. We got 2,500 people there at Tividale. Then he wanted to use his involvement with former players to hold an auction and comedy night. He got Gordon Banks down with a copy of the World Cup and several other ex-professionals.

"Derek was fantastic and it was a terrific night. In about three months we raised £15,000 and a lot of that was down to Derek. He was very considerate and compassionate and that overrode everything. He was calling people he had fallen out with five or ten years previously, pulling in favours and just begging. Derek didn't bow down to anybody but when he needed to he would.

"In those five months Derek would ring me literally every week and ask me about Ian's health. He supported him when we had a meeting with the National Health Trust and was as passionate as anybody in trying to convince them why a young man should not be denied treatment for an illness that was killing him. He involved some solicitors who worked with XPro and tried to challenge the health authority from a legal standpoint so we could get the drug 100 per cent funded."

By the time Dougan had helped raise sponsorship for a charity walk, the money raised was approaching £60,000. "In the end we have played the game," says Dunkley, "and moved Ian to Bromsgrove, where he can get the drug."

Dunkley concludes: "I have never met anyone like Derek. Some days I would be at his house and he would be having coughing fits or wouldn't get around too well because of his feet, yet he had so much fight left in him. It was such a shock when the call came through that we had lost him."

Cartwright and his family were hit hard by news of the death of someone they had all come to love and admire. "There was no real reason for Derek to do this for me," Cartwright admits. "But he was passionate about things like that and maybe that is what kept him going at the end. I was so proud of him and I sent a message to the London Wolves explaining how much my children and I thought of him.

"One time, even though he was poorly, he had grabbed me and pulled my head onto his shoulder and said 'we'll never give up. I will be gone before you but we will get through this'. On the day it came on the news that he had died, my children started to cry."

Dougan's concern for Cartwright and his work with XPro was symptomatic of the anger he reserved for administrators who had prevented his generation of footballers earning the salaries they deserved and the care they had earned. It certainly was not an indication of bitterness or envy towards the modern millionaire footballers.

His niece Josephine Long says: "Derek was a big player in his day but you would never hear him being resentful towards the equivalent players who earn so much money now. He was not a vicious man."

Dougan himself said in 2006: "I get continually asked to respond to two issues. One is George Best, the other is 'wouldn't you love to be playing today?' I can't put the clock back. I miss two things. I miss the regular training and I miss the camaraderie in the dressing room because footballers can be very interesting, very talented and very intelligent." But he did add: "I am envious of the state of the football pitches. They are unbelievable."

It was Best's death in 2005 that gave Dougan one of the most poignant and public duties of his later life: the role of pall bearer at his Irish teammate's funeral. He had never lost respect and affection for the man he once saw sign so many autographs for children that he had two blisters on his fingers. "He's very much maligned," Dougan once said. "I've seen him do things for mentally handicapped kids, for kids with disabilities, but unfortunately it never makes the news."

On the day itself, as thousands stood in the December rain outside Stormont, Belfast's parliamentary buildings, Dougan commented: "It is a privilege and pleasure to be here today. The Irish really do things properly. They are coming out in their droves because they think they owe George Best something because he gave them ten years of producing dazzling form that will never be repeated in this country." Within a year and a half, it was Dougan for whom a funeral route would be lined.

Derek Dougan's death took the public by surprise, knowing him as they did as an apparently tireless campaigner. He had even sparred with politicians on live television as recently as a 2006 edition of David Dimbleby's BBC current affairs show *Question Time*, where he sat as a representative of the United Kingdom Independence Party.[23]

For those close to him, there was shock and grief, of course, but they had witnessed his health battles of the last several years. For Merlyn Humphreys, there was a period of soul-searching before being comforted by medical experts that there was nothing she could have seen or should have done that would have changed Dougan's fate. For the fans who had cheered him from the terraces, there was one last chance to prove that he'd been wrong to believe they had fallen out of love with him.

Wolves stalwart Geoff Palmer says: "There were fans crying at

---

23   This was something of an about-turn for man who had been a spokesman for the pro-EEC lobby three decades earlier. After being introduced to the party by Doug Hope, he had first spoken up for them during a general election campaign, when he had expressed regret at his previous stance on Europe.

the funeral. And look at all the people who came to speak on his behalf. I don't think he ever lost anything in their eyes. I often used to see him in the petrol station and it took him ages to get served because everyone wanted to stop and talk to him."

Kenny Hibbitt, another who shared in so many of Dougan's greatest moments on the field, adds: "The amount of people at the funeral and all the press cuttings gave him a fantastic send-off. There was so much admiration for him. Nothing that happened [in the 1980s] ever detracted from him being a hero at Wolves."

From football followers and commentators, there was the usual assessment in death of a person's contribution in life. What can never be refuted was that Dougan was an embryonic component of so much that is taken for granted in today's football – from shirt sponsorship and freedom of contract to the more frivolous areas of television panels, shaven-headed players and flamboyant goal celebrations.

It would be an exaggeration to say that certain things would never have happened without him because evolution will find its way. Yet every generation needs the shoulders of predecessors to stand upon, and Dougan bore more weight than most in the game's development.

And, despite the battles and the bitching and all the pages he penned about what was wrong with his profession, he had great fun along the way. "He said himself he had a fantastic life," says his niece Josephine. "He played football and George Best was his mate. What more do you want? He was not materialistic. He was happy watching football and happy singing."

Merlyn Humphreys chose the inclusion of the old Nat King Cole hit *Unforgettable* in Dougan's funeral service after hearing him singing it around the house one day. "I said to him: 'That's you, that is. You'll be unforgettable one day'."

One day? For better or worse, in times of joy or controversy – in sunshine or in shadow – he always was.

POSTSCRIPT

More than three years after his death, Derek Dougan was still able to start a row in a committee room. Late in 2010 it was announced that, in the following January, he would be inducted into the Wolverhampton Wanderers Hall of Fame, along with former teammate Kenny Hibbitt.

"We ask the fans to send in their nominations and they are considered by a semi-independent committee which contains journalists, fans' representatives and members of the Former Players' Association," Matt Grayson, the club's head of marketing, explained.

"Derek Dougan was considered a substantial enough player to be in the Hall of Fame, it is just sad he could not be here to see it. He was such a colourful character on the pitch as a player. These days the modern sportsman is accused of not breaking a smile, but Derek combined a sense of fun with skill and was a hugely successful player for us."

The club's chief executive, Jez Moxey, described Dougan as an "iconic Wolves figure, always entertaining both on and off the pitch and a major crowd favourite in his own right".

However, those comments hid the facts behind Dougan's election. To have such an honour bestowed upon him seemed like the final act of reconciliation with the club he served for so many years but with whom he had a difficult relationship in the later years of his life.

Yet Merlyn Humphreys, who had led the campaign for his nomination, argued that it had been a far from easy passage, with the vote on Dougan's nomination being swung only by the persuasiveness of some of his ex-teammates on the voting committee, notably Derek Parkin. "Whatever else you say about Derek, he was one hell of a footballer," the former full-back stated after the vote. "When you were out there on the pitch with him, he was just incredible."

On the night of the ceremonies in the club's banqueting suite, Martin O'Neill reprised the role he had played at Dougan's funeral, speaking warmly of his relationship with his former Northern Ireland colleague. "I absolutely loved the fella," he told the audience, who also saw former club owner Sir Jack Hayward honoured.

Fellow-inductee Hibbitt added his own tribute and long-serving goalkeeper Phil Parkes explained how the ultra-fit Dougan was less bothered about warming up on the field before games then he was conducting the Molineux crowd as they chanted his name. "He was the ultimate showman; the Eric Cantona of his day," Parkes concluded.

Later in 2011, came the moment that Dougan had foreseen several years earlier, with the granting of charitable status to XPro. Co-founder Bob Runham described a tortuous process of 24 interviews over an 18-month period before the organisation was able to add the officially registered charity number of 1136193 to its masthead.

Official recognition as a charity allowed XPro to extend automatic membership to any former professional footballer, meaning that by the end of the year it could boast access to 30,000 potential recruits. England's most capped player, goalkeeper Peter Shilton, was serving as president, alongside former Stoke centre-back Denis Smith as chairman and another ex-Potter, Geoff Scott, as chief executive. Notable names recruited as patrons included Ian Rush, Iain Dowie and Don Hutchison, while television personality Nick Hancock was among the trustees.

"I am fully behind XPro's initiative to help former professional footballers," said Rush upon his appointment. "It is comforting to know that the charity is on hand with help and advice for ex-players who may need assistance."

Even Sir Alex Ferguson was singing the praises of Dougan's brainchild: "Football needs XPro and I send the charity my very best wishes in hoping they establish a place in the football community. I hope those who hold this game of ours close to their heart will support XPro in any way they can."

Just as Dougan had said all along, XPro was proving that it could co-exist with, and complement, the rest of the football community. "We are no longer seen as a threat to the PFA," said Runham. "Doog would be proud to be proved right."

And, Runham might have added, he would never have thought that he was anything else.

BIBLIOGRAPHY

Bagchi, Rob and Paul Rogerson *The Unforgiven: The Story of Don Revie's Leeds United* (Aurum, 2002)

Burtenshaw, Norman *Whose Side Are You On, Ref?* (Arthur Baker,1973)

Dougan, Derek *Attack!* (Pelham Books, 1969)

Dougan, Derek *Doog* (All Seasons Publishing, 1980)

Dougan, Derek *How Not to Run Football* (All Seasons Publishing, 1981)

Dougan, Derek *The Footballer* (Allison & Busby, 1974)

Dougan, Derek *The Sash He Never Wore* (Allison & Busby, 1972)

Dougan, Derek *The Sash He Never Wore – 25 Years On* (Lagan Books,1997)

Dougan, Derek and Pat Murphy *The Games of our Lives* (J.M. Dent & Sons, 1983)

Dougan, Derek and Percy Young *On the Spot: Football as a Profession* (Stanley Paul, 1975)

Ellis, Doug *Deadly Doug: Behind the Scenes at Villa Park (Blake Publishing, 2005)*

Glanville, Brian *The Story of the World Cup* (Faber and Faber, 2001)

Glanville, Brian *World Football Handbook* (Mayflower, various years)

Graham, George *The Glory and the Grief* (Andre Deutsch, 1995)
Gray, Andy *Gray Matters: My Autobiography* (MacMillan, 2004)

Hewitt, Paolo and Mark Baxter *The Fashion of Football*
    (Mainstream, 2004)
Hill, Jimmy *The Jimmy Hill Story: My Autobiography* (Hodder &
    Stoughton, 1998)
Hugman, Barry J. *Football League Players Records 1946-92* (Tony
    Williams Publications, 1992)

Imlach, Gary *My Father and Other Working Class Football Heroes*
    (Yellow Jersey Press, 2005)
Inglis, Simon *The Football Grounds of England and Wales* (Collins
    Willow, 1983)

Jackman, Mike *The Essential History of Blackburn Rovers* (Headline,
    2001)
James, Gary *Football With a Smile: The Authorised Biography of Joe
    Mercer* (ACL & Polar, 1993)

Lansley, Peter *Running with Wolves* (Thomas Publications, 2004)

McIlroy, Jimmy *Right Inside Soccer* (Nicholas Kaye, 1960)
McKittrick, David and David McVea *Making Sense of the Troubles*
    (Penguin, 2001)
Morgan, Phil *The Wolverhampton Wanderers Football Book* (Stanley
    Paul, 1970)

Neill, Terry *Confessions of a Football Manager* (Sidgwick and
    Jackson,1985)

Simpson, Dawson *The Whites, A History of Distillery Football
    Club1880-2004* (Dawson Simpson, 2004)

Taylor, Rogan and Andrew Ward *Kicking and Screaming: An Oral
    History of Football in England* (Robson Books, 1995)
Tossell, David *Big Mal: The High Life and Troubled Times of
    Malcolm Allison, Football Legend* (Mainstream, 2008)

BIBLIOGRAPHY

Tossell, David *Playing for Uncle Sam: The Brits' Story of the North American Soccer League* (Mainstream, 2003)

Tossell, David *Seventy-One Guns: The Year of the First Arsenal Double* (Mainstream, 2002)

Westcott, Chris *Joker in the Pack: The Ernie Hunt Story* (Tempus, 2004)

The following publications and periodicals were also of valuable assistance:
Belfast Telegraph, Belfast Newsletter, Birmingham Mail, Leicester Mercury, Portsmouth Evening News, Peterborough Evening Telegraph, Peterborough Standard, Wolverhampton Express and Star and various UK national daily newspapers. *Rothmans Football Yearbook, Shoot!, Goal, Charles Buchan's Football Monthly, Foul.*